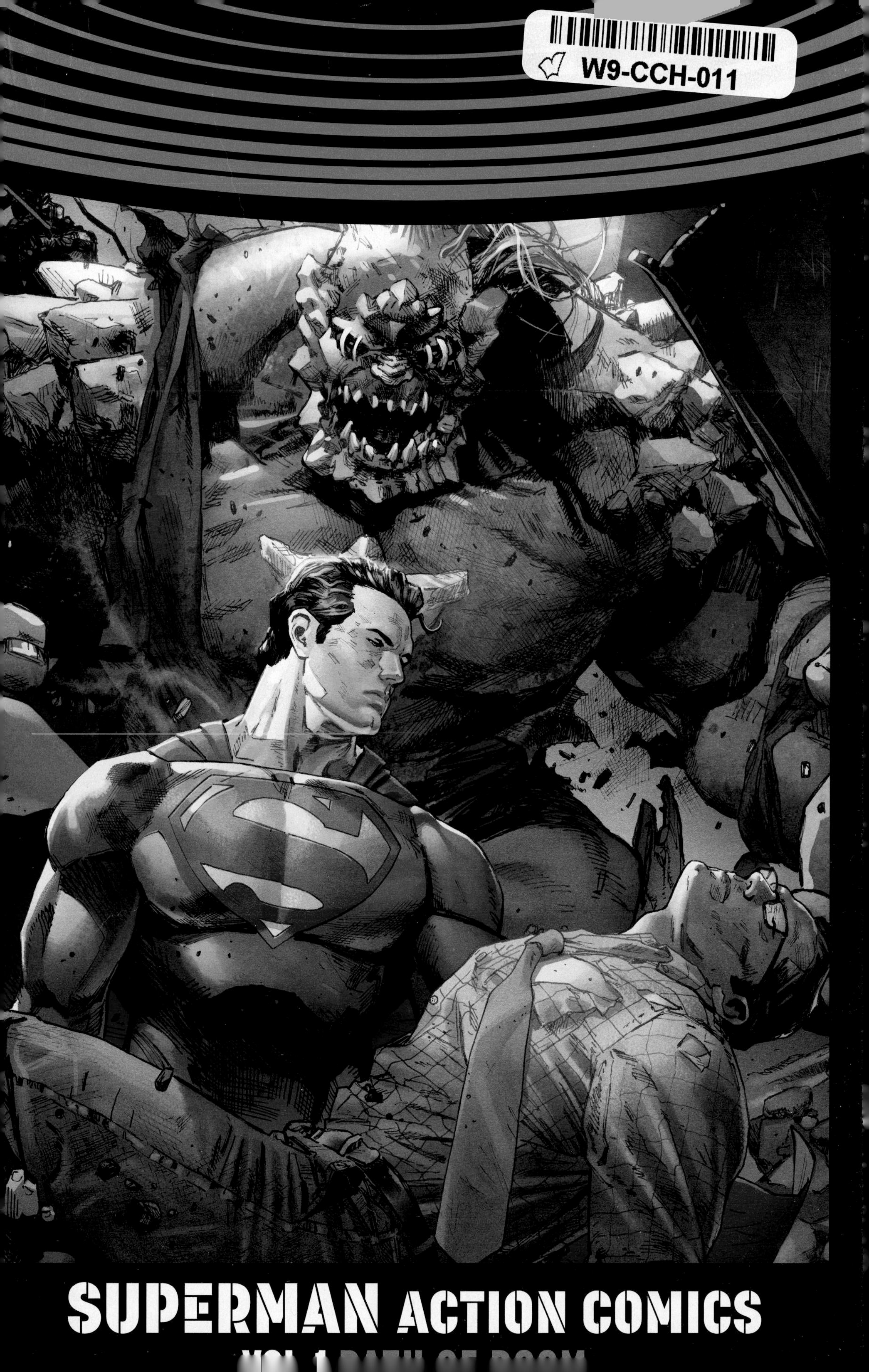

SUPERMAN ACTION COMICS

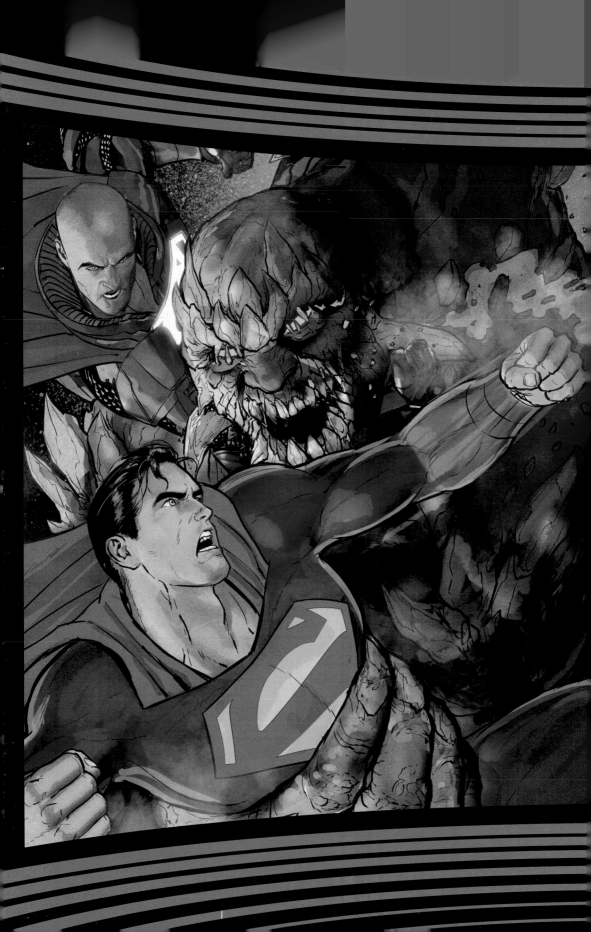

SUPERMAN ACTION COMICS
VOL.1 PATH OF DOOM

DAN JURGENS
writer

PATCH ZIRCHER * **TYLER KIRKHAM** * **STEPHEN SEGOVIA** * **ART THIBERT**
artists

TOMEU MOREY * **ULISES ARREOLA** * **ARIF PRIANTO**
colorists

ROB LEIGH
letterer

RYAN SOOK
collection cover artist

IVAN REIS * **JOE PRADO** * **MIKEL JANÍN** * **CLAY MANN**
DAN JURGENS * **SONIA OBACK** * **ALEJANDRO SANCHEZ**
original series covers

SUPERMAN created by **JERRY SIEGEL** and **JOE SHUSTER**
By special arrangement with the Jerry Siegel family

MIKE COTTON Editor - Original Series • **PAUL KAMINSKI** Associate Editor - Original Series
JEB WOODARD Group Editor - Collected Editions • **SCOTT NYBAKKEN** Editor - Collected Edition
STEVE COOK Design Director - Books • **DAMIAN RYLAND** Publication Design

BOB HARRAS Senior VP - Editor-in-Chief, DC Comics

DIANE NELSON President • **DAN DiDIO** Publisher • **JIM LEE** Publisher • **GEOFF JOHNS** President & Chief Creative Officer
AMIT DESAI Executive VP - Business & Marketing Strategy, Direct to Consumer & Global Franchise Management • **SAM ADES** Senior VP - Direct to Consumer
BOBBIE CHASE VP - Talent Development • **MARK CHIARELLO** Senior VP - Art, Design & Collected Editions
JOHN CUNNINGHAM Senior VP - Sales & Trade Marketing • **ANNE DePIES** Senior VP - Business Strategy, Finance & Administration
DON FALLETTI VP - Manufacturing Operations • **LAWRENCE GANEM** VP - Editorial Administration & Talent Relations
ALISON GILL Senior VP - Manufacturing & Operations • **HANK KANALZ** Senior VP - Editorial Strategy & Administration
JAY KOGAN VP - Legal Affairs • **THOMAS LOFTUS** VP - Business Affairs
JACK MAHAN VP - Business Affairs • **NICK J. NAPOLITANO** VP - Manufacturing Administration
EDDIE SCANNELL VP - Consumer Marketing • **COURTNEY SIMMONS** Senior VP - Publicity & Communications
JIM (SKI) SOKOLOWSKI VP - Comic Book Specialty Sales & Trade Marketing • **NANCY SPEARS** VP - Mass, Book, Digital Sales & Trade Marketing

SUPERMAN: ACTION COMICS VOL. 1 – PATH OF DOOM

Published by DC Comics. Compilation and all new material Copyright © 2017 DC Comics. All Rights Reserved.

Originally published in single magazine form in ACTION COMICS 957-962. Copyright © 2016 DC Comics. All Rights Reserved.
All characters, their distinctive likenesses and related elements featured in this publication are trademarks of DC Comics.
The stories, characters and incidents featured in this publication are entirely fictional. DC Comics does not read or accept unsolicited ideas, stories or artwork.

DC Comics, 2900 West Alameda Ave., Burbank, CA 91505. Printed by LSC Communications, Salem, VA, USA. 1/13/17.
First Printing. ISBN: 978-1-4012-6804-6

Library of Congress Cataloging-in-Publication Data is available.

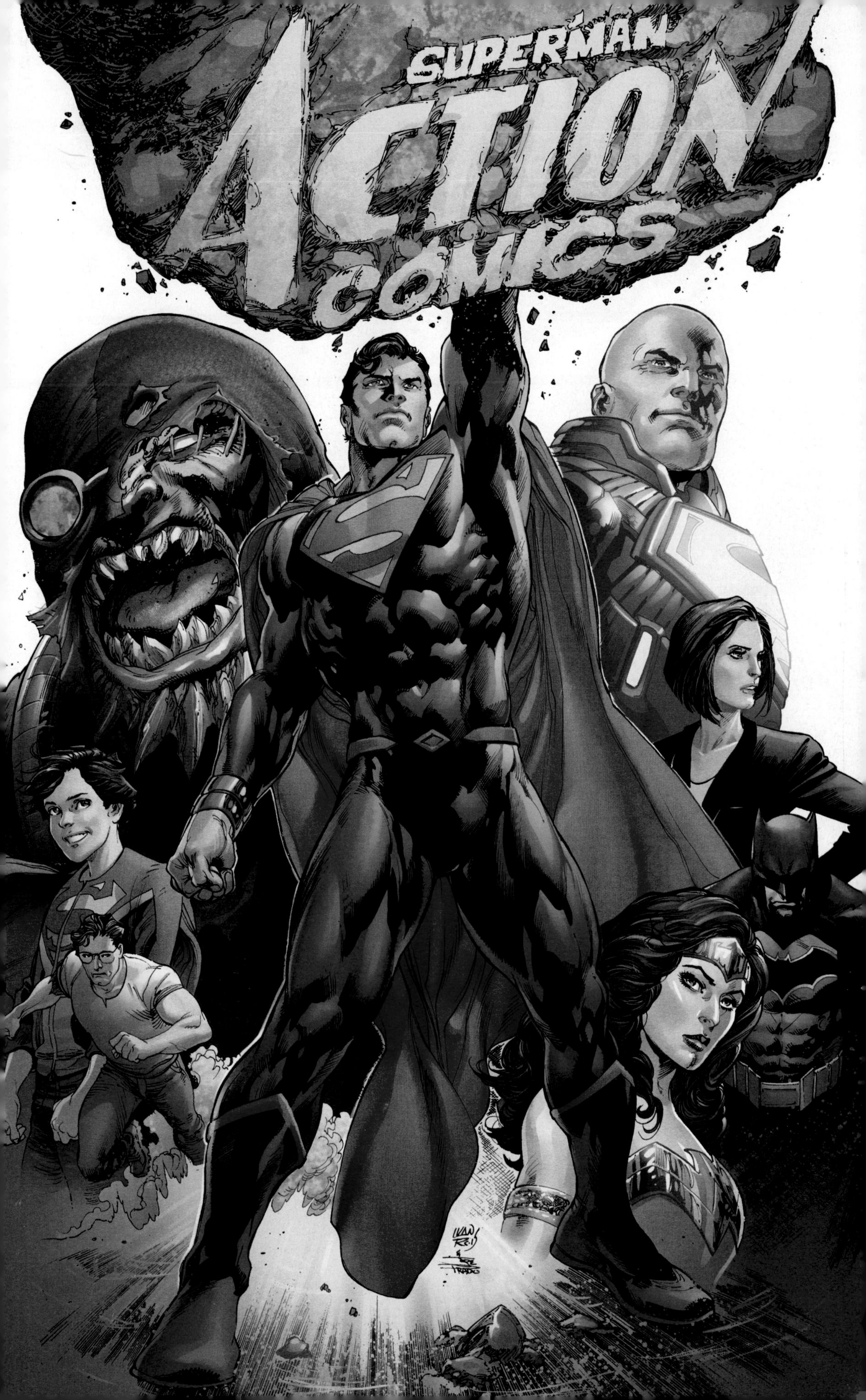
SUPERMAN
ACTION
COMICS

ACTION COMICS #957

IVAN REIS, JOE PRADO and SONIA OBACK cover artists

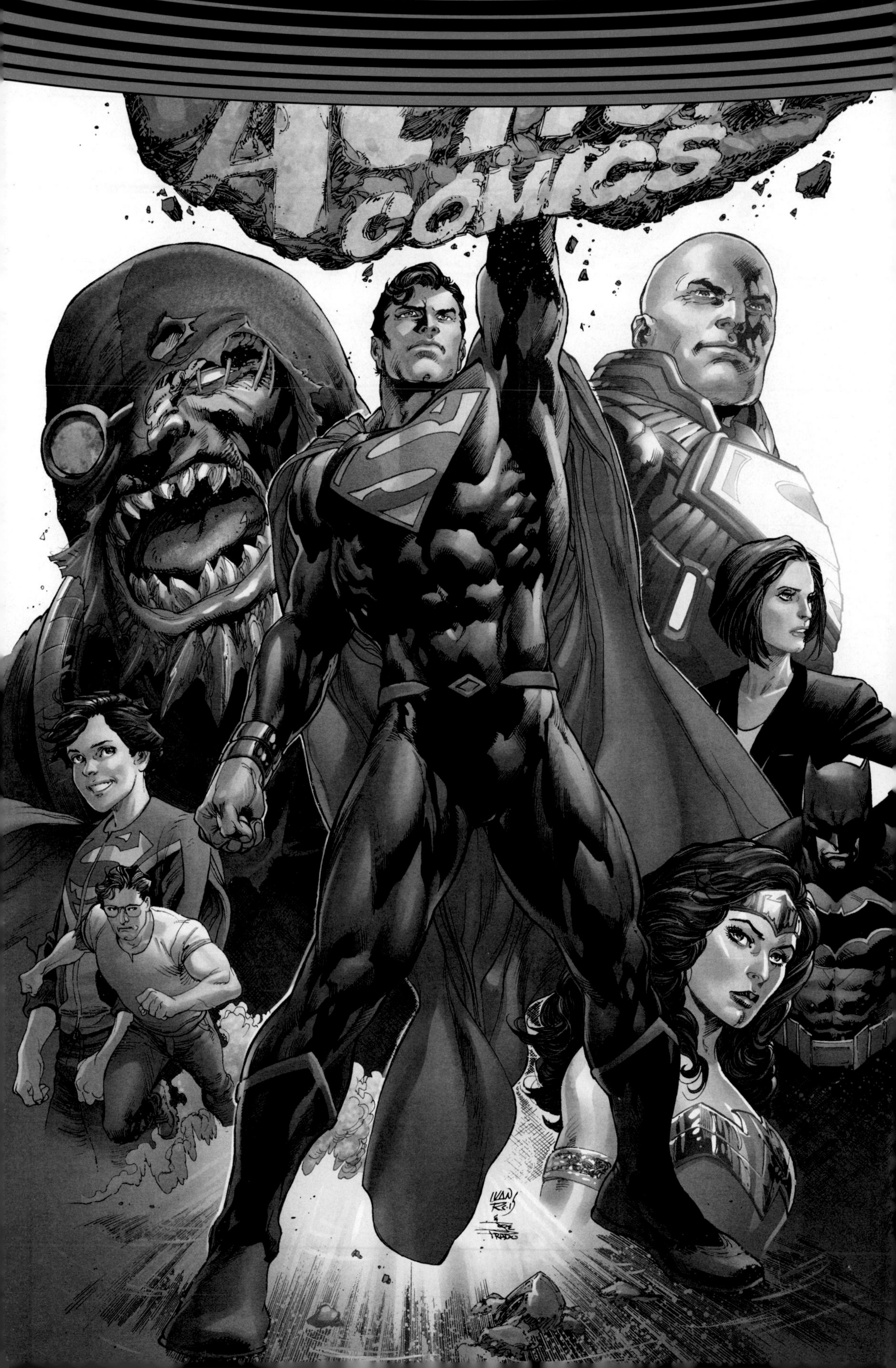
COMICS

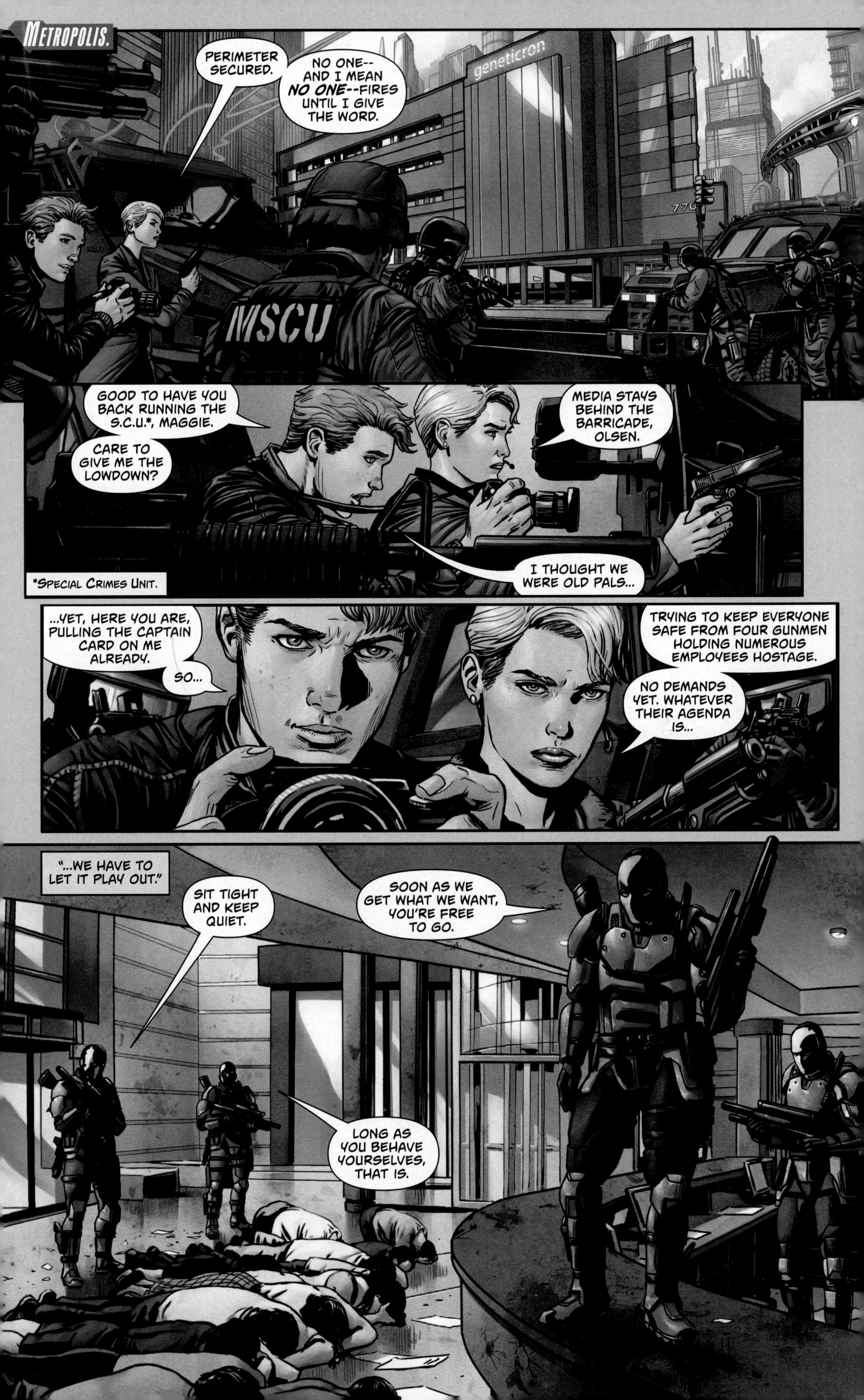
METROPOLIS.
PERIMETER SECURED.
NO ONE-- AND I MEAN NO ONE--FIRES UNTIL I GIVE THE WORD.
geneticron
MSCU
770
GOOD TO HAVE YOU BACK RUNNING THE S.C.U.*, MAGGIE.
CARE TO GIVE ME THE LOWDOWN?
MEDIA STAYS BEHIND THE BARRICADE, OLSEN.
I THOUGHT WE WERE OLD PALS...
*SPECIAL CRIMES UNIT.
...YET, HERE YOU ARE, PULLING THE CAPTAIN CARD ON ME ALREADY.
SO...
TRYING TO KEEP EVERYONE SAFE FROM FOUR GUNMEN HOLDING NUMEROUS EMPLOYEES HOSTAGE.
NO DEMANDS YET. WHATEVER THEIR AGENDA IS...
"...WE HAVE TO LET IT PLAY OUT."
SIT TIGHT AND KEEP QUIET.
SOON AS WE GET WHAT WE WANT, YOU'RE FREE TO GO.
LONG AS YOU BEHAVE YOURSELVES, THAT IS.

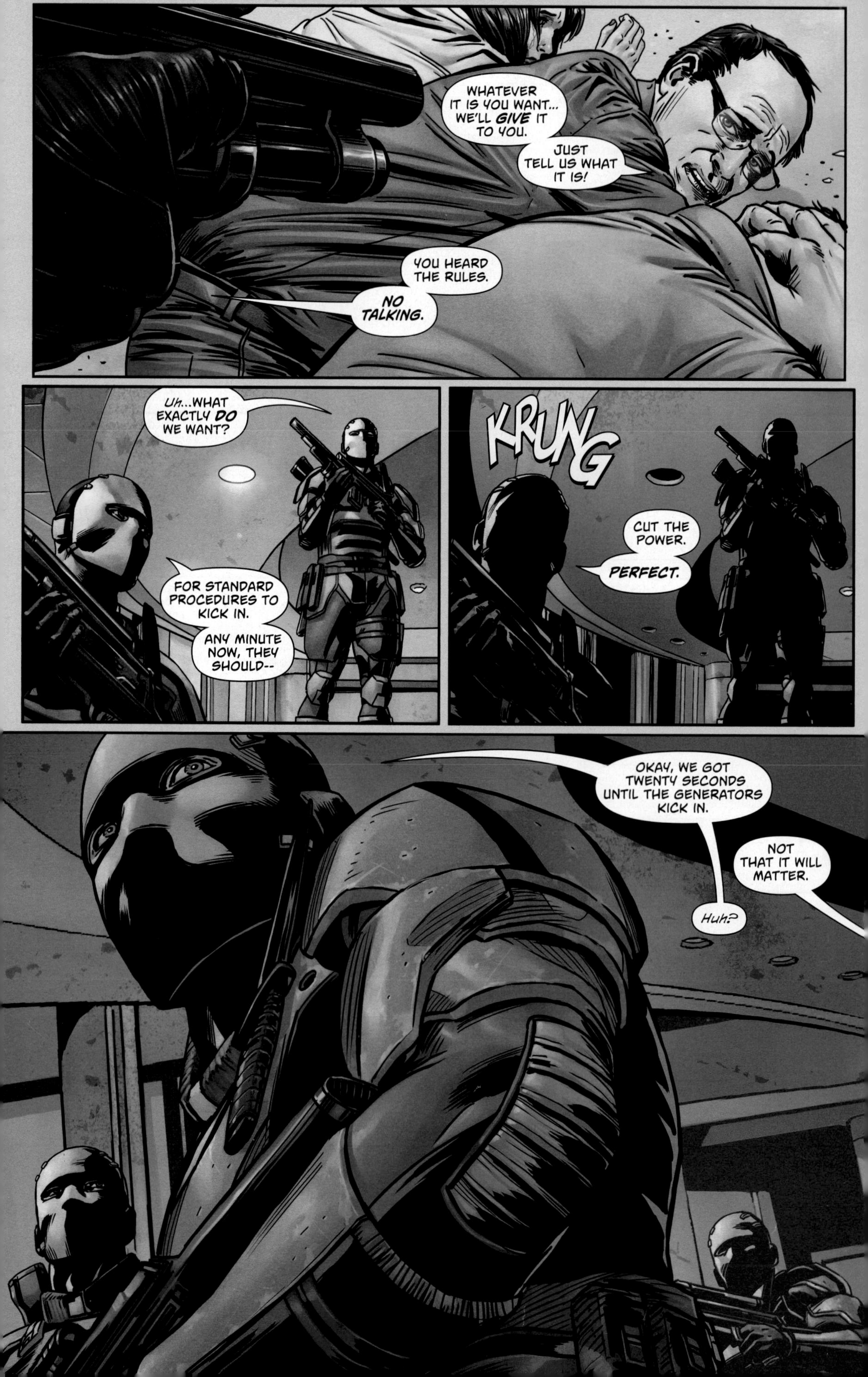
WHATEVER IT IS YOU WANT... WE'LL GIVE IT TO YOU.
JUST TELL US WHAT IT IS!
YOU HEARD THE RULES.
NO TALKING.
Uh...WHAT EXACTLY DO WE WANT?
FOR STANDARD PROCEDURES TO KICK IN.
ANY MINUTE NOW, THEY SHOULD--
KRUNG
CUT THE POWER.
PERFECT.
OKAY, WE GOT TWENTY SECONDS UNTIL THE GENERATORS KICK IN.
NOT THAT IT WILL MATTER.
Huh?

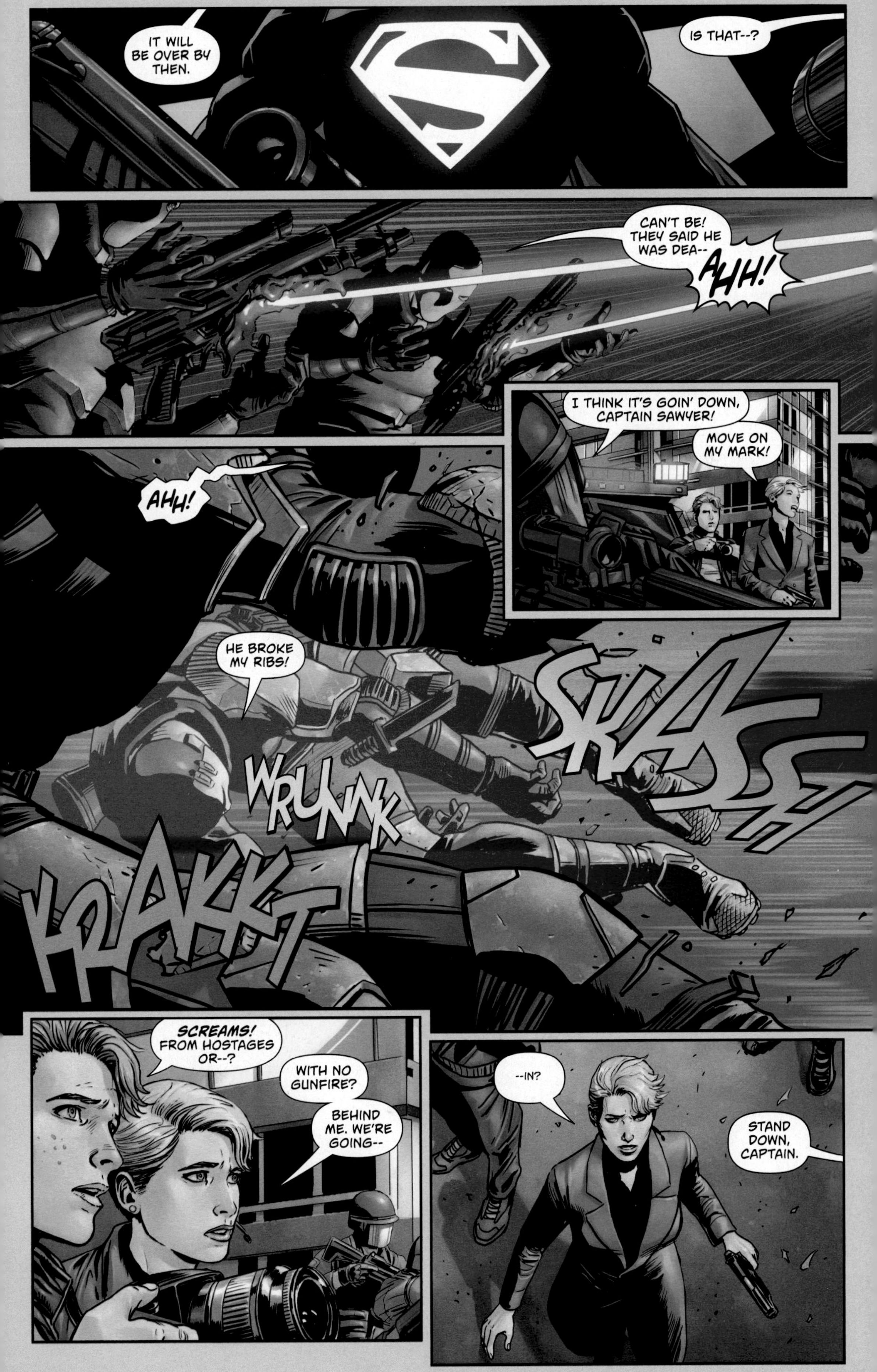
IT WILL BE OVER BY THEN.
IS THAT--?
CAN'T BE! THEY SAID HE WAS DEA--
AHH!
I THINK IT'S GOIN' DOWN, CAPTAIN SAWYER!
MOVE ON MY MARK!
AHH!
HE BROKE MY RIBS!
SKASSH
WRUNNK
KRAKKT
SCREAMS! FROM HOSTAGES OR--?
WITH NO GUNFIRE?
BEHIND ME. WE'RE GOING--
--IN?
STAND DOWN, CAPTAIN.

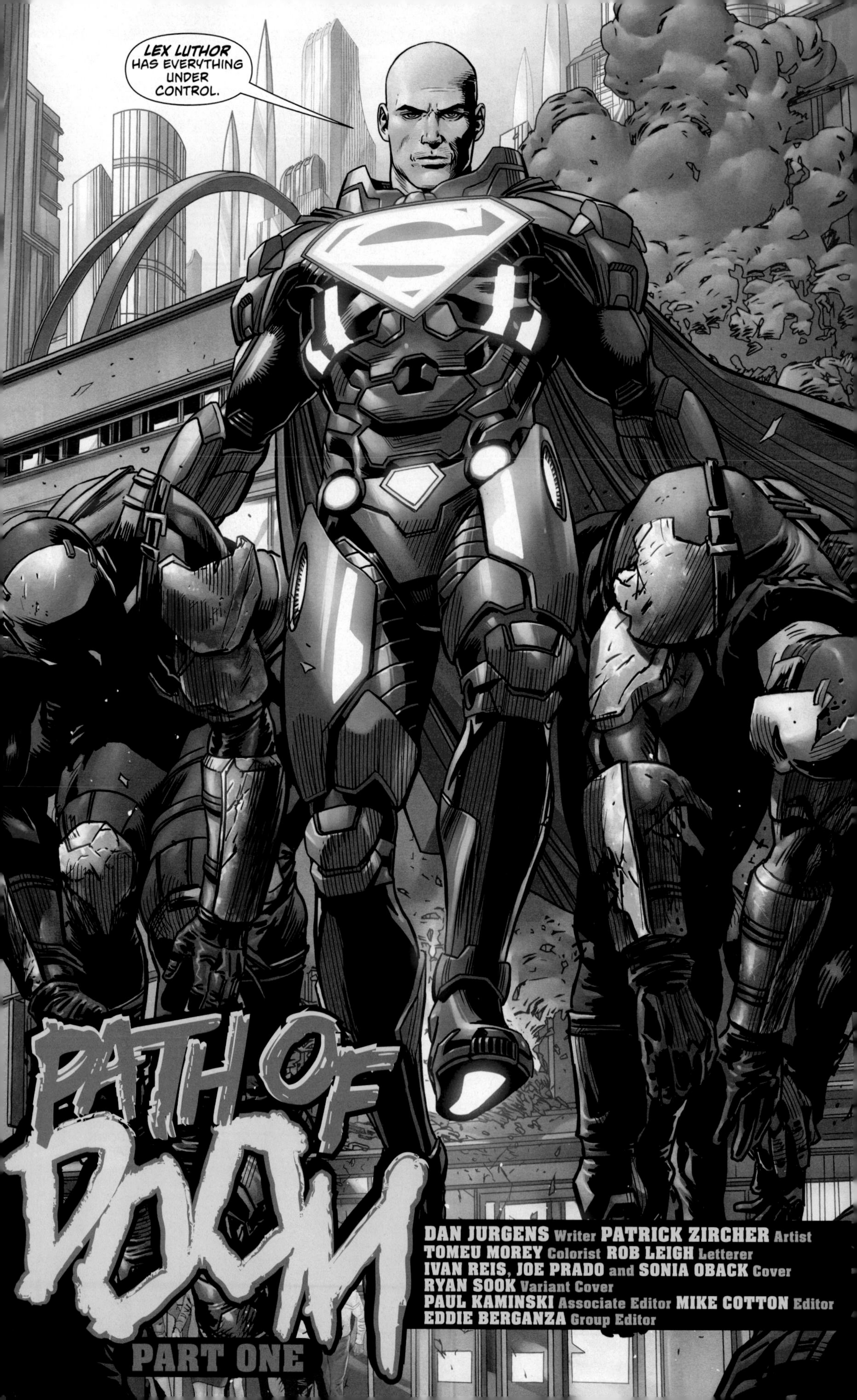
LEX LUTHOR HAS EVERYTHING UNDER CONTROL.
PATH OF DOOM
PART ONE
DAN JURGENS Writer PATRICK ZIRCHER Artist
TOMEU MOREY Colorist ROB LEIGH Letterer
IVAN REIS, JOE PRADO and SONIA OBACK Cover
RYAN SOOK Variant Cover
PAUL KAMINSKI Associate Editor MIKE COTTON Editor
EDDIE BERGANZA Group Editor

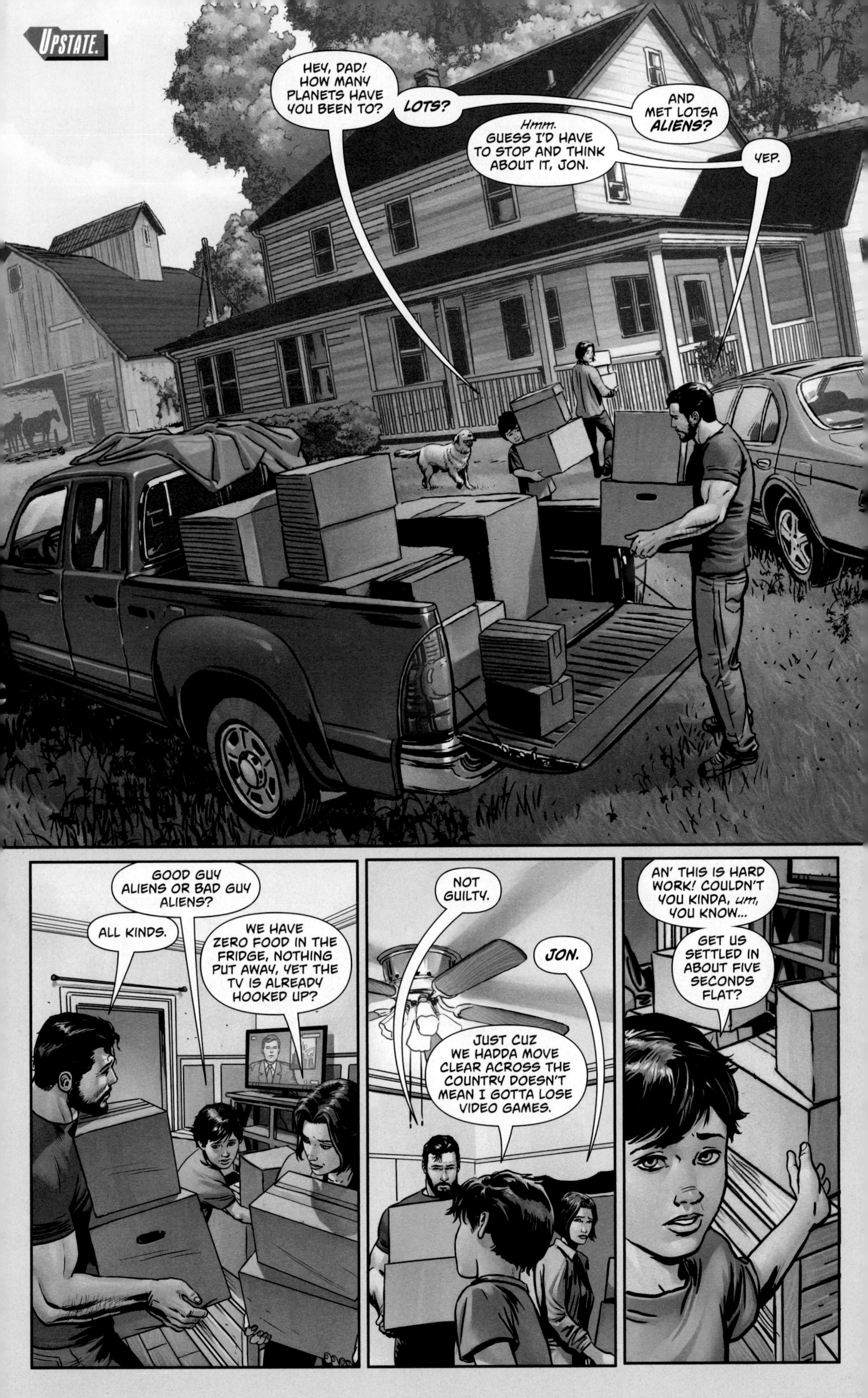
UPSTATE.
HEY, DAD! HOW MANY PLANETS HAVE YOU BEEN TO?
LOTS?
AND MET LOTSA ALIENS?
Hmm. GUESS I'D HAVE TO STOP AND THINK ABOUT IT, JON.
YEP.
GOOD GUY ALIENS OR BAD GUY ALIENS?
ALL KINDS.
WE HAVE ZERO FOOD IN THE FRIDGE, NOTHING PUT AWAY, YET THE TV IS ALREADY HOOKED UP?
NOT GUILTY.
JON.
JUST CUZ WE HADDA MOVE CLEAR ACROSS THE COUNTRY DOESN'T MEAN I GOTTA LOSE VIDEO GAMES.
AN' THIS IS HARD WORK! COULDN'T YOU KINDA, um, YOU KNOW...
GET US SETTLED IN ABOUT FIVE SECONDS FLAT?

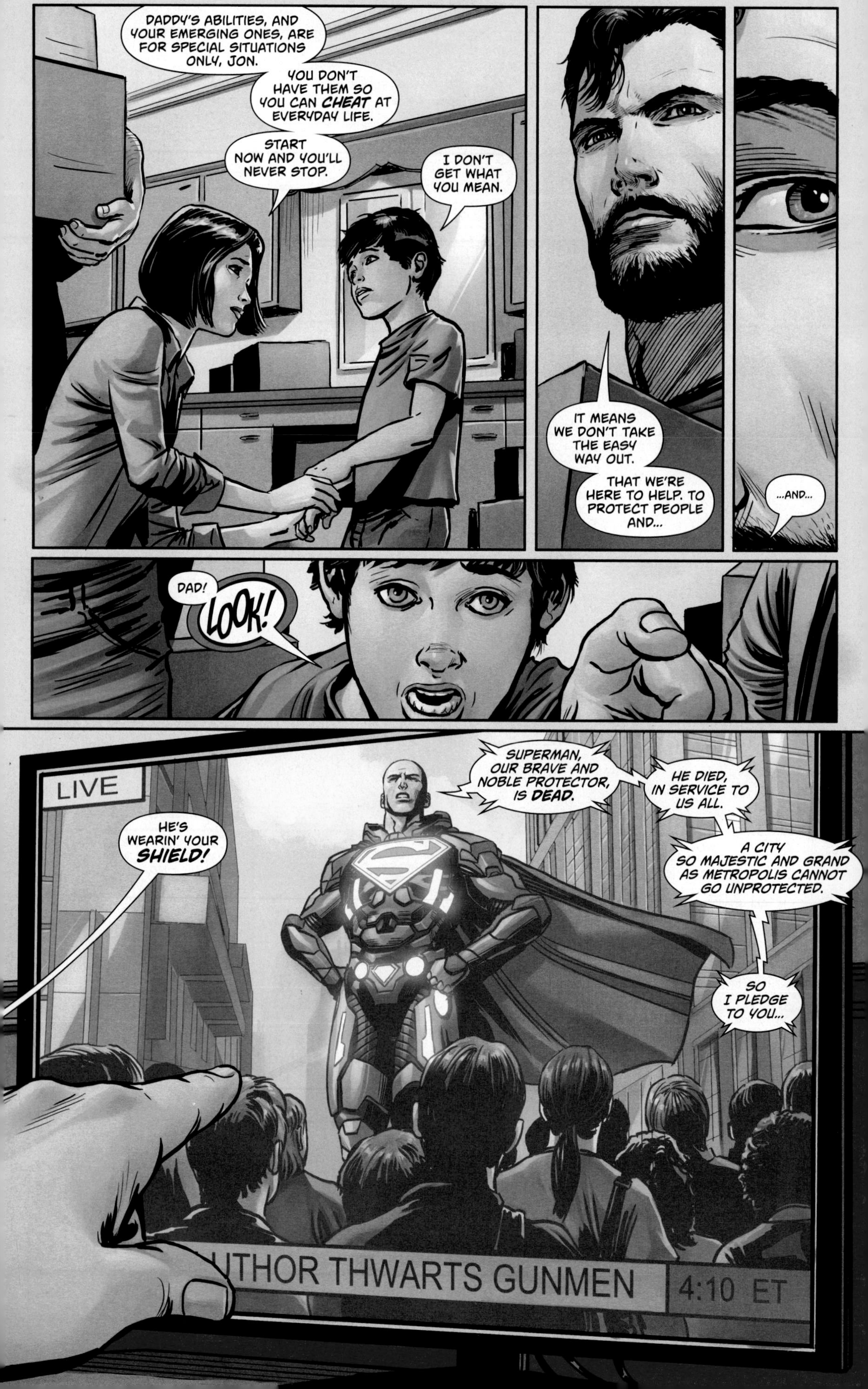

DADDY'S ABILITIES, AND YOUR EMERGING ONES, ARE FOR SPECIAL SITUATIONS ONLY, JON.
YOU DON'T HAVE THEM SO YOU CAN CHEAT AT EVERYDAY LIFE.
START NOW AND YOU'LL NEVER STOP.
I DON'T GET WHAT YOU MEAN.
IT MEANS WE DON'T TAKE THE EASY WAY OUT.
THAT WE'RE HERE TO HELP. TO PROTECT PEOPLE AND...
...AND...
DAD!
LOOK!
LIVE
SUPERMAN, OUR BRAVE AND NOBLE PROTECTOR, IS DEAD.
HE DIED, IN SERVICE TO US ALL.
HE'S WEARIN' YOUR SHIELD!
A CITY SO MAJESTIC AND GRAND AS METROPOLIS CANNOT GO UNPROTECTED.
SO I PLEDGE TO YOU...
UTHOR THWARTS GUNMEN
4:10 ET

...HERE AND NOW...

CLARK? WAIT!

...THAT AS LONG AS I AM HERE...

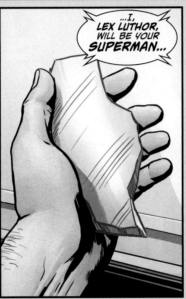

...I, LEX LUTHOR, WILL BE YOUR SUPERMAN...

...AND METROPOLIS WILL BE SAFE UNDER MY PROTECTION.

CLARK?

YOU AND I BOTH KNOW WHAT LUTHOR IS, LOIS.

HE DESTROYS LIVES. INFLICTS CHAOS.

ON OUR WORLD, YES. BUT WE TALKED ABOUT THIS. YOU INVESTIGATED THIS LEX LUTHOR AND FOUND NOTHING.

OUR WORK NEEDS TO STAY A SECRET, FOR JON'S SAKE.

WE'VE COME SO FAR, IS THIS LITTLE GAME OF HIS WORTH MAKING YOU GO PUBLIC?

YOU DON'T BELIEVE HE'S INNOCENT ANY MORE THAN I DO.

MAYBE NOT.

BUT WITHOUT PROOF...

I'VE COME TO ACCEPT THAT THIS WORLD'S SUPERMAN IS DEAD, LOIS.

I CAN'T LET LUTHOR TAKE HIS PLACE.

IT'S TIME TO COME OUT OF THE SHADOWS.

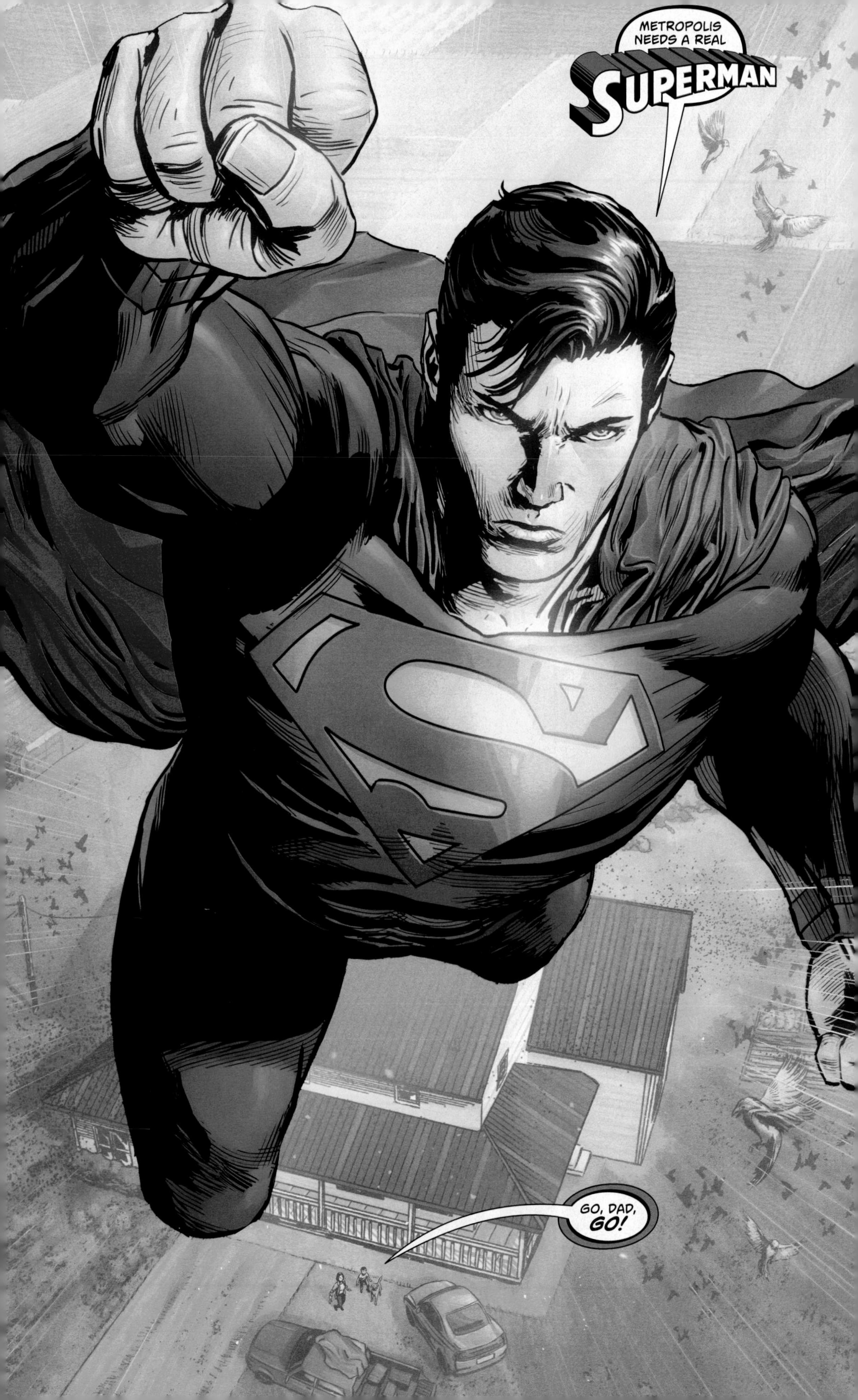
METROPOLIS NEEDS A REAL SUPERMAN
GO, DAD, GO!

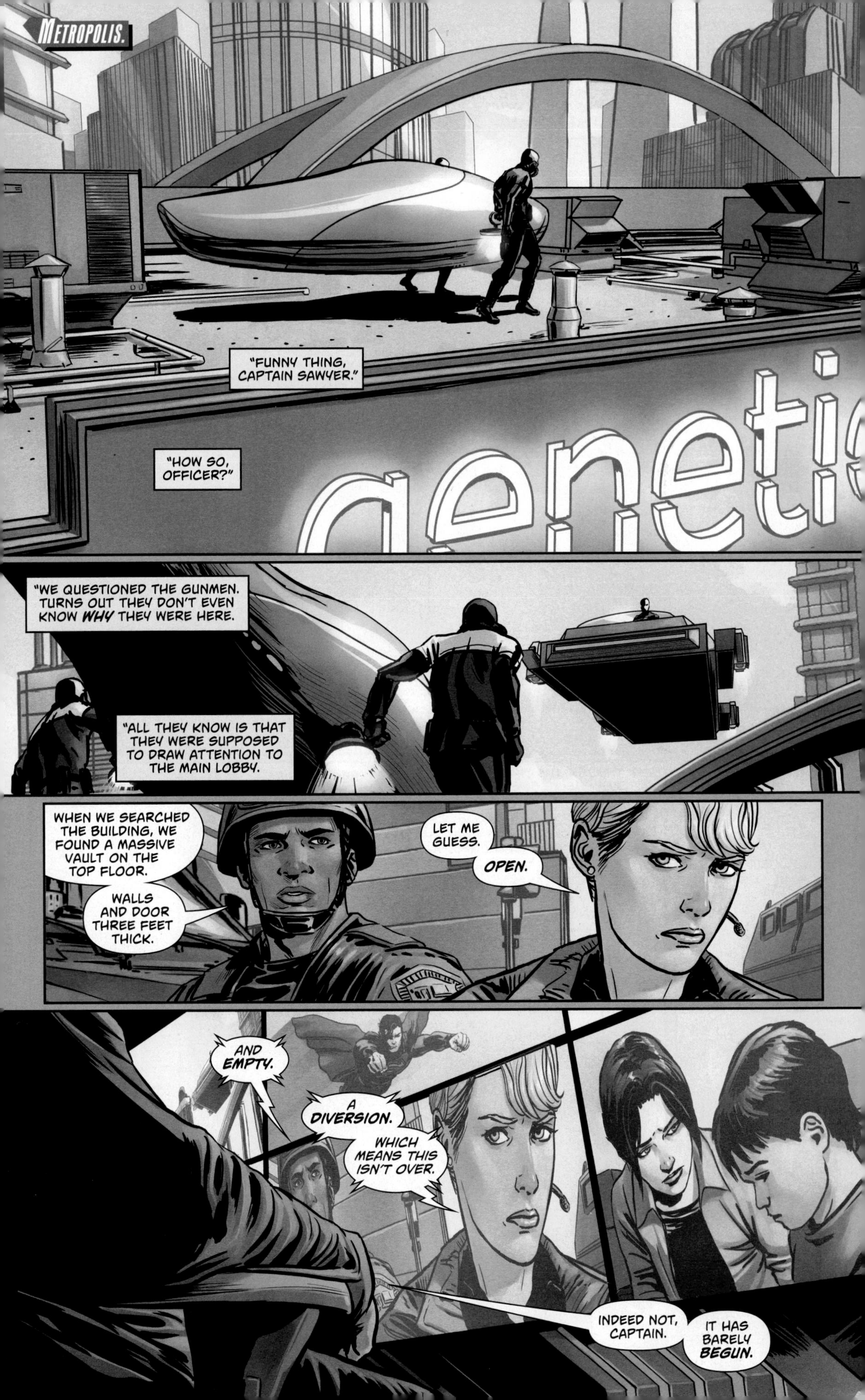
METROPOLIS.
"FUNNY THING, CAPTAIN SAWYER."
"HOW SO, OFFICER?"
genetic
"WE QUESTIONED THE GUNMEN. TURNS OUT THEY DON'T EVEN KNOW WHY THEY WERE HERE.
"ALL THEY KNOW IS THAT THEY WERE SUPPOSED TO DRAW ATTENTION TO THE MAIN LOBBY.
WHEN WE SEARCHED THE BUILDING, WE FOUND A MASSIVE VAULT ON THE TOP FLOOR.
WALLS AND DOOR THREE FEET THICK.
LET ME GUESS. OPEN.
AND EMPTY.
A DIVERSION.
WHICH MEANS THIS ISN'T OVER.
INDEED NOT, CAPTAIN.
IT HAS BARELY BEGUN.

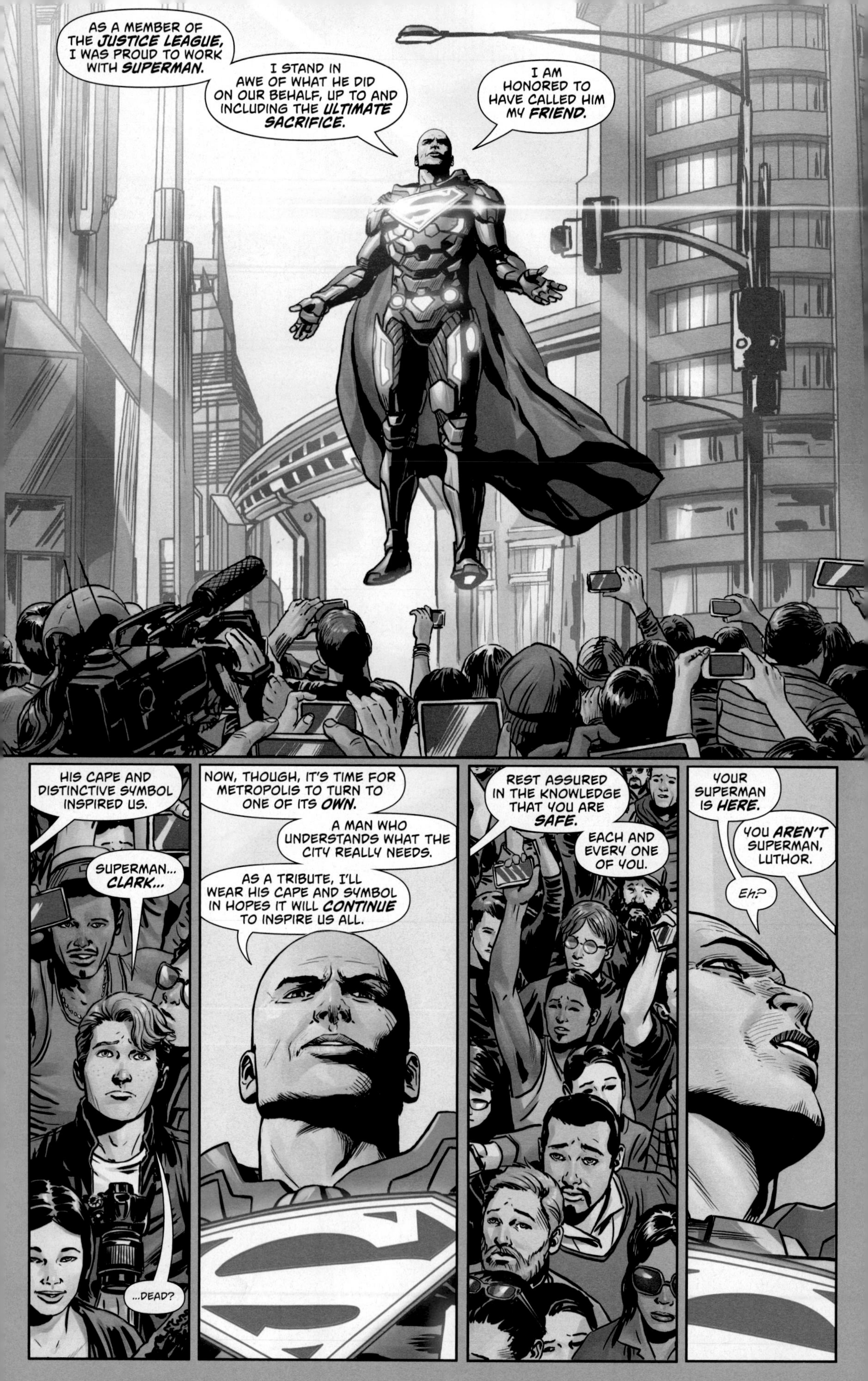

AS A MEMBER OF THE JUSTICE LEAGUE, I WAS PROUD TO WORK WITH SUPERMAN.
I STAND IN AWE OF WHAT HE DID ON OUR BEHALF, UP TO AND INCLUDING THE ULTIMATE SACRIFICE.
I AM HONORED TO HAVE CALLED HIM MY FRIEND.
HIS CAPE AND DISTINCTIVE SYMBOL INSPIRED US.
SUPERMAN... CLARK...
...DEAD?
NOW, THOUGH, IT'S TIME FOR METROPOLIS TO TURN TO ONE OF ITS OWN.
A MAN WHO UNDERSTANDS WHAT THE CITY REALLY NEEDS.
AS A TRIBUTE, I'LL WEAR HIS CAPE AND SYMBOL IN HOPES IT WILL CONTINUE TO INSPIRE US ALL.
REST ASSURED IN THE KNOWLEDGE THAT YOU ARE SAFE.
EACH AND EVERY ONE OF YOU.
YOUR SUPERMAN IS HERE.
YOU AREN'T SUPERMAN, LUTHOR.
Eh?

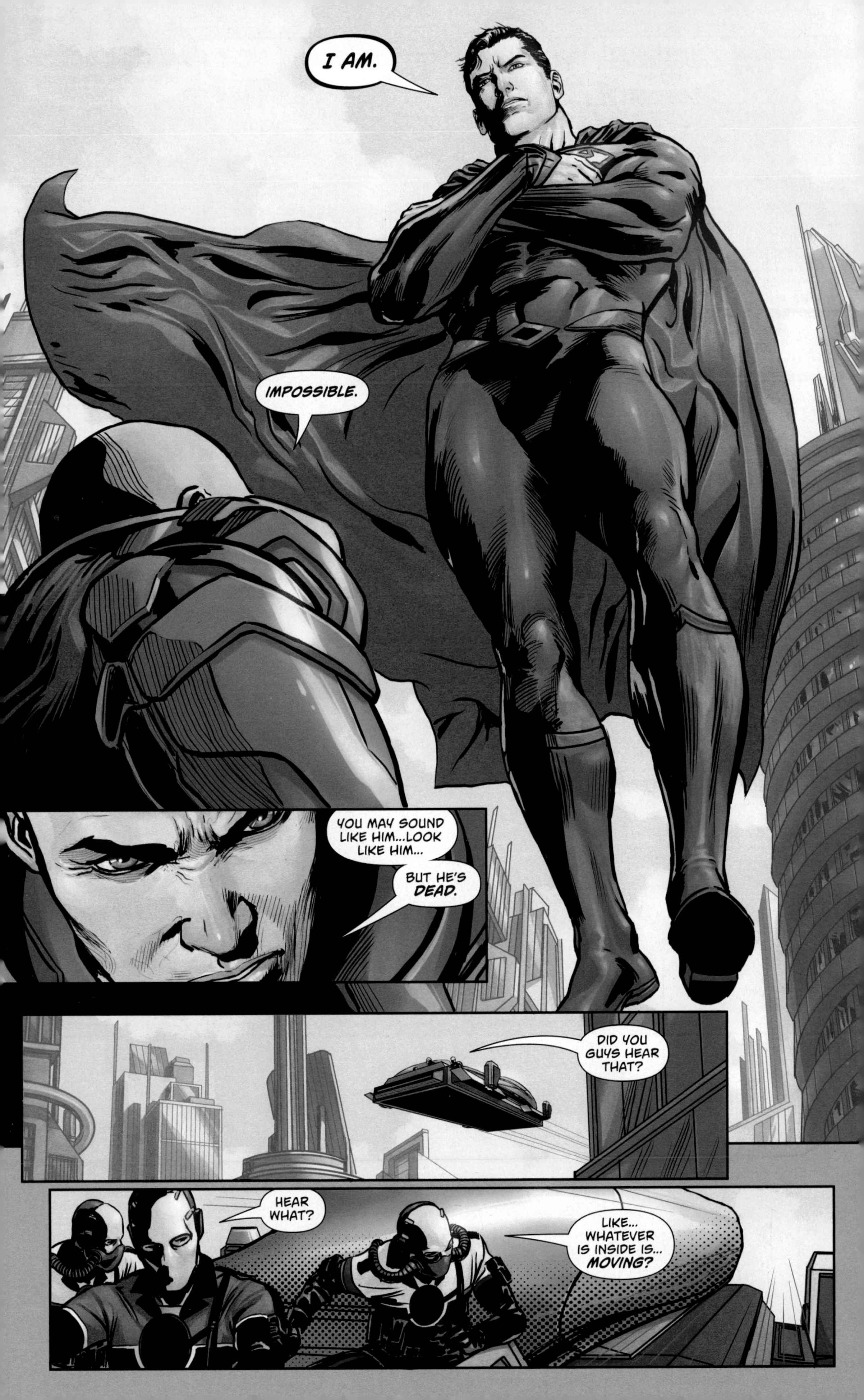
I AM.
IMPOSSIBLE.
YOU MAY SOUND LIKE HIM...LOOK LIKE HIM...
BUT HE'S DEAD.
DID YOU GUYS HEAR THAT?
HEAR WHAT?
LIKE... WHATEVER IS INSIDE IS... MOVING?

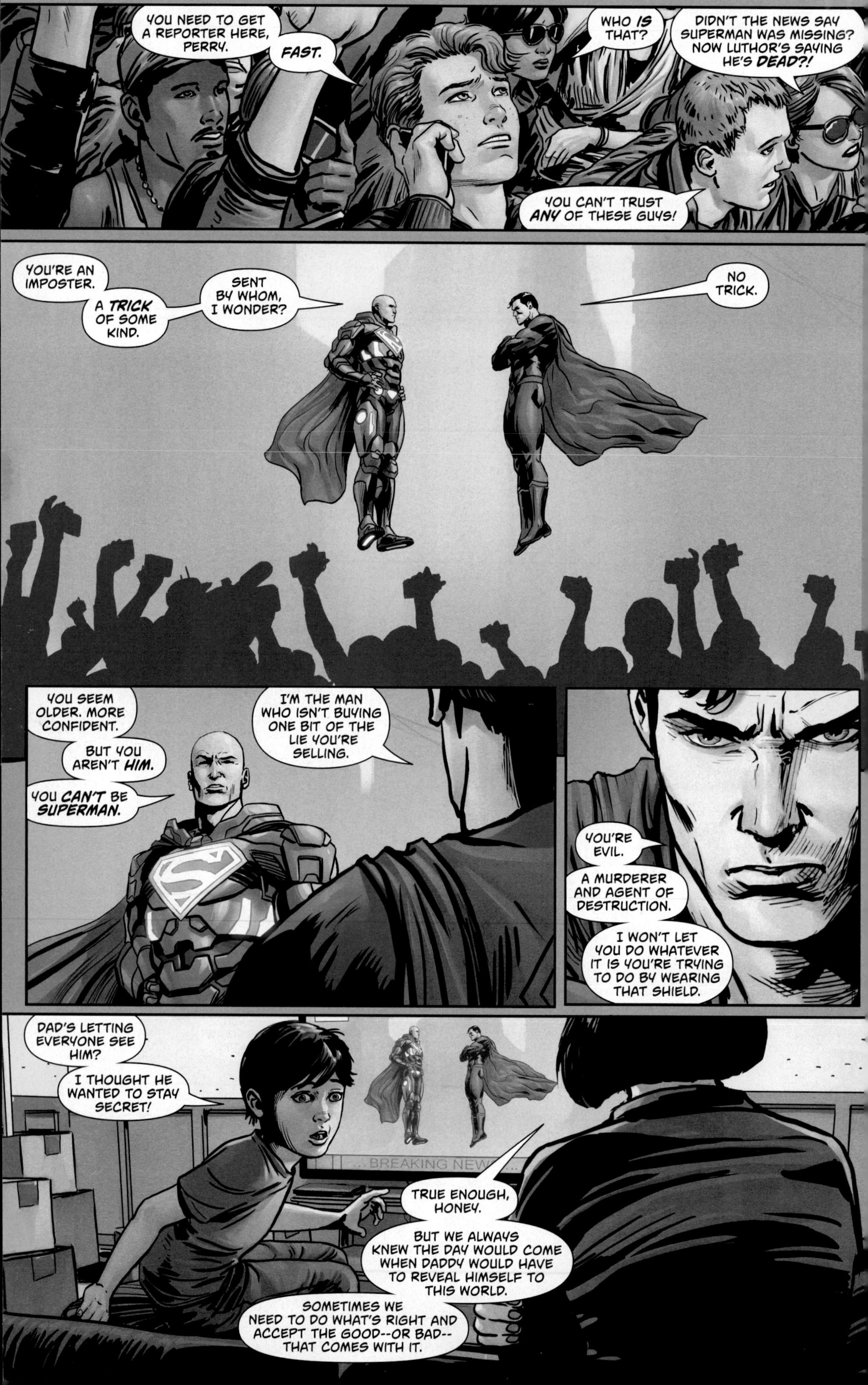

YOU NEED TO GET A REPORTER HERE, PERRY.
FAST.
WHO IS THAT?
DIDN'T THE NEWS SAY SUPERMAN WAS MISSING? NOW LUTHOR'S SAYING HE'S DEAD?!
YOU CAN'T TRUST ANY OF THESE GUYS!
YOU'RE AN IMPOSTER.
A TRICK OF SOME KIND.
SENT BY WHOM, I WONDER?
NO TRICK.
YOU SEEM OLDER. MORE CONFIDENT.
BUT YOU AREN'T HIM.
YOU CAN'T BE SUPERMAN.
I'M THE MAN WHO ISN'T BUYING ONE BIT OF THE LIE YOU'RE SELLING.
YOU'RE EVIL.
A MURDERER AND AGENT OF DESTRUCTION.
I WON'T LET YOU DO WHATEVER IT IS YOU'RE TRYING TO DO BY WEARING THAT SHIELD.
DAD'S LETTING EVERYONE SEE HIM?
I THOUGHT HE WANTED TO STAY SECRET!
...BREAKING NEW...
TRUE ENOUGH, HONEY.
BUT WE ALWAYS KNEW THE DAY WOULD COME WHEN DADDY WOULD HAVE TO REVEAL HIMSELF TO THIS WORLD.
SOMETIMES WE NEED TO DO WHAT'S RIGHT AND ACCEPT THE GOOD--OR BAD--THAT COMES WITH IT.

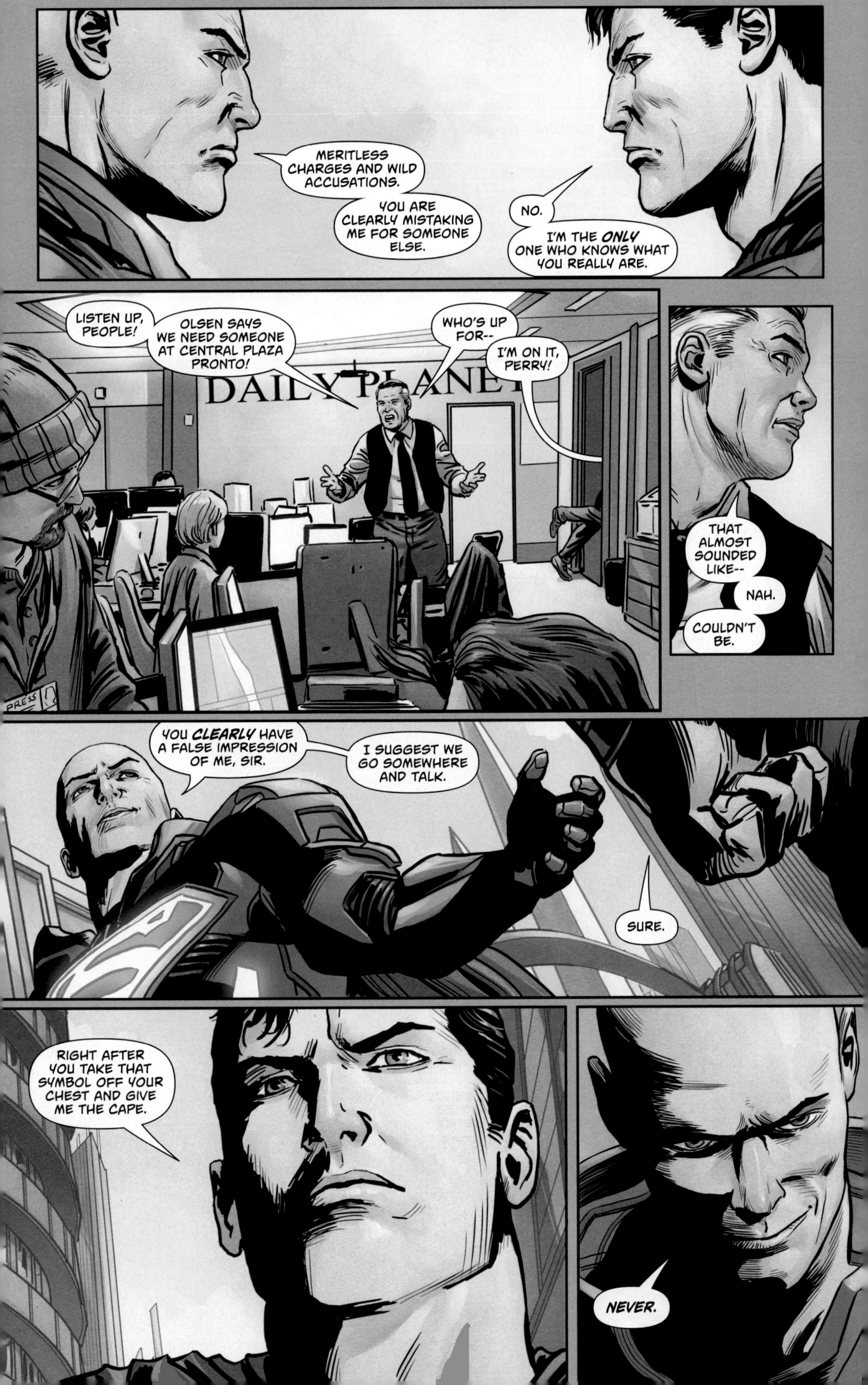
MERITLESS CHARGES AND WILD ACCUSATIONS.
YOU ARE CLEARLY MISTAKING ME FOR SOMEONE ELSE.
NO.
I'M THE *ONLY* ONE WHO KNOWS WHAT YOU REALLY ARE.
LISTEN UP, PEOPLE!
OLSEN SAYS WE NEED SOMEONE AT CENTRAL PLAZA PRONTO!
WHO'S UP FOR--
I'M ON IT, PERRY!
DAILY PLANET
PRESS
THAT ALMOST SOUNDED LIKE--
NAH.
COULDN'T BE.
YOU *CLEARLY* HAVE A FALSE IMPRESSION OF ME, SIR.
I SUGGEST WE GO SOMEWHERE AND TALK.
SURE.
RIGHT AFTER YOU TAKE THAT SYMBOL OFF YOUR CHEST AND GIVE ME THE CAPE.
NEVER.

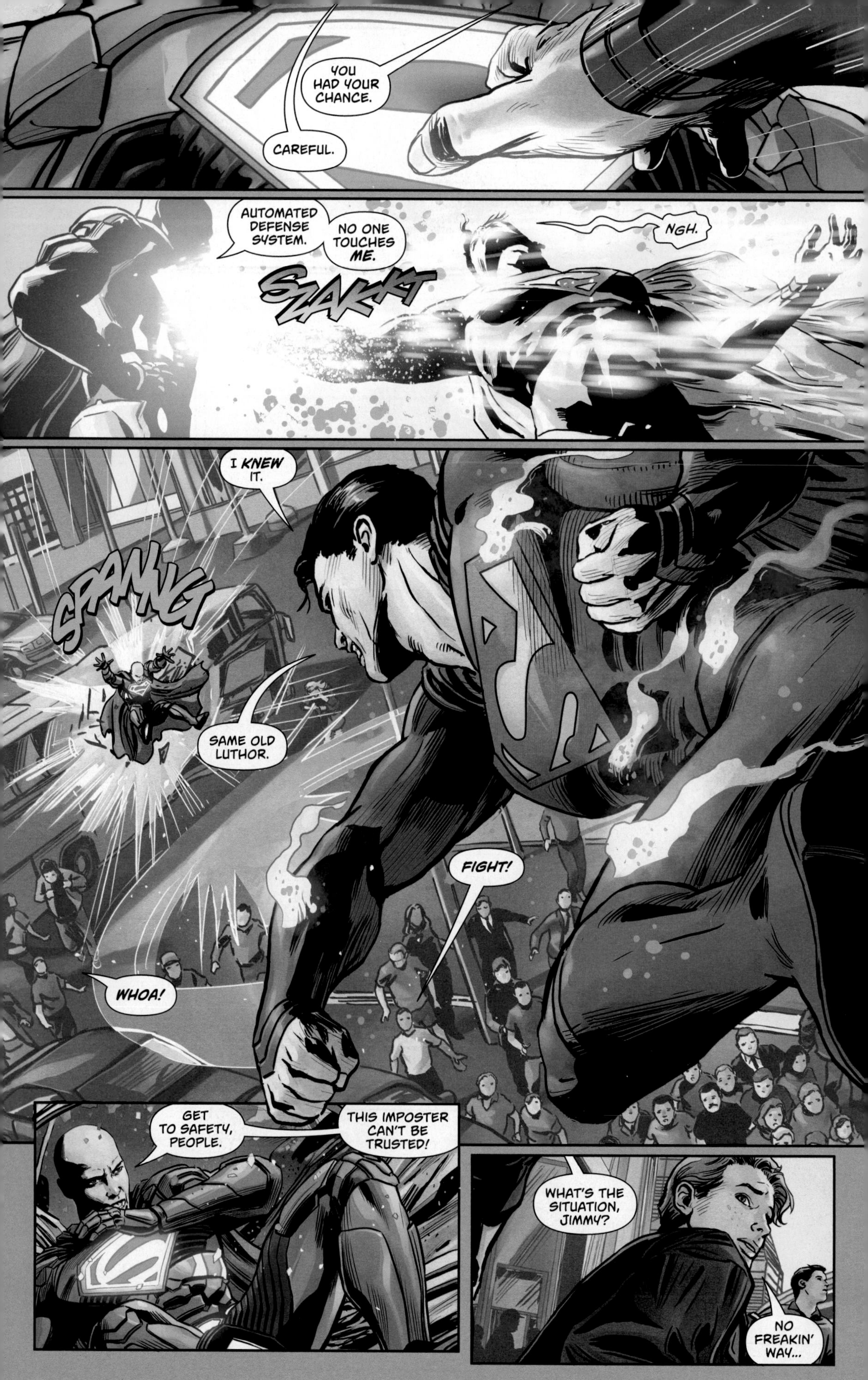
YOU HAD YOUR CHANCE.
CAREFUL.
AUTOMATED DEFENSE SYSTEM.
NO ONE TOUCHES ME.
NGH.
SZAKKT
I KNEW IT.
SPANNG
SAME OLD LUTHOR.
FIGHT!
WHOA!
GET TO SAFETY, PEOPLE.
THIS IMPOSTER CAN'T BE TRUSTED!
WHAT'S THE SITUATION, JIMMY?
NO FREAKIN' WAY...

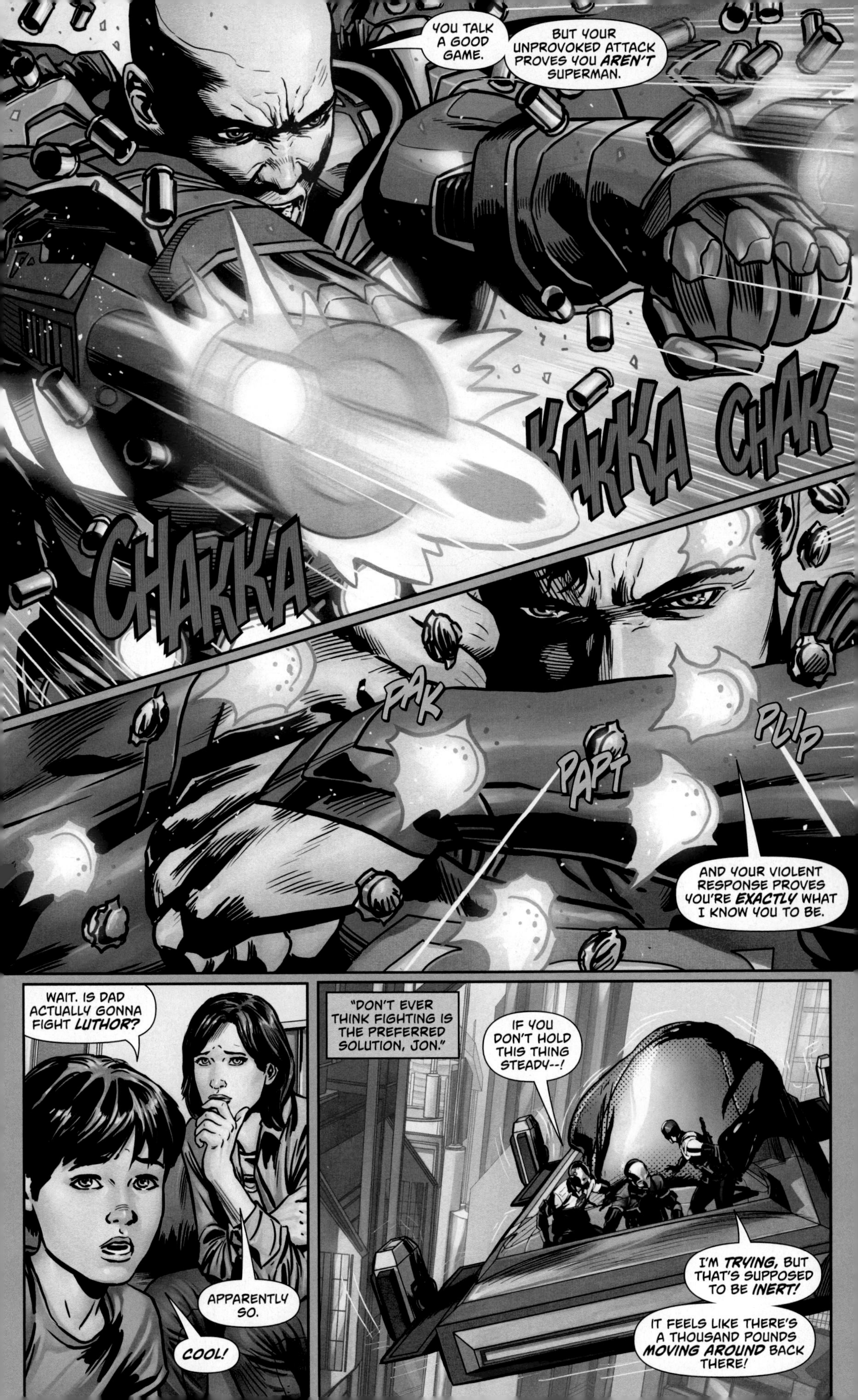
YOU TALK A GOOD GAME.
BUT YOUR UNPROVOKED ATTACK PROVES YOU *AREN'T* SUPERMAN.
KAKKA CHAK
CHAKKA
PAK
PLIP
PAPT
AND YOUR VIOLENT RESPONSE PROVES YOU'RE *EXACTLY* WHAT I KNOW YOU TO BE.
WAIT. IS DAD ACTUALLY GONNA FIGHT *LUTHOR?*
APPARENTLY SO.
COOL!
"DON'T EVER THINK FIGHTING IS THE PREFERRED SOLUTION, JON."
IF YOU DON'T HOLD THIS THING STEADY--!
I'M *TRYING*, BUT THAT'S SUPPOSED TO BE *INERT!*
IT FEELS LIKE THERE'S A THOUSAND POUNDS *MOVING AROUND* BACK THERE!

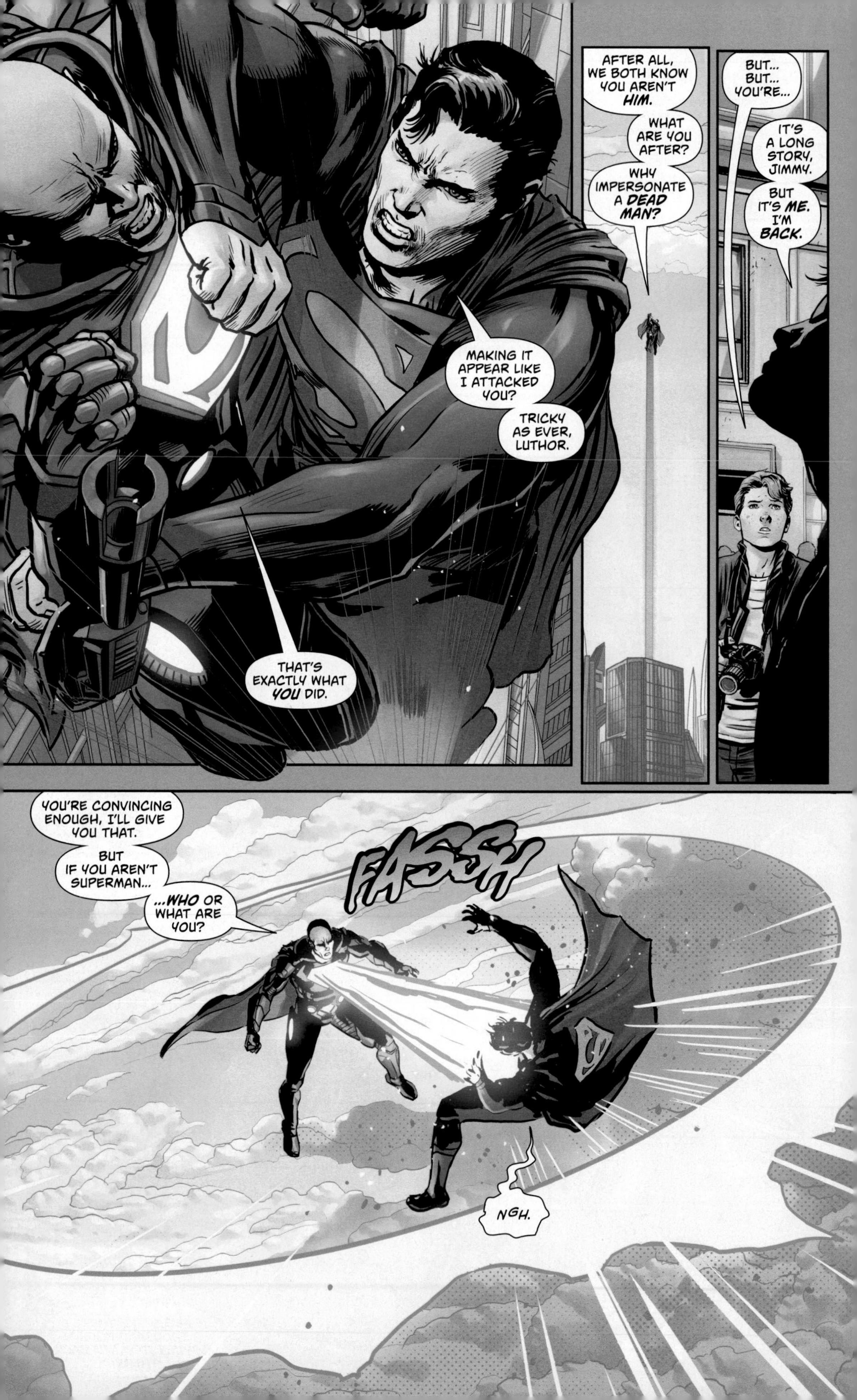
MAKING IT APPEAR LIKE I ATTACKED YOU?
TRICKY AS EVER, LUTHOR.
THAT'S EXACTLY WHAT YOU DID.
AFTER ALL, WE BOTH KNOW YOU AREN'T HIM.
WHAT ARE YOU AFTER?
WHY IMPERSONATE A DEAD MAN?
BUT... BUT... YOU'RE...
IT'S A LONG STORY, JIMMY.
BUT IT'S ME. I'M BACK.
YOU'RE CONVINCING ENOUGH, I'LL GIVE YOU THAT.
BUT IF YOU AREN'T SUPERMAN...
...WHO OR WHAT ARE YOU?
FASSH
NGH.

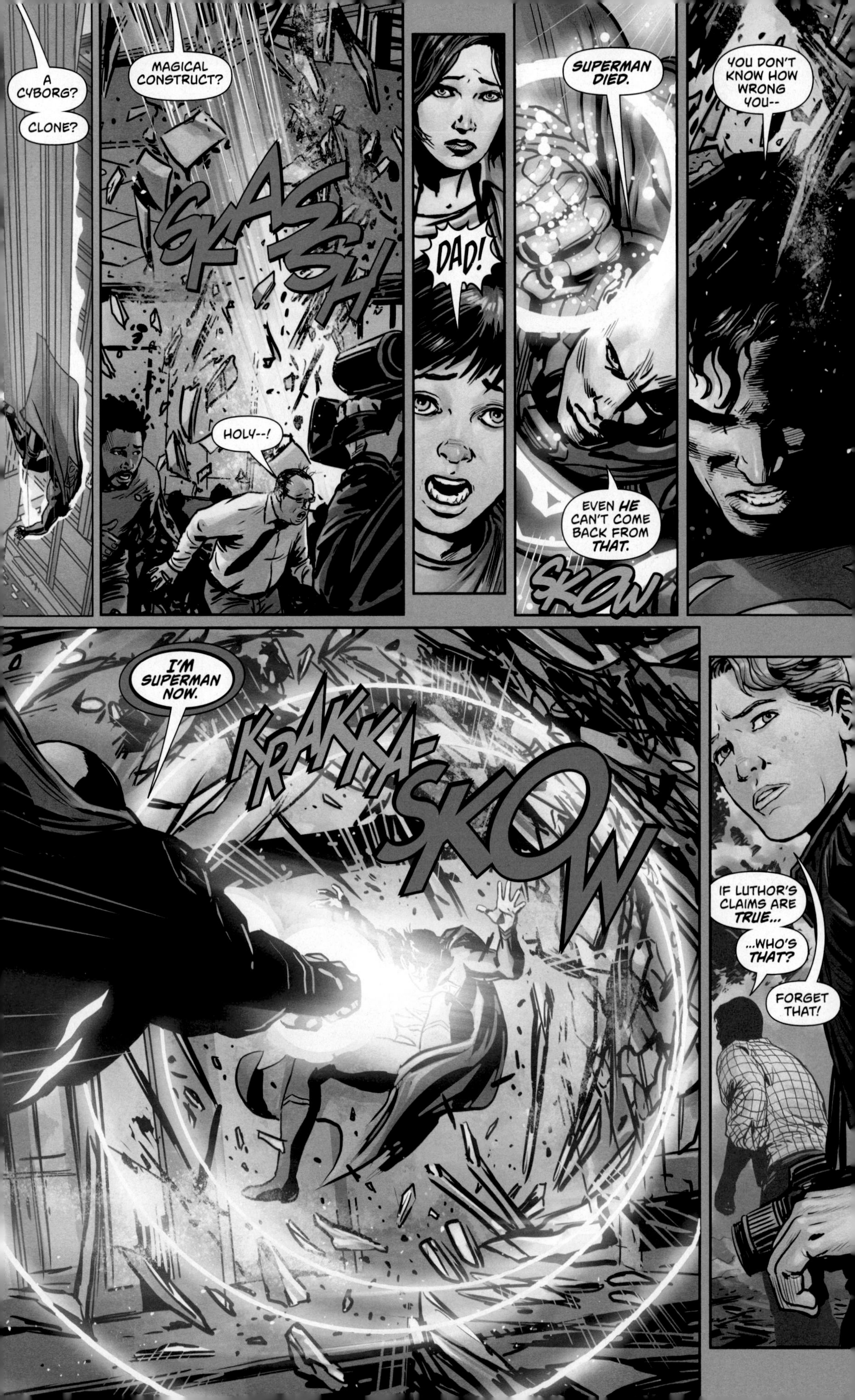
A CYBORG?
CLONE?
MAGICAL CONSTRUCT?
SKASSH
HOLY--!
DAD!
SUPERMAN DIED.
EVEN HE CAN'T COME BACK FROM THAT.
SKOW
YOU DON'T KNOW HOW WRONG YOU--
I'M SUPERMAN NOW.
KRAKKA-SKOW
IF LUTHOR'S CLAIMS ARE TRUE...
...WHO'S THAT?
FORGET THAT!

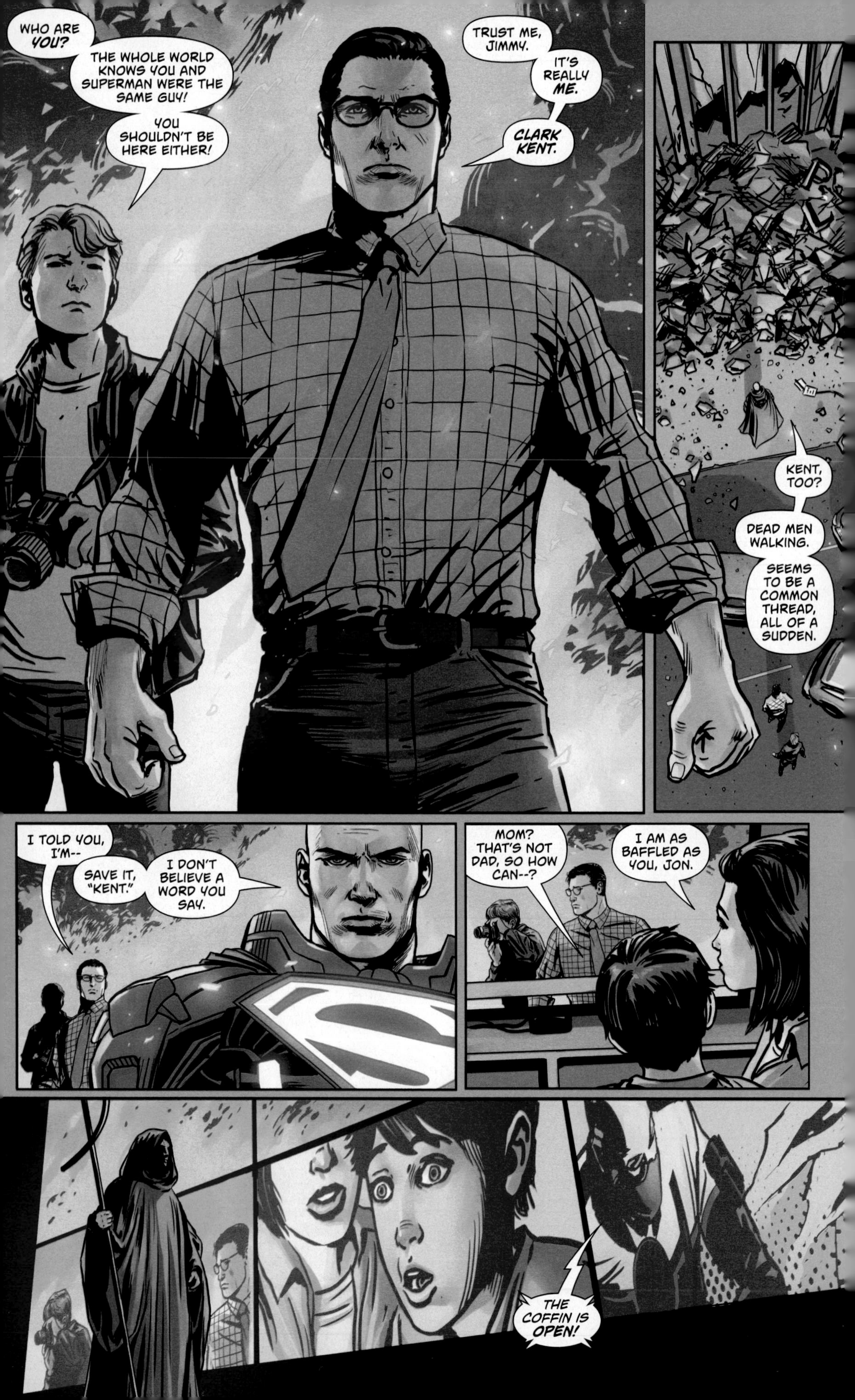
WHO ARE YOU?
THE WHOLE WORLD KNOWS YOU AND SUPERMAN WERE THE SAME GUY!
YOU SHOULDN'T BE HERE EITHER!
TRUST ME, JIMMY.
IT'S REALLY ME.
CLARK KENT.
KENT, TOO?
DEAD MEN WALKING.
SEEMS TO BE A COMMON THREAD, ALL OF A SUDDEN.
I TOLD YOU, I'M--
SAVE IT, "KENT."
I DON'T BELIEVE A WORD YOU SAY.
MOM? THAT'S NOT DAD, SO HOW CAN--?
I AM AS BAFFLED AS YOU, JON.
THE COFFIN IS OPEN!

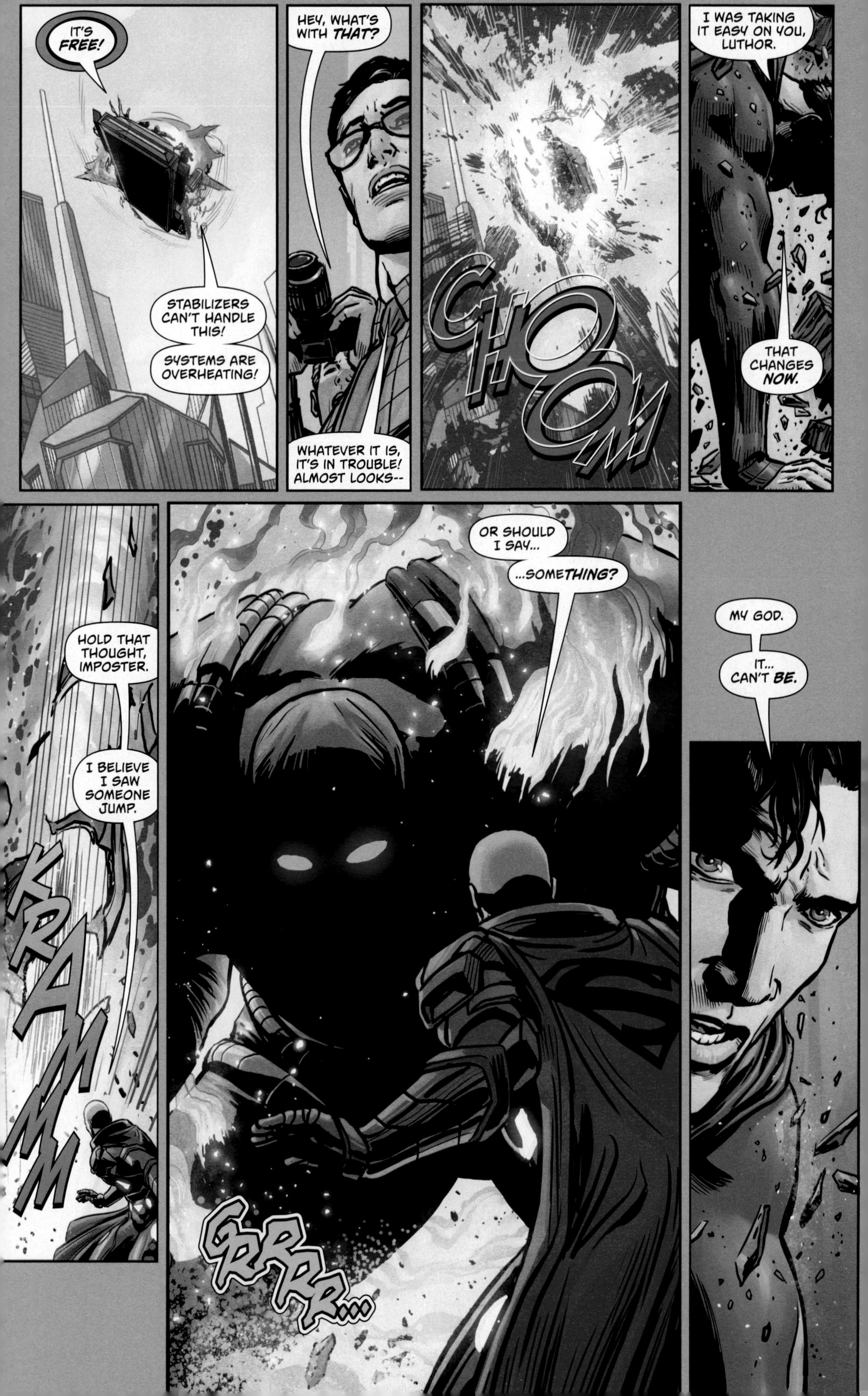
IT'S FREE!
STABILIZERS CAN'T HANDLE THIS!
SYSTEMS ARE OVERHEATING!
HEY, WHAT'S WITH THAT?
WHATEVER IT IS, IT'S IN TROUBLE! ALMOST LOOKS--
CHOOM
I WAS TAKING IT EASY ON YOU, LUTHOR.
THAT CHANGES NOW.
HOLD THAT THOUGHT, IMPOSTER.
I BELIEVE I SAW SOMEONE JUMP.
KRAMMM
OR SHOULD I SAY...
...SOMETHING?
GRRRR...
MY GOD.
IT... CAN'T BE.

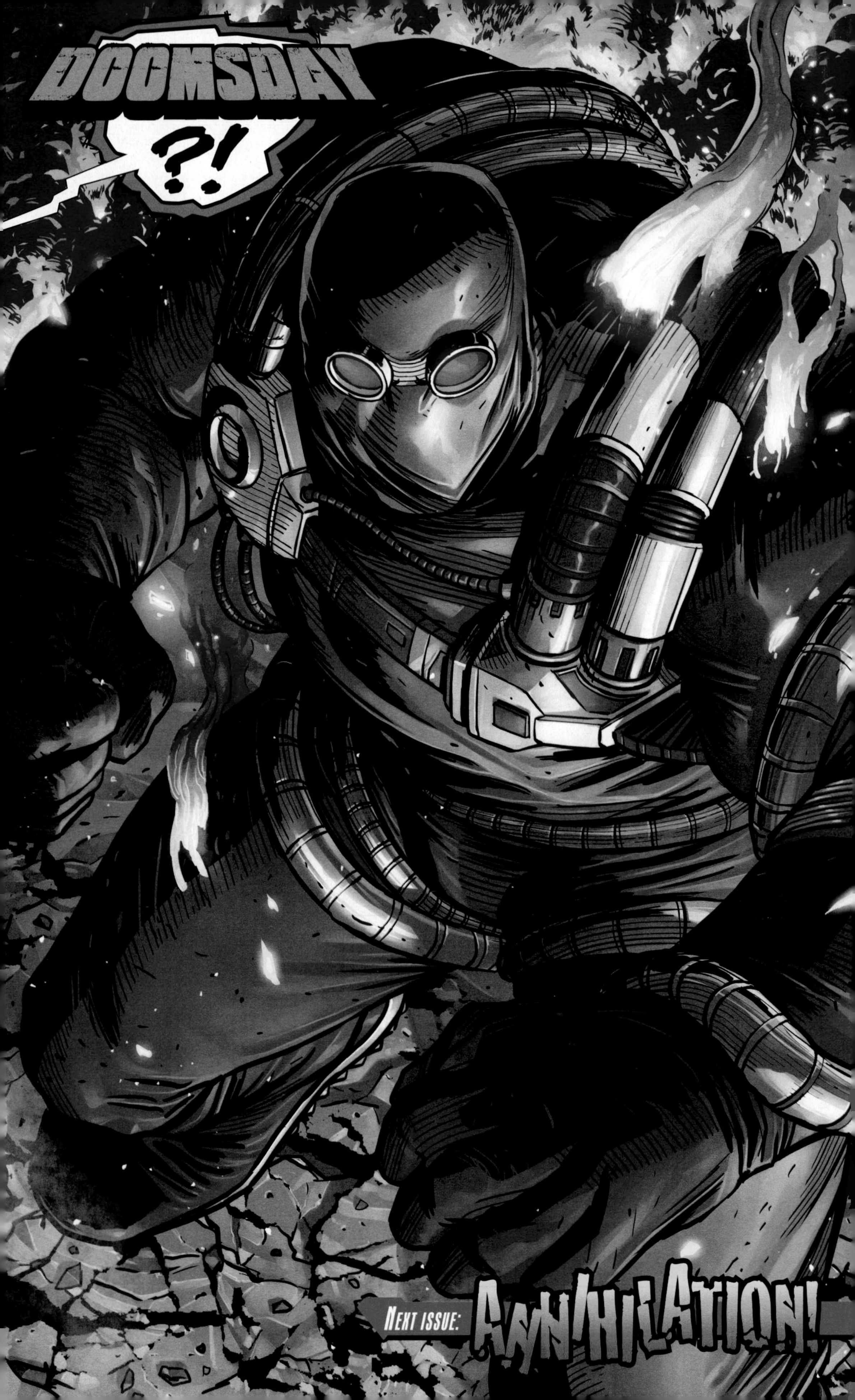
DOOMSDAY
?!
NEXT ISSUE: ANNIHILATION!

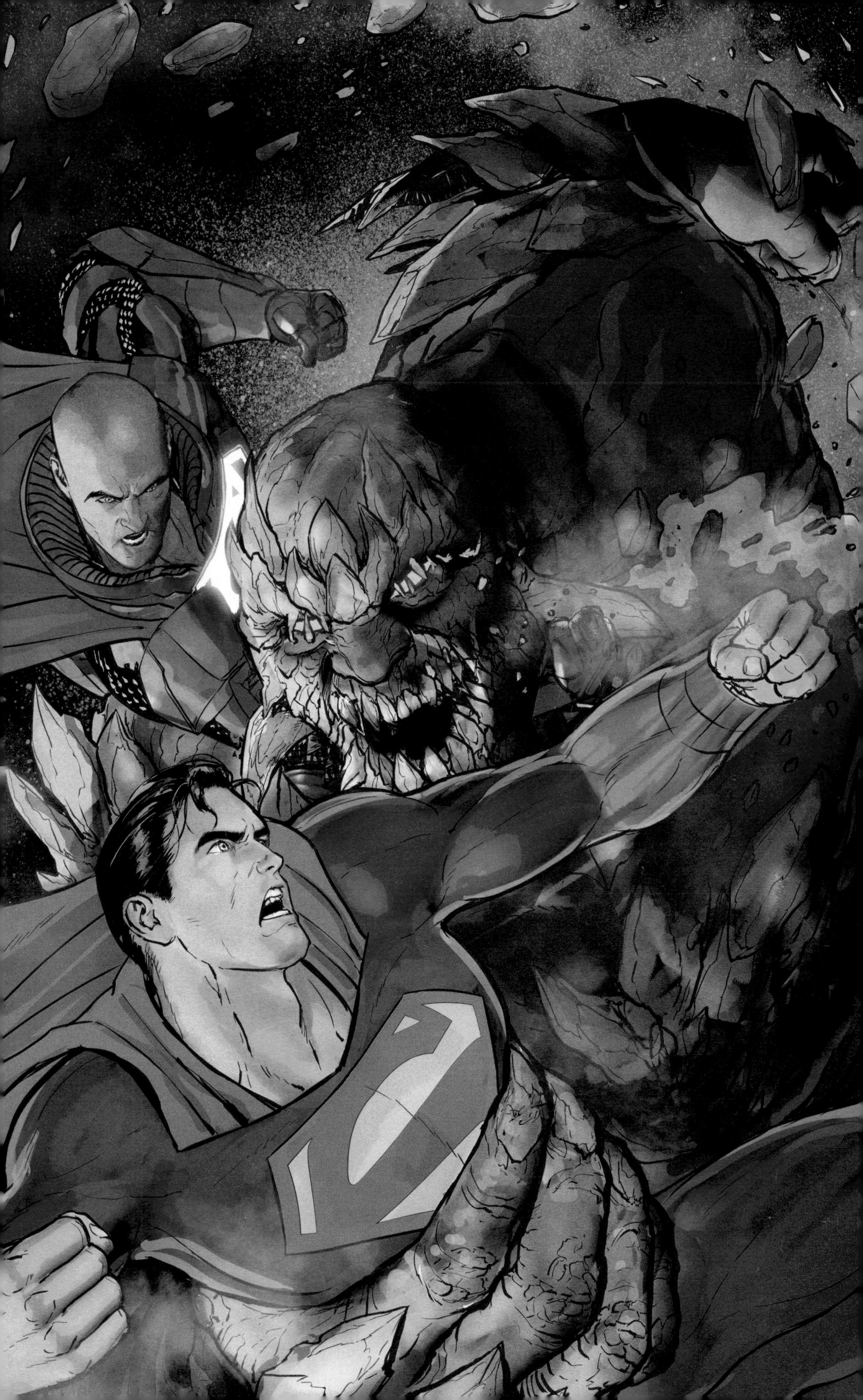

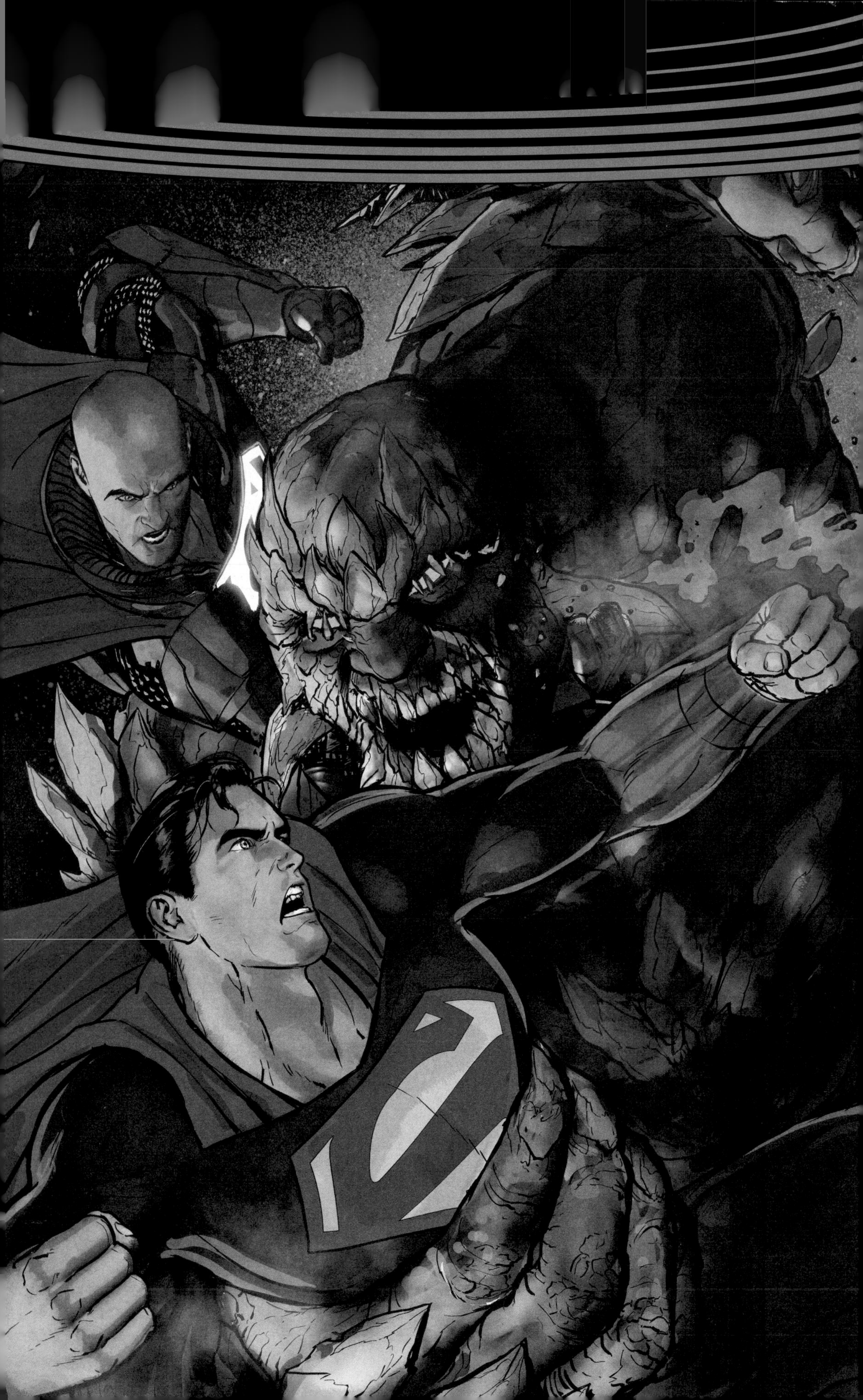

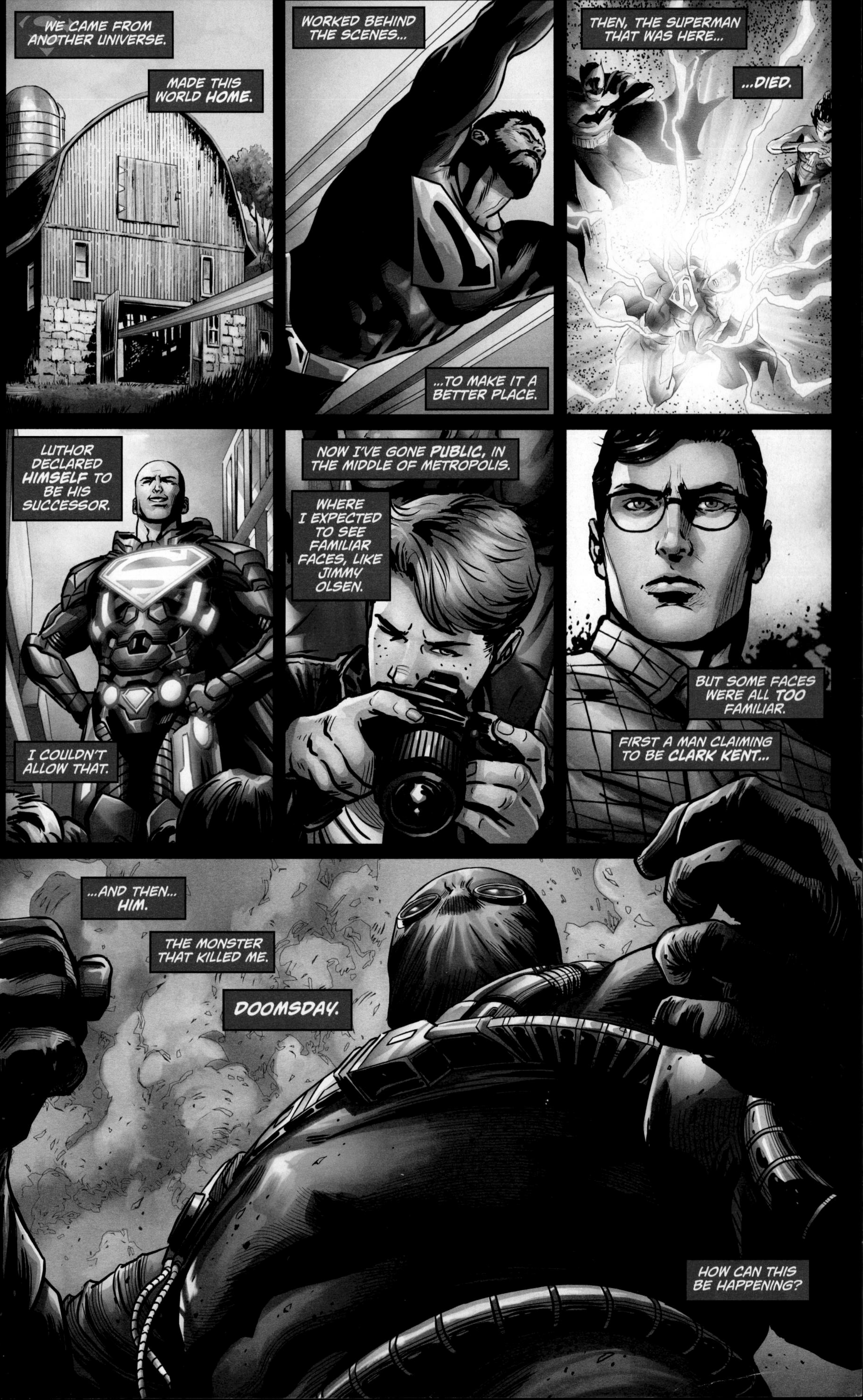
WE CAME FROM ANOTHER UNIVERSE.
MADE THIS WORLD HOME.
WORKED BEHIND THE SCENES...
...TO MAKE IT A BETTER PLACE.
THEN, THE SUPERMAN THAT WAS HERE...
...DIED.
LUTHOR DECLARED HIMSELF TO BE HIS SUCCESSOR.
I COULDN'T ALLOW THAT.
NOW I'VE GONE PUBLIC, IN THE MIDDLE OF METROPOLIS.
WHERE I EXPECTED TO SEE FAMILIAR FACES, LIKE JIMMY OLSEN.
BUT SOME FACES WERE ALL TOO FAMILIAR.
FIRST A MAN CLAIMING TO BE CLARK KENT...
...AND THEN... HIM.
THE MONSTER THAT KILLED ME.
DOOMSDAY.
HOW CAN THIS BE HAPPENING?

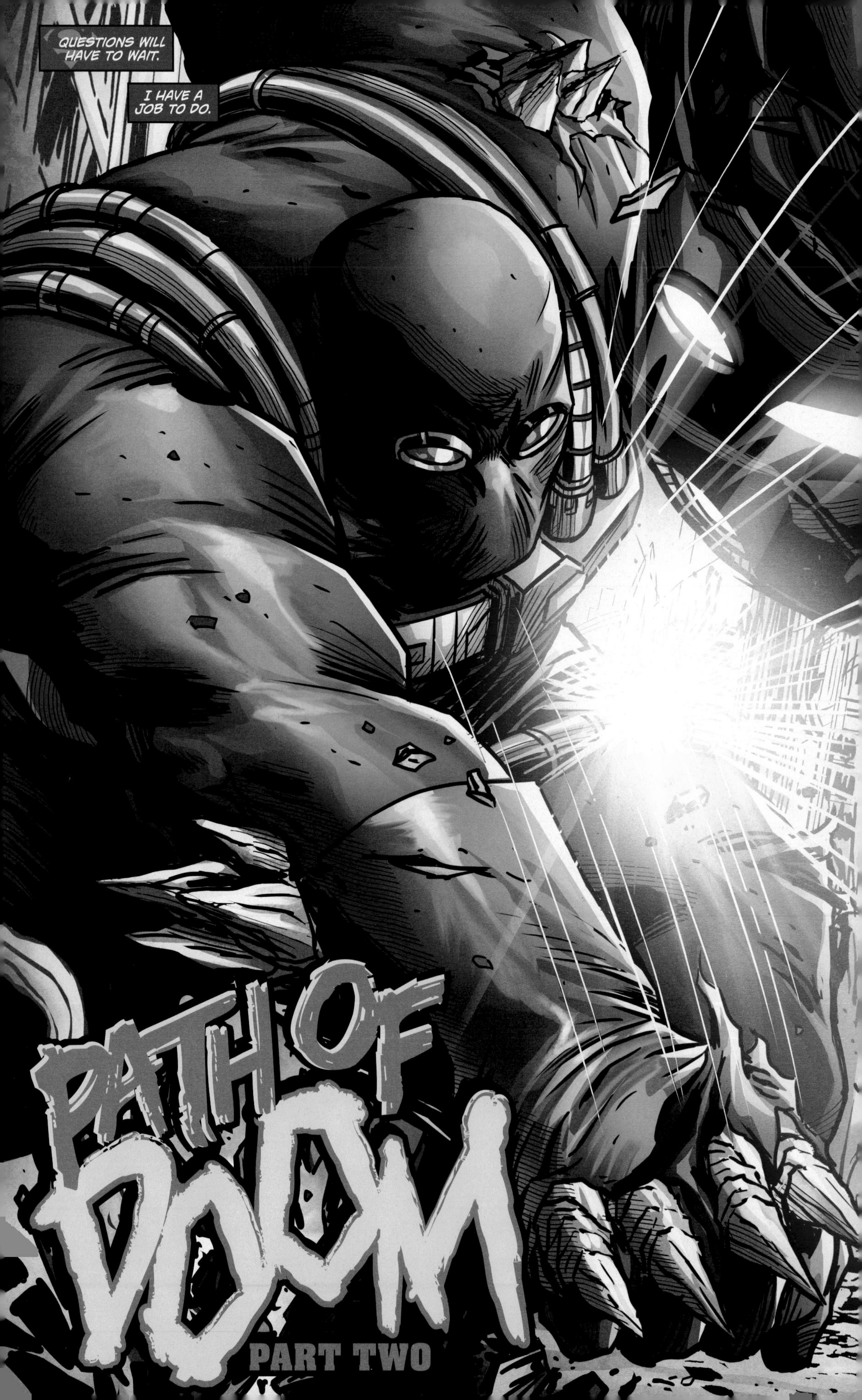
QUESTIONS WILL HAVE TO WAIT.
I HAVE A JOB TO DO.
PATH OF DOOM
PART TWO

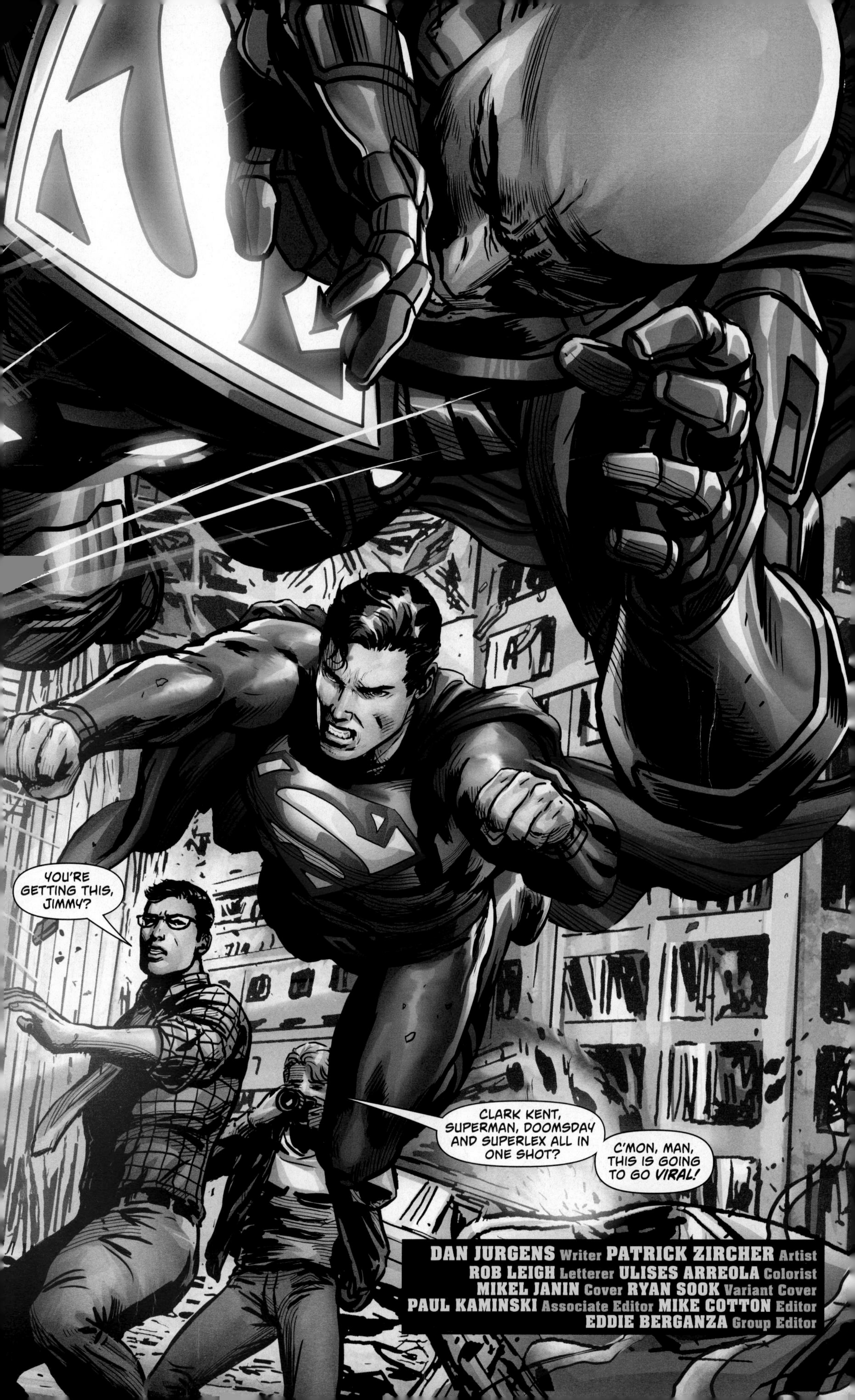
YOU'RE GETTING THIS, JIMMY?
CLARK KENT, SUPERMAN, DOOMSDAY AND SUPERLEX ALL IN ONE SHOT?
C'MON, MAN, THIS IS GOING TO GO VIRAL!
DAN JURGENS Writer PATRICK ZIRCHER Artist
ROB LEIGH Letterer ULISES ARREOLA Colorist
MIKEL JANIN Cover RYAN SOOK Variant Cover
PAUL KAMINSKI Associate Editor MIKE COTTON Editor
EDDIE BERGANZA Group Editor

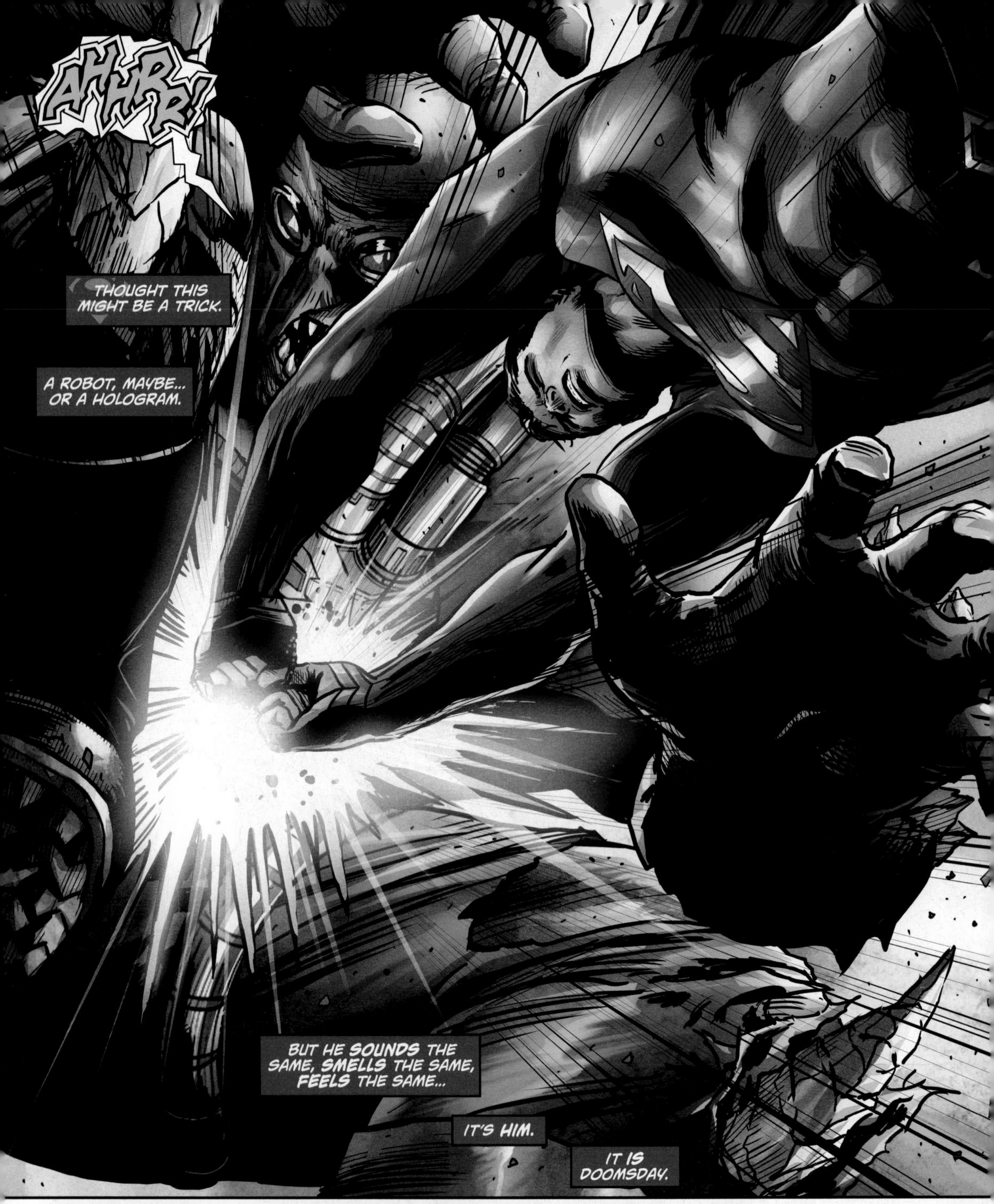
AHHRR!
THOUGHT THIS MIGHT BE A TRICK.
A ROBOT, MAYBE... OR A HOLOGRAM.
BUT HE **SOUNDS** THE SAME, **SMELLS** THE SAME, **FEELS** THE SAME...
IT'S **HIM.**
IT **IS** DOOMSDAY.

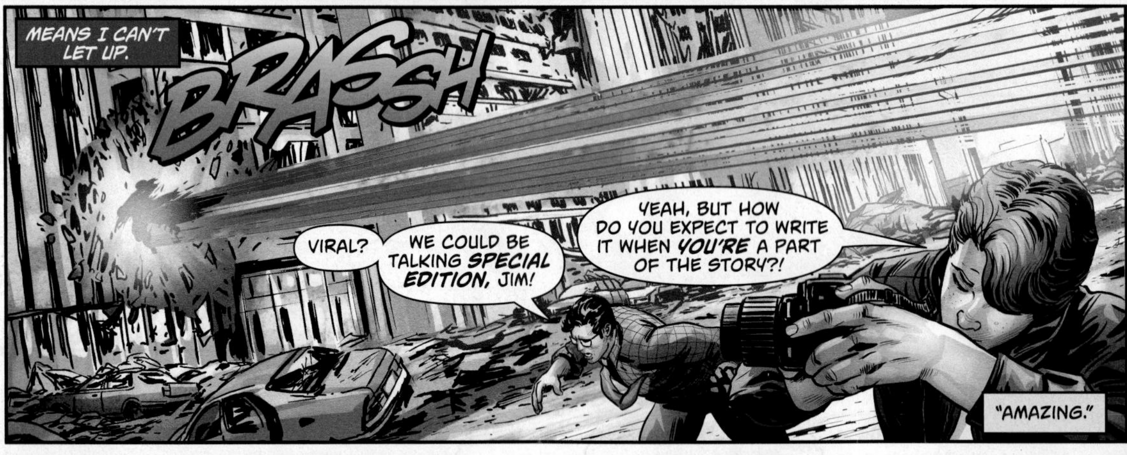
MEANS I CAN'T LET UP.
BRASSH
VIRAL?
WE COULD BE TALKING ***SPECIAL EDITION,*** JIM!
YEAH, BUT HOW DO YOU EXPECT TO WRITE IT WHEN ***YOU'RE*** A PART OF THE STORY?!
"AMAZING."

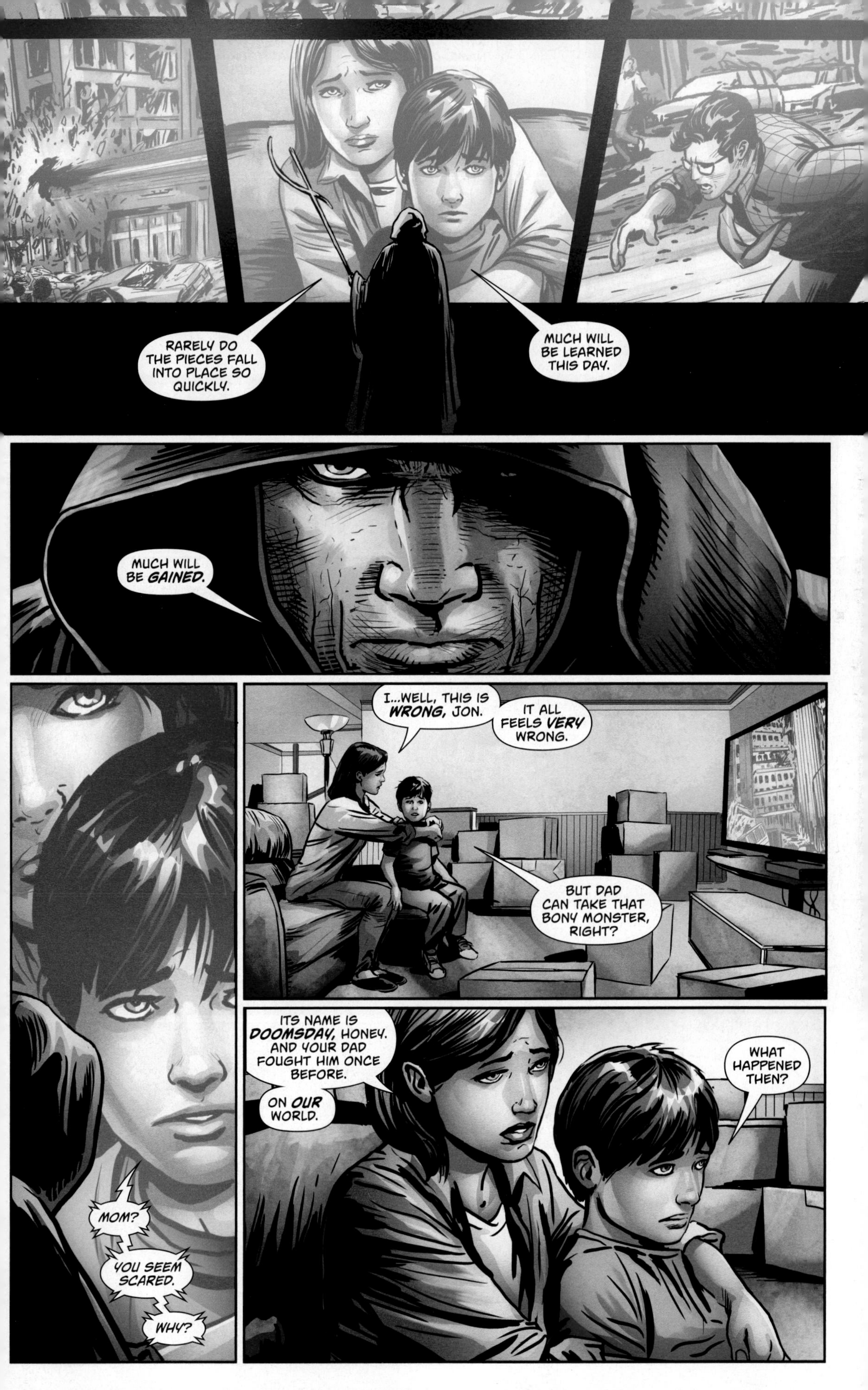
RARELY DO THE PIECES FALL INTO PLACE SO QUICKLY.
MUCH WILL BE LEARNED THIS DAY.
MUCH WILL BE *GAINED.*
MOM?
YOU SEEM SCARED.
WHY?
I...WELL, THIS IS *WRONG,* JON.
IT ALL FEELS *VERY* WRONG.
BUT DAD CAN TAKE THAT BONY MONSTER, RIGHT?
ITS NAME IS *DOOMSDAY,* HONEY. AND YOUR DAD FOUGHT HIM ONCE BEFORE.
ON *OUR* WORLD.
WHAT HAPPENED THEN?

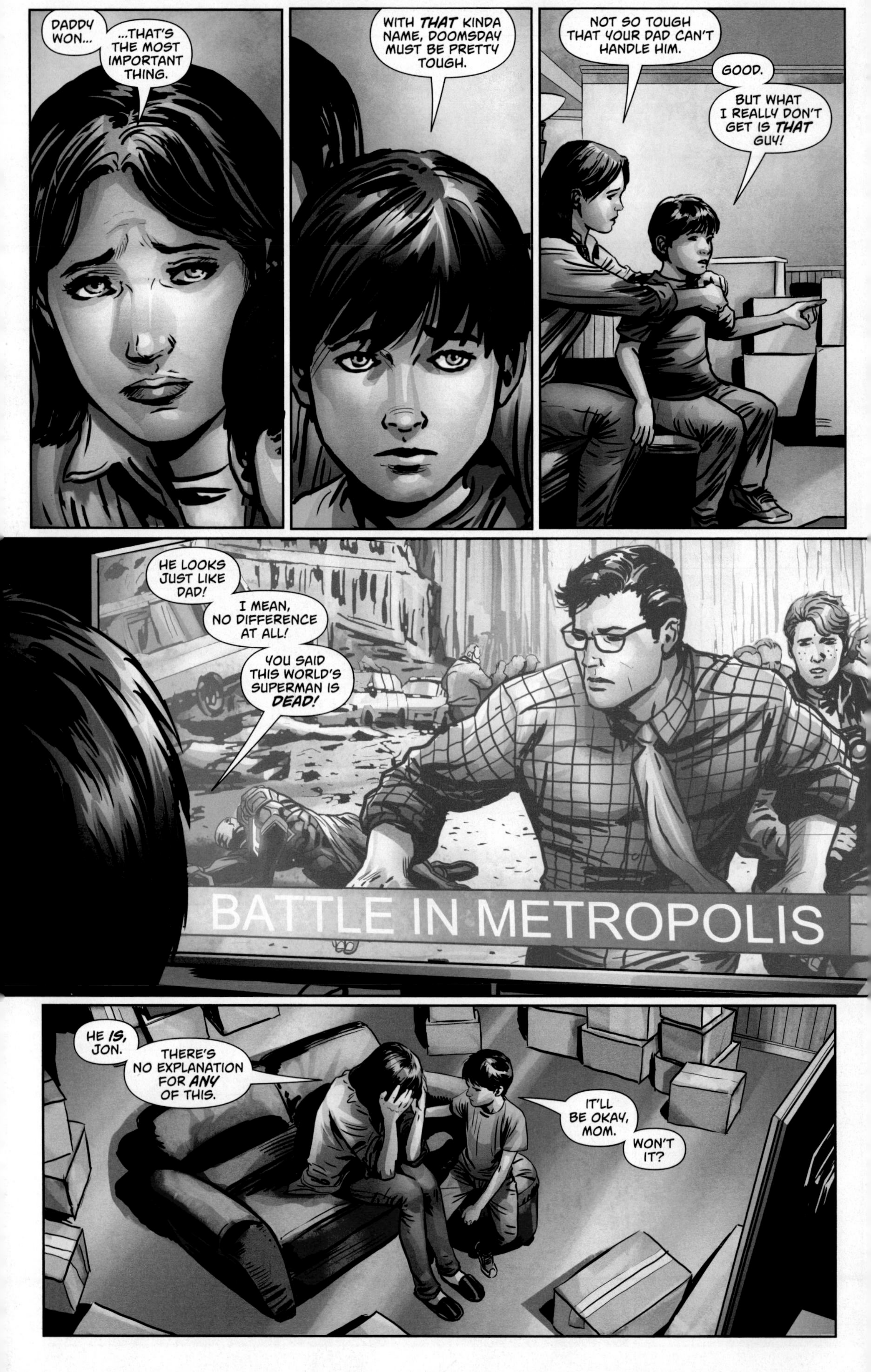
DADDY WON...
...THAT'S THE MOST IMPORTANT THING.
WITH THAT KINDA NAME, DOOMSDAY MUST BE PRETTY TOUGH.
NOT SO TOUGH THAT YOUR DAD CAN'T HANDLE HIM.
GOOD.
BUT WHAT I REALLY DON'T GET IS THAT GUY!
HE LOOKS JUST LIKE DAD!
I MEAN, NO DIFFERENCE AT ALL!
YOU SAID THIS WORLD'S SUPERMAN IS DEAD!
BATTLE IN METROPOLIS
HE IS, JON.
THERE'S NO EXPLANATION FOR ANY OF THIS.
IT'LL BE OKAY, MOM.
WON'T IT?

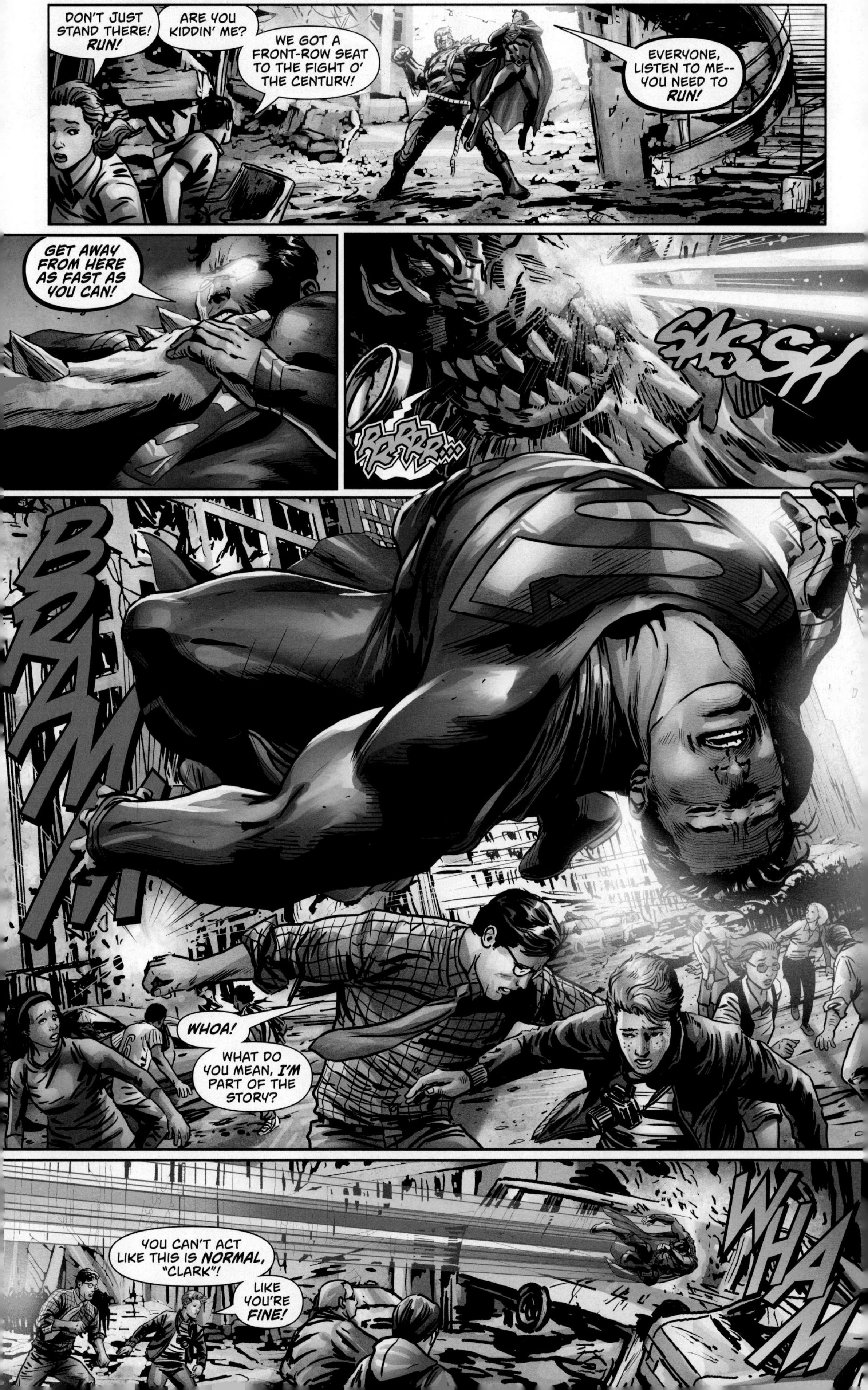
DON'T JUST STAND THERE! RUN!
ARE YOU KIDDIN' ME?
WE GOT A FRONT-ROW SEAT TO THE FIGHT O' THE CENTURY!
EVERYONE, LISTEN TO ME-- YOU NEED TO RUN!
GET AWAY FROM HERE AS FAST AS YOU CAN!
BRAM
WHOA!
WHAT DO YOU MEAN, I'M PART OF THE STORY?
YOU CAN'T ACT LIKE THIS IS NORMAL, "CLARK"!
LIKE YOU'RE FINE!
WHAM

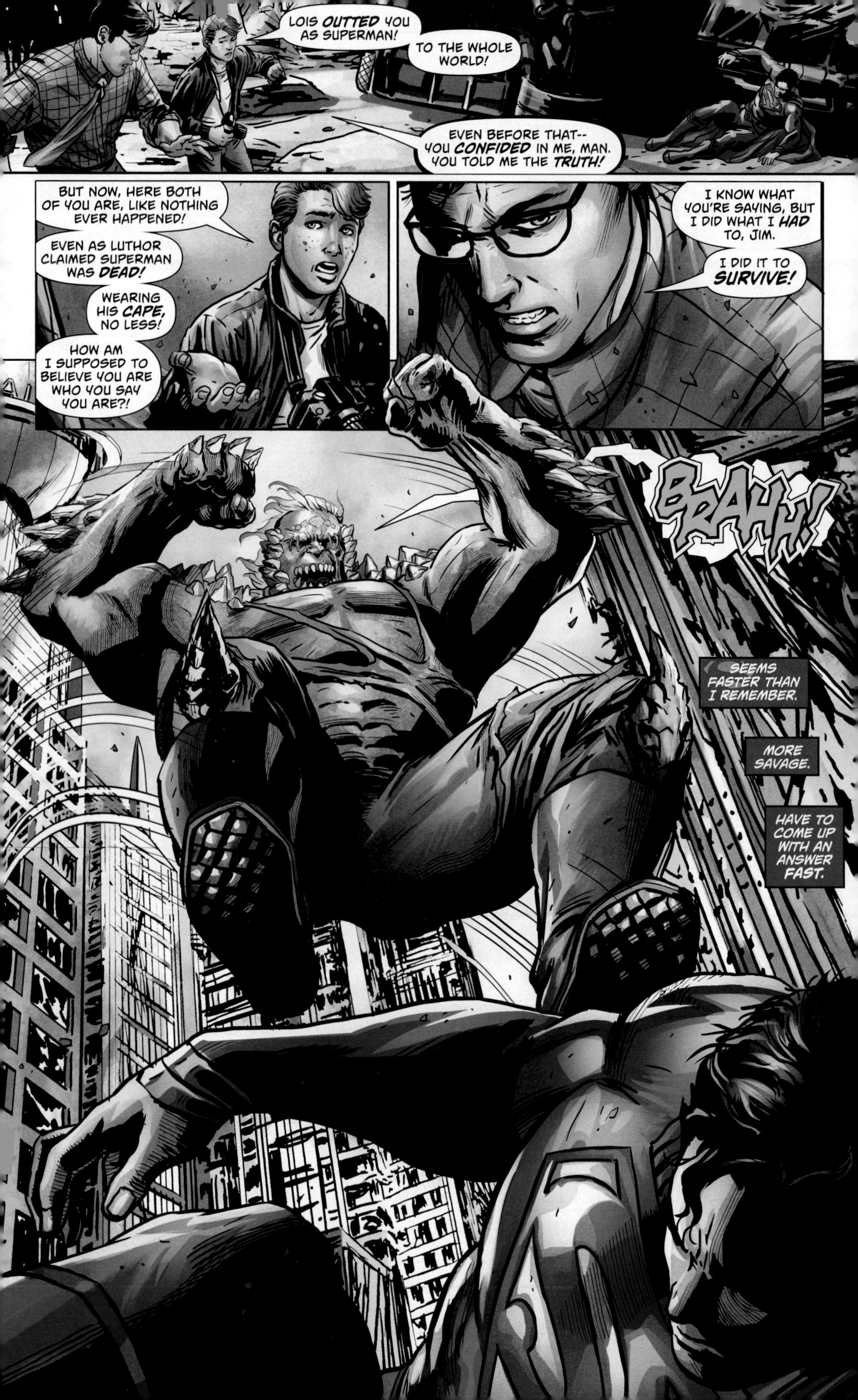
LOIS OUTTED YOU AS SUPERMAN!
TO THE WHOLE WORLD!
EVEN BEFORE THAT-- YOU CONFIDED IN ME, MAN. YOU TOLD ME THE TRUTH!
BUT NOW, HERE BOTH OF YOU ARE, LIKE NOTHING EVER HAPPENED!
EVEN AS LUTHOR CLAIMED SUPERMAN WAS DEAD!
WEARING HIS CAPE, NO LESS!
HOW AM I SUPPOSED TO BELIEVE YOU ARE WHO YOU SAY YOU ARE?!
I KNOW WHAT YOU'RE SAYING, BUT I DID WHAT I HAD TO, JIM.
I DID IT TO SURVIVE!
BRAHH!
SEEMS FASTER THAN I REMEMBER.
MORE SAVAGE.
HAVE TO COME UP WITH AN ANSWER FAST.

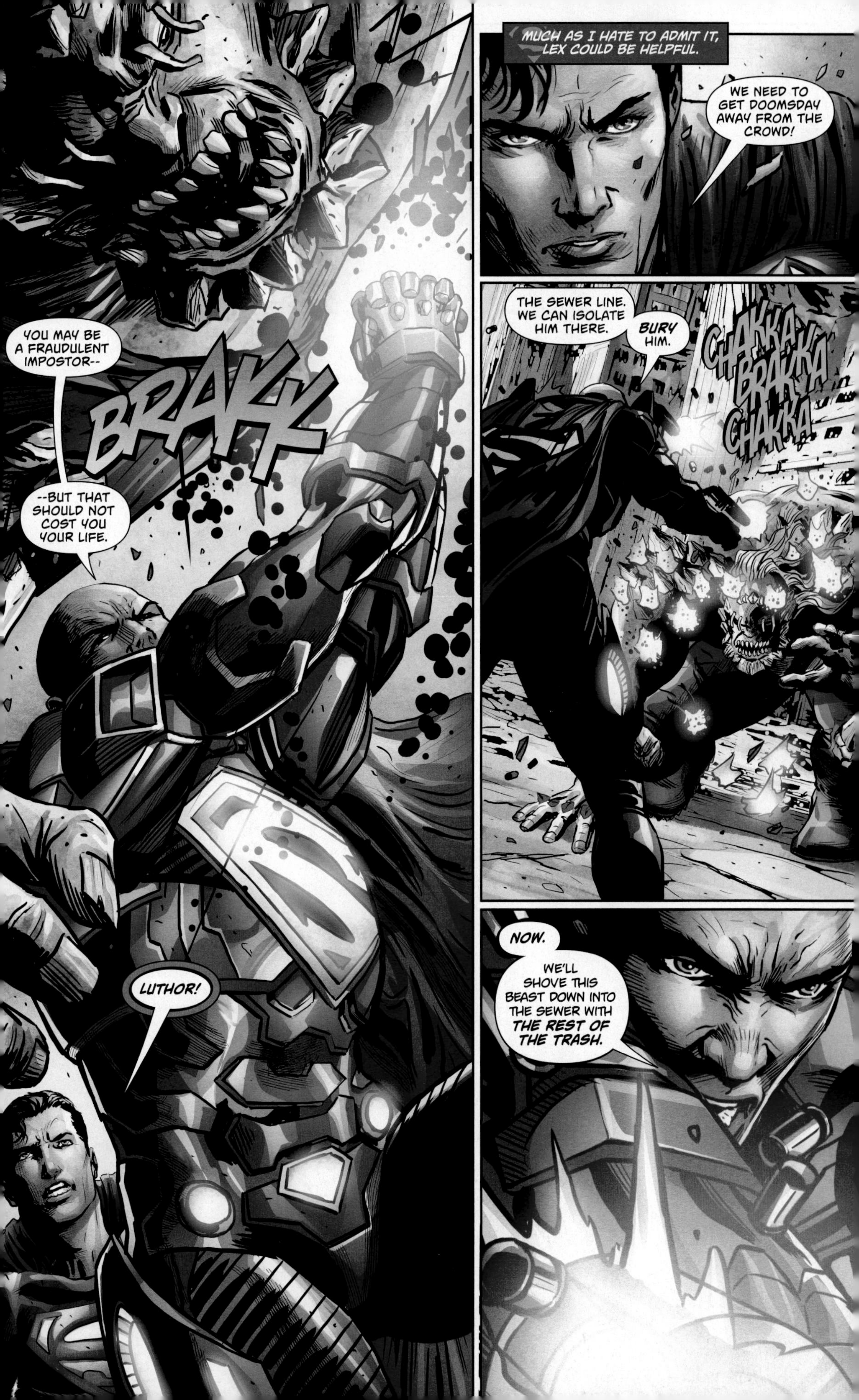
YOU MAY BE A FRAUDULENT IMPOSTOR--
BRAKK
--BUT THAT SHOULD NOT COST YOU YOUR LIFE.
LUTHOR!
MUCH AS I HATE TO ADMIT IT, LEX COULD BE HELPFUL.
WE NEED TO GET DOOMSDAY AWAY FROM THE CROWD!
THE SEWER LINE. WE CAN ISOLATE HIM THERE.
BURY HIM.
CHAKKA BRAKKA CHAKKA
NOW.
WE'LL SHOVE THIS BEAST DOWN INTO THE SEWER WITH THE REST OF THE TRASH.

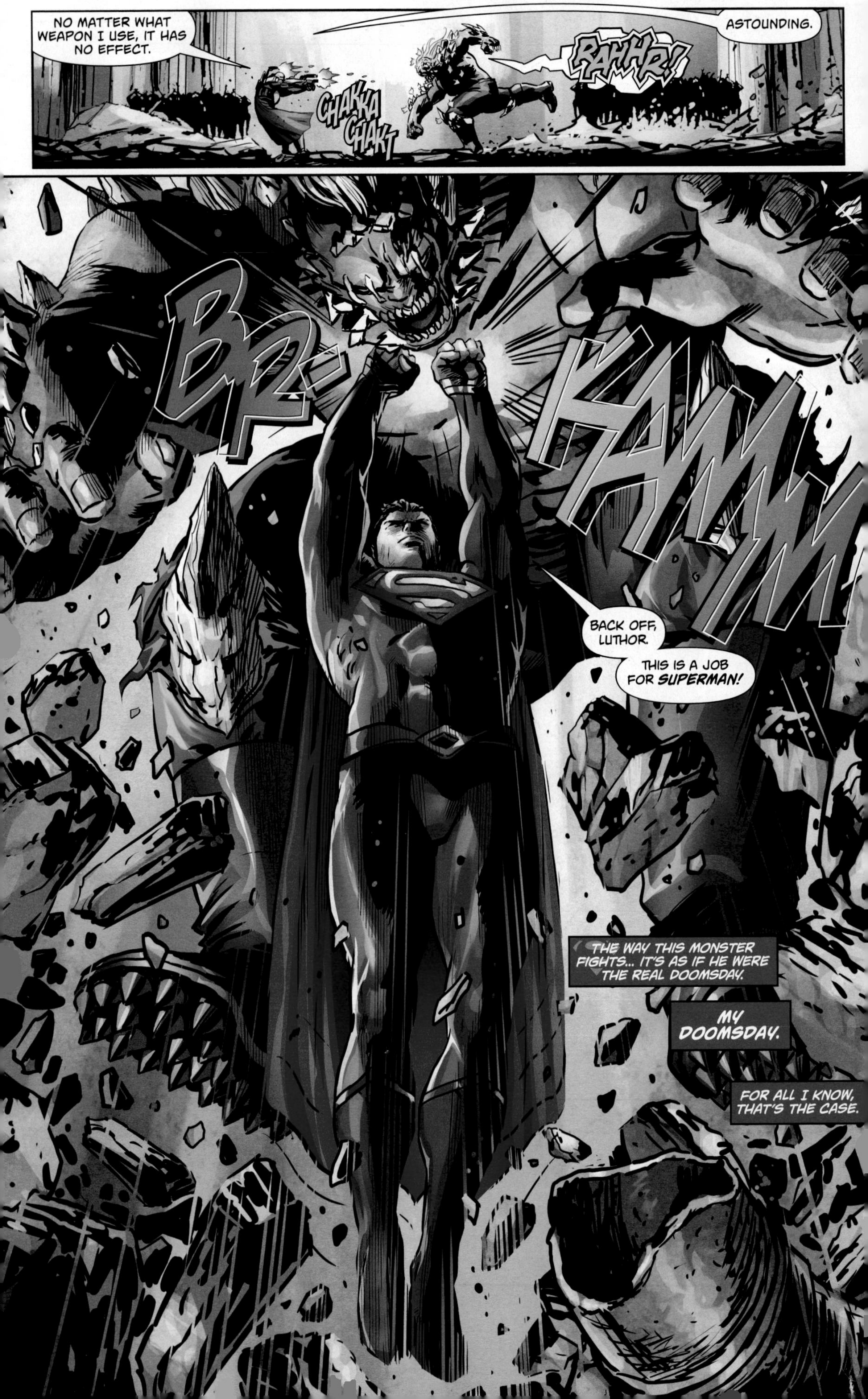
NO MATTER WHAT WEAPON I USE, IT HAS NO EFFECT.
ASTOUNDING.
CHAKKA CHAKT
RAHHR!
BA-KAMM
BACK OFF, LUTHOR.
THIS IS A JOB FOR SUPERMAN!
THE WAY THIS MONSTER FIGHTS... IT'S AS IF HE WERE THE REAL DOOMSDAY.
MY DOOMSDAY.
FOR ALL I KNOW, THAT'S THE CASE.

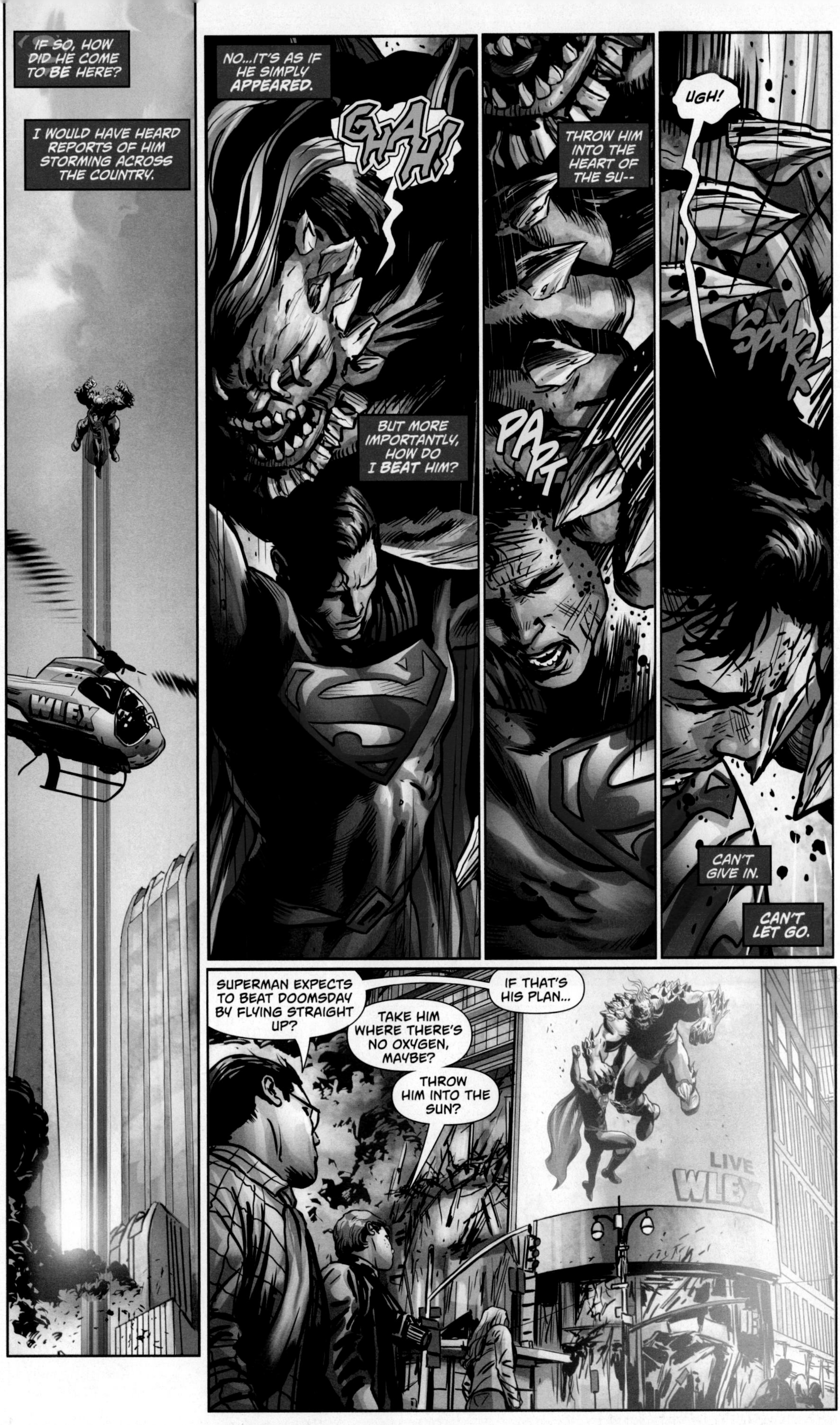
IF SO, HOW DID HE COME TO BE HERE?
I WOULD HAVE HEARD REPORTS OF HIM STORMING ACROSS THE COUNTRY.
WLEX
NO...IT'S AS IF HE SIMPLY APPEARED.
GWAH!
BUT MORE IMPORTANTLY, HOW DO I BEAT HIM?
THROW HIM INTO THE HEART OF THE SU--
PAPT
UGH!
SPAK
CAN'T GIVE IN.
CAN'T LET GO.
SUPERMAN EXPECTS TO BEAT DOOMSDAY BY FLYING STRAIGHT UP?
IF THAT'S HIS PLAN...
TAKE HIM WHERE THERE'S NO OXYGEN, MAYBE?
THROW HIM INTO THE SUN?
LIVE
WLEX

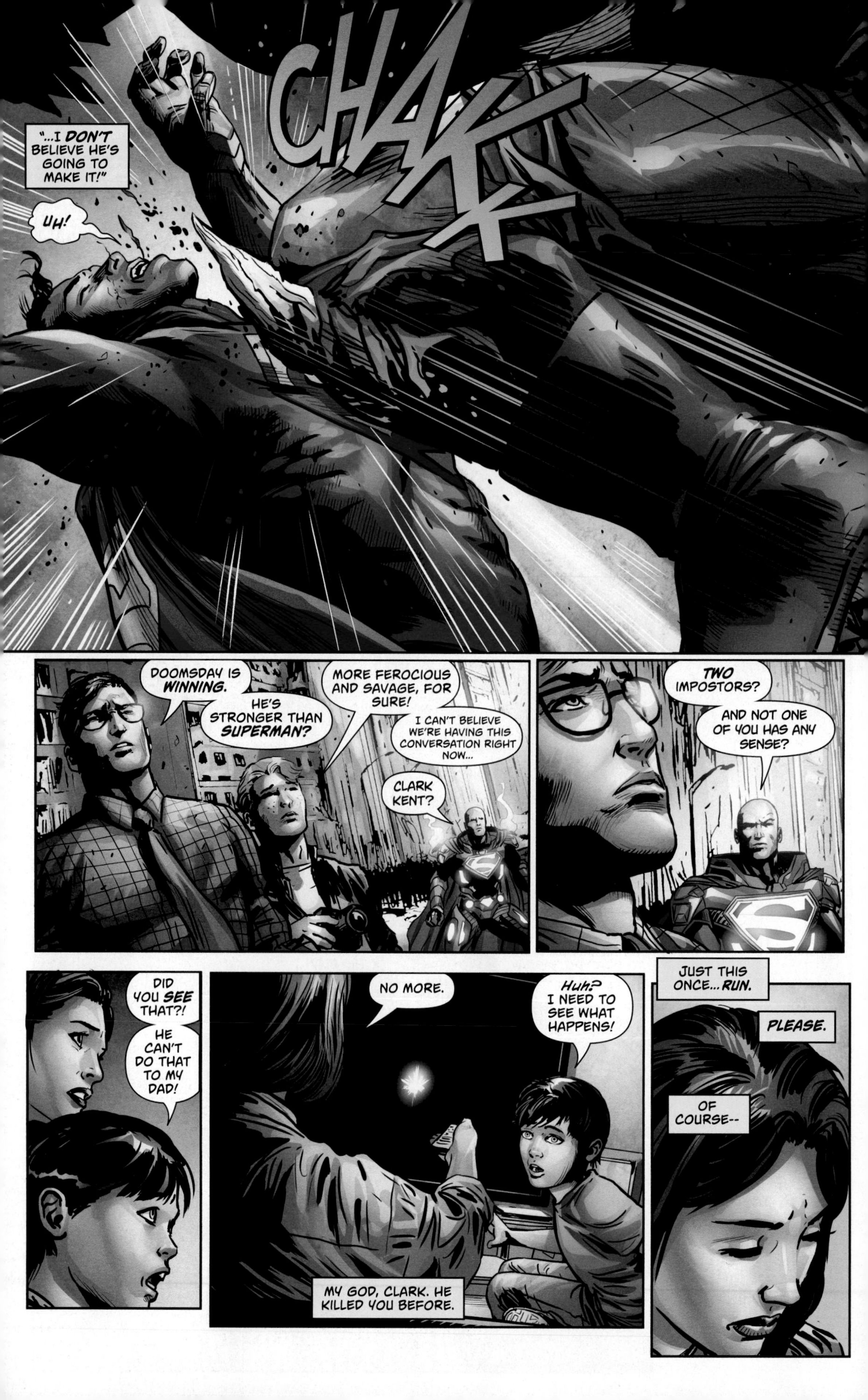
CHAKK
"...I DON'T BELIEVE HE'S GOING TO MAKE IT!"
UH!
DOOMSDAY IS WINNING.
HE'S STRONGER THAN SUPERMAN?
MORE FEROCIOUS AND SAVAGE, FOR SURE!
I CAN'T BELIEVE WE'RE HAVING THIS CONVERSATION RIGHT NOW...
CLARK KENT?
TWO IMPOSTORS?
AND NOT ONE OF YOU HAS ANY SENSE?
DID YOU SEE THAT?!
HE CAN'T DO THAT TO MY DAD!
NO MORE.
Huh? I NEED TO SEE WHAT HAPPENS!
MY GOD, CLARK. HE KILLED YOU BEFORE.
JUST THIS ONCE... RUN.
PLEASE.
OF COURSE--

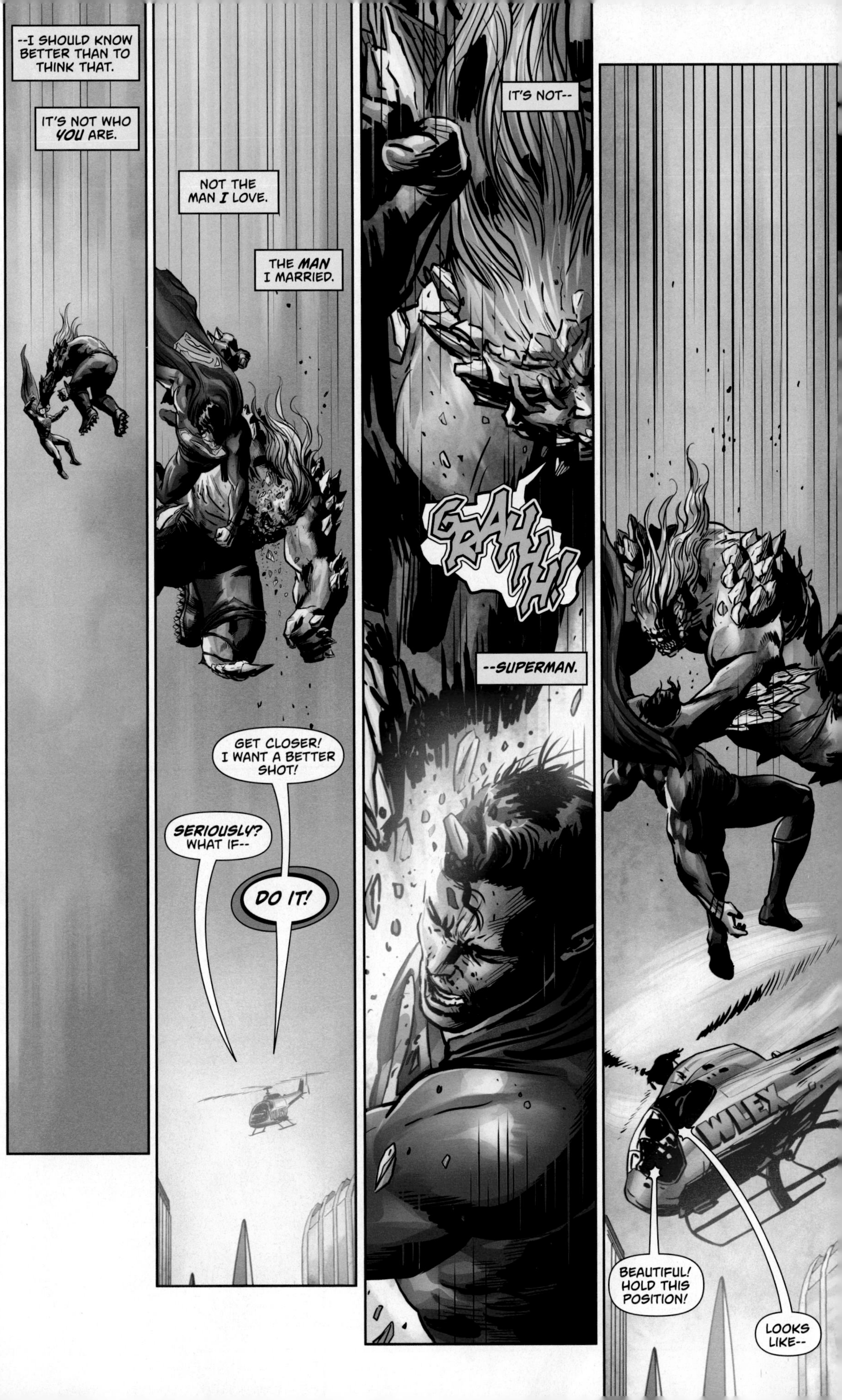
--I SHOULD KNOW BETTER THAN TO THINK THAT.
IT'S NOT WHO *YOU* ARE.
NOT THE MAN *I* LOVE.
THE *MAN* I MARRIED.
GET CLOSER! I WANT A BETTER SHOT!
SERIOUSLY? WHAT IF--
DO IT!
IT'S NOT--
GRAHHH!
--*SUPERMAN.*
WLEX
BEAUTIFUL! HOLD THIS POSITION!
LOOKS LIKE--

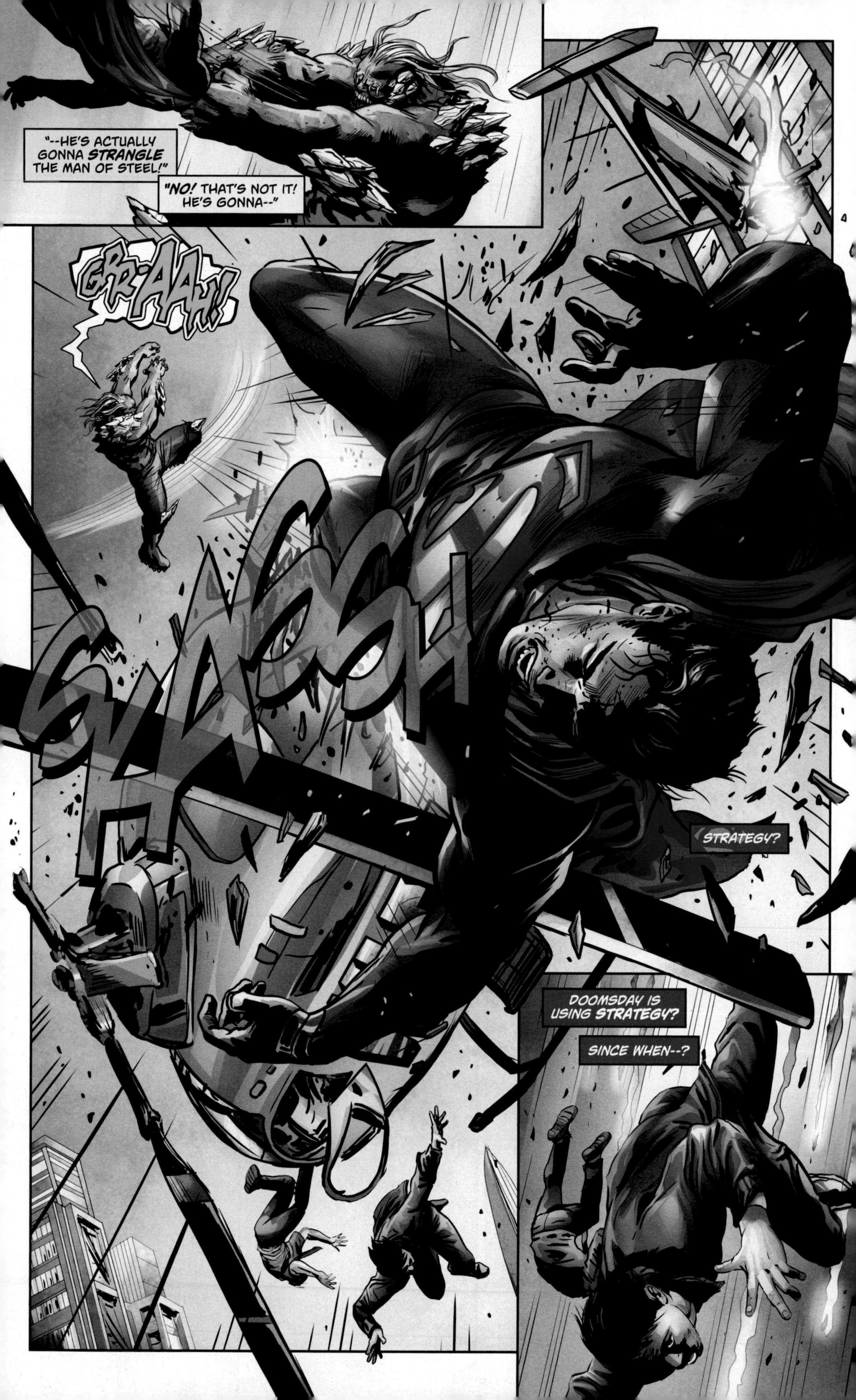
"--HE'S ACTUALLY GONNA STRANGLE THE MAN OF STEEL!"
"NO! THAT'S NOT IT! HE'S GONNA--"
GR-AAH!
SHASSH
STRATEGY?
DOOMSDAY IS USING STRATEGY?
SINCE WHEN--?

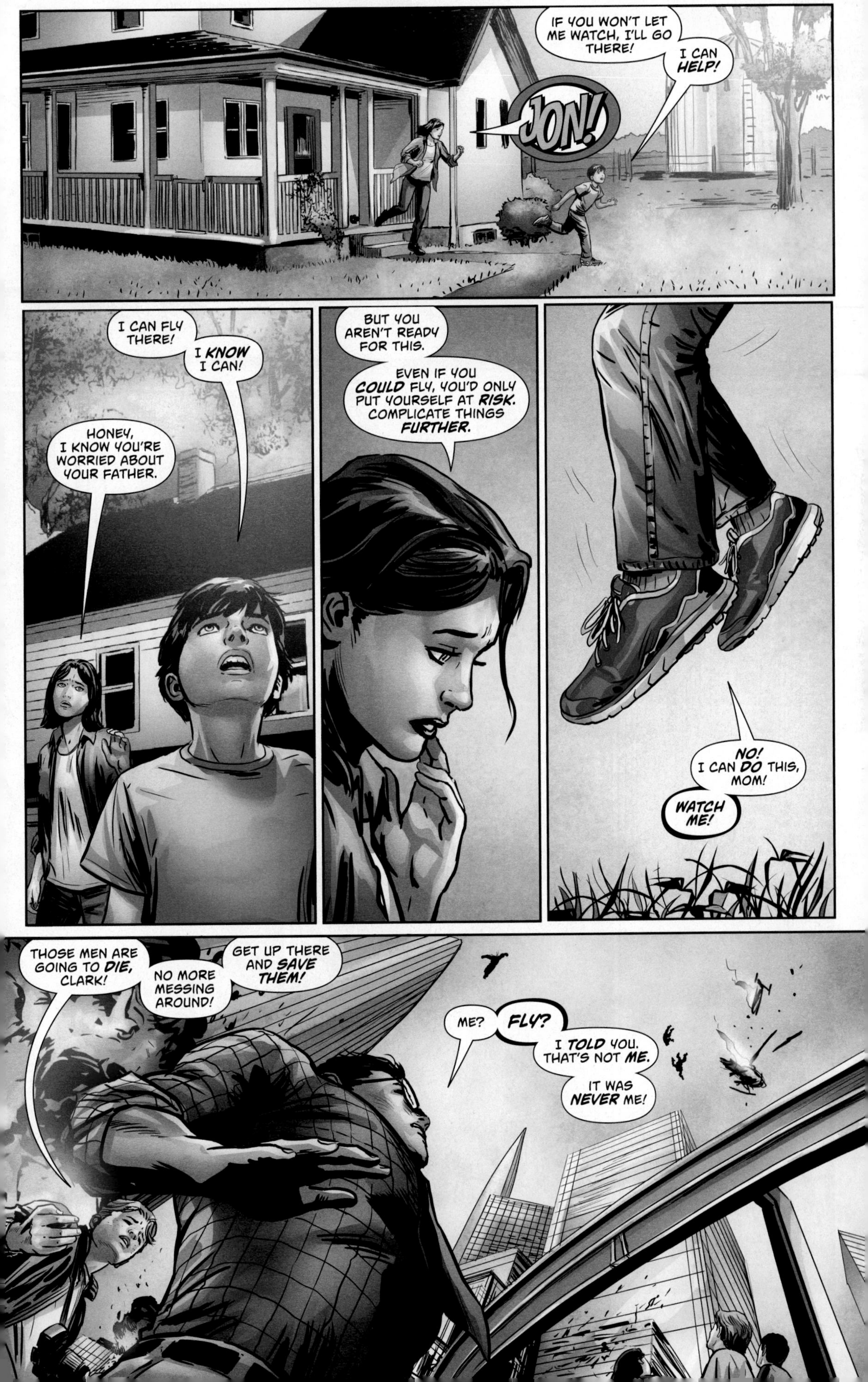
IF YOU WON'T LET ME WATCH, I'LL GO THERE!
I CAN HELP!
JON!
I CAN FLY THERE!
I KNOW I CAN!
HONEY, I KNOW YOU'RE WORRIED ABOUT YOUR FATHER.
BUT YOU AREN'T READY FOR THIS.
EVEN IF YOU COULD FLY, YOU'D ONLY PUT YOURSELF AT RISK. COMPLICATE THINGS FURTHER.
NO! I CAN DO THIS, MOM!
WATCH ME!
THOSE MEN ARE GOING TO DIE, CLARK!
NO MORE MESSING AROUND!
GET UP THERE AND SAVE THEM!
ME?
FLY?
I TOLD YOU. THAT'S NOT ME.
IT WAS NEVER ME!

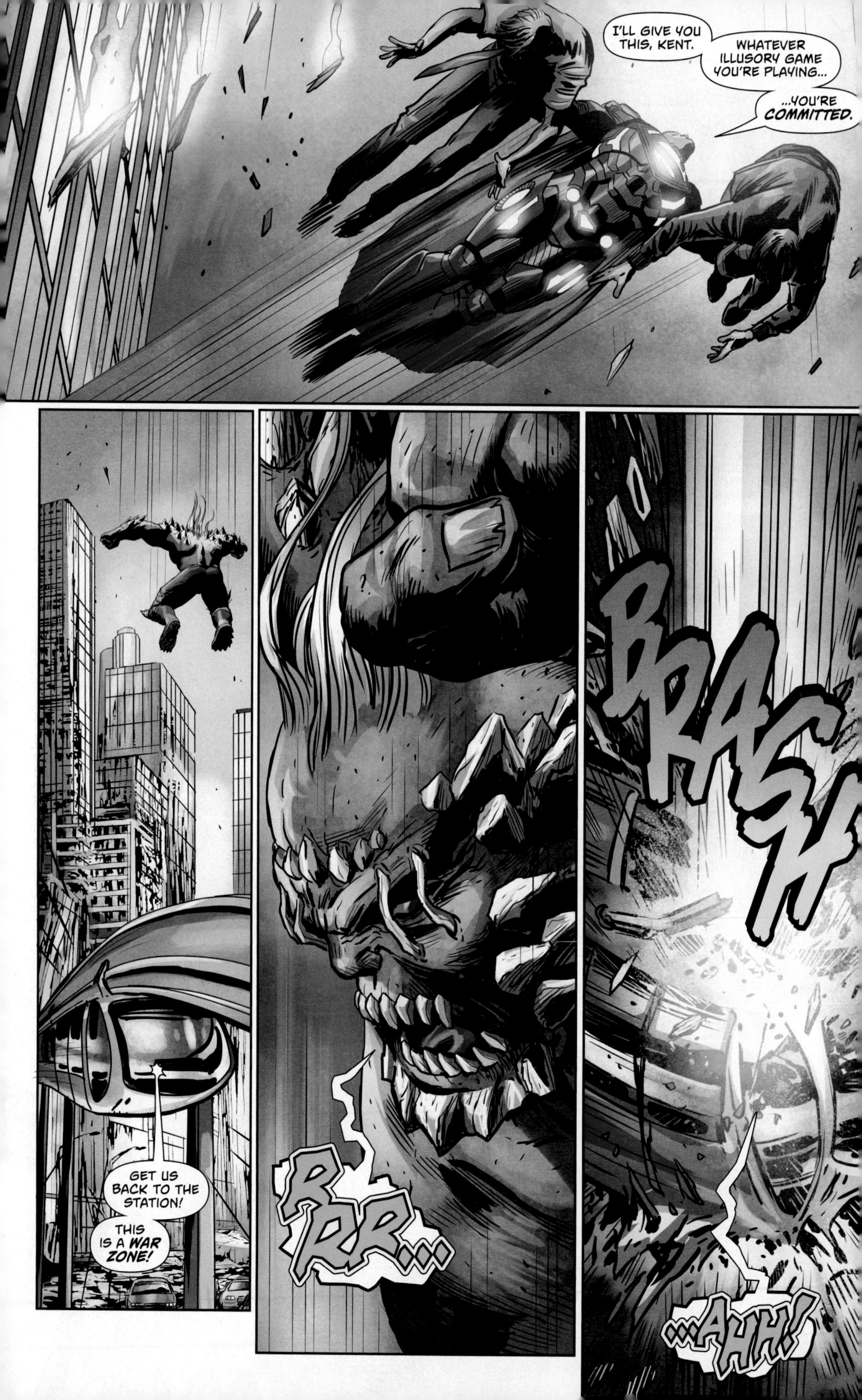

I'LL GIVE YOU THIS, KENT.
WHATEVER ILLUSORY GAME YOU'RE PLAYING...
...YOU'RE COMMITTED.
GET US BACK TO THE STATION!
THIS IS A WAR ZONE!
RRR...
BRASH
...AHH!

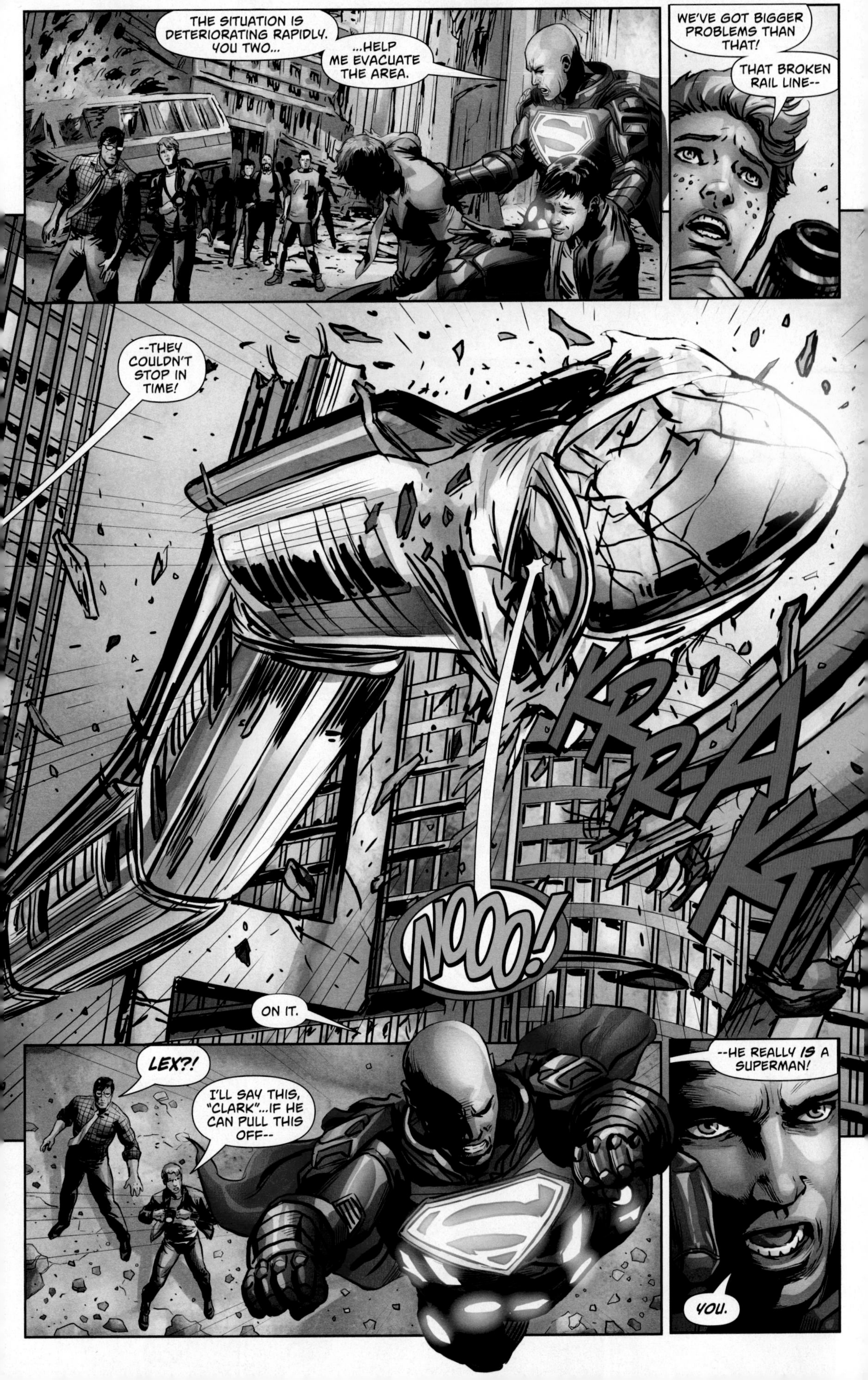
THE SITUATION IS DETERIORATING RAPIDLY. YOU TWO...
...HELP ME EVACUATE THE AREA.
WE'VE GOT BIGGER PROBLEMS THAN THAT!
THAT BROKEN RAIL LINE--
--THEY COULDN'T STOP IN TIME!
KR-R-AKT
NOOO!
ON IT.
LEX?!
I'LL SAY THIS, "CLARK"...IF HE CAN PULL THIS OFF--
--HE REALLY IS A SUPERMAN!
YOU.

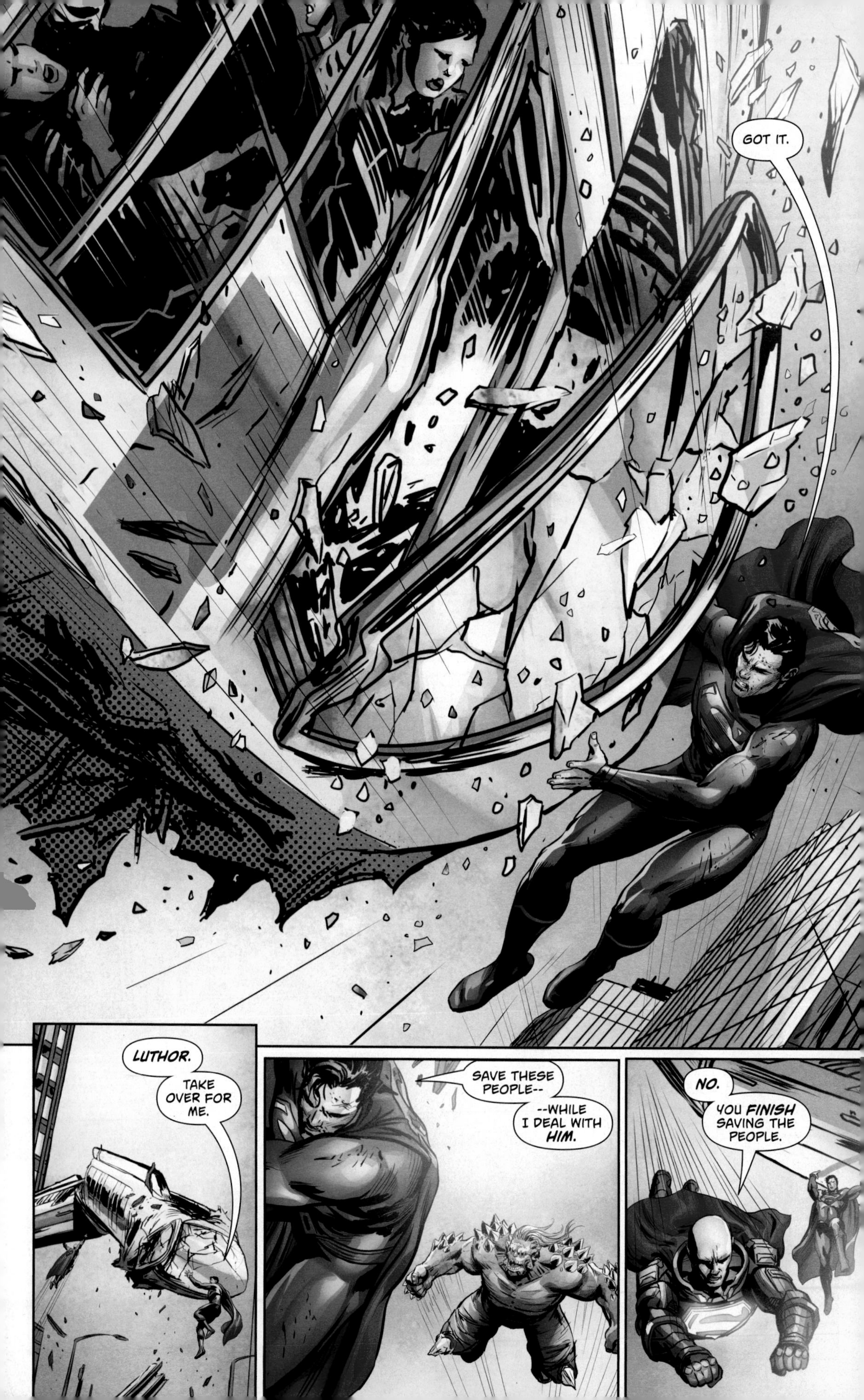
GOT IT.
LUTHOR.
TAKE OVER FOR ME.
SAVE THESE PEOPLE--
--WHILE I DEAL WITH HIM.
NO.
YOU FINISH SAVING THE PEOPLE.

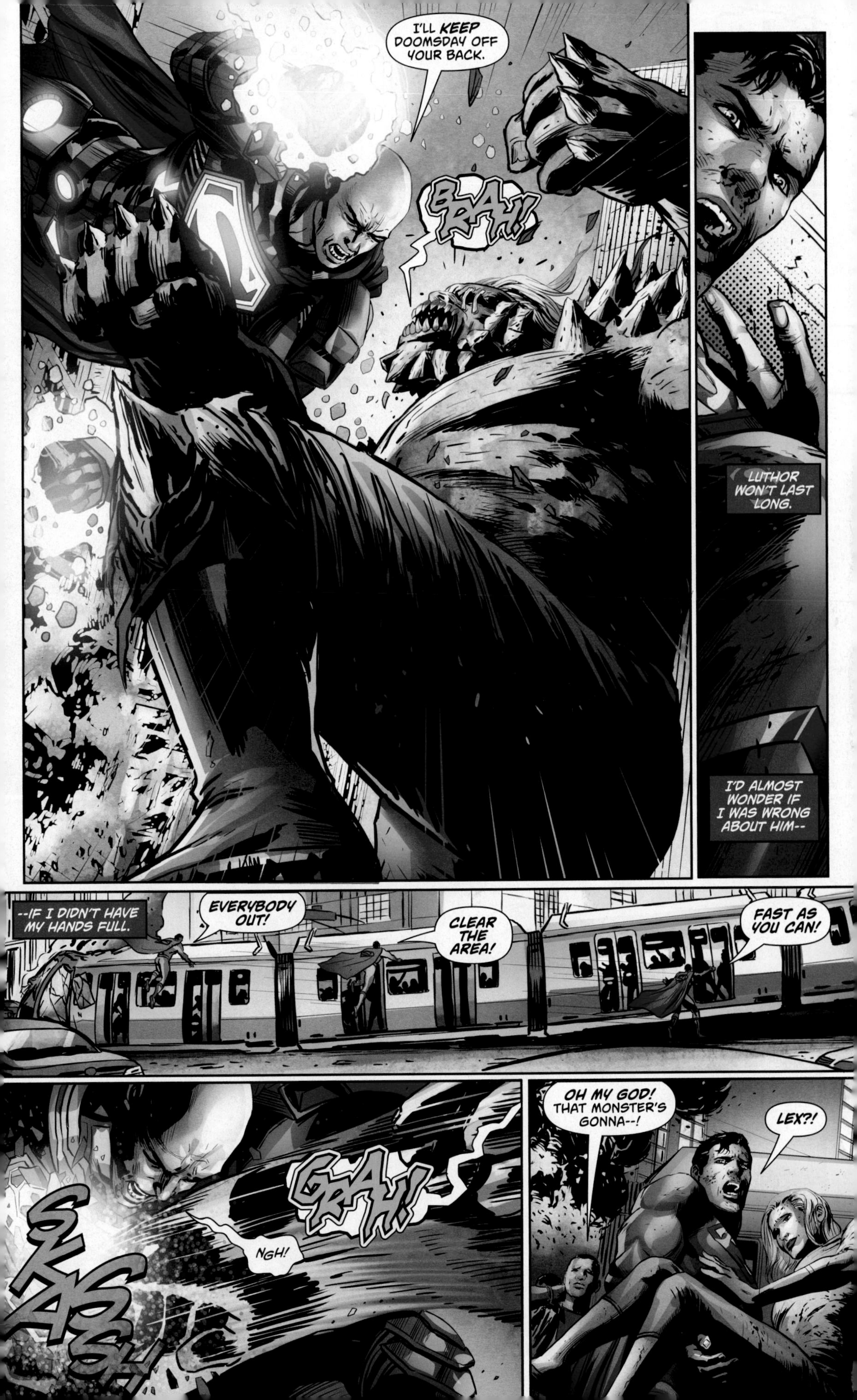
I'LL KEEP DOOMSDAY OFF YOUR BACK.
BRAH!
LUTHOR WON'T LAST LONG.
I'D ALMOST WONDER IF I WAS WRONG ABOUT HIM--
--IF I DIDN'T HAVE MY HANDS FULL.
EVERYBODY OUT!
CLEAR THE AREA!
FAST AS YOU CAN!
SKASH
GRAH!
NGH!
OH MY GOD! THAT MONSTER'S GONNA--!
LEX?!

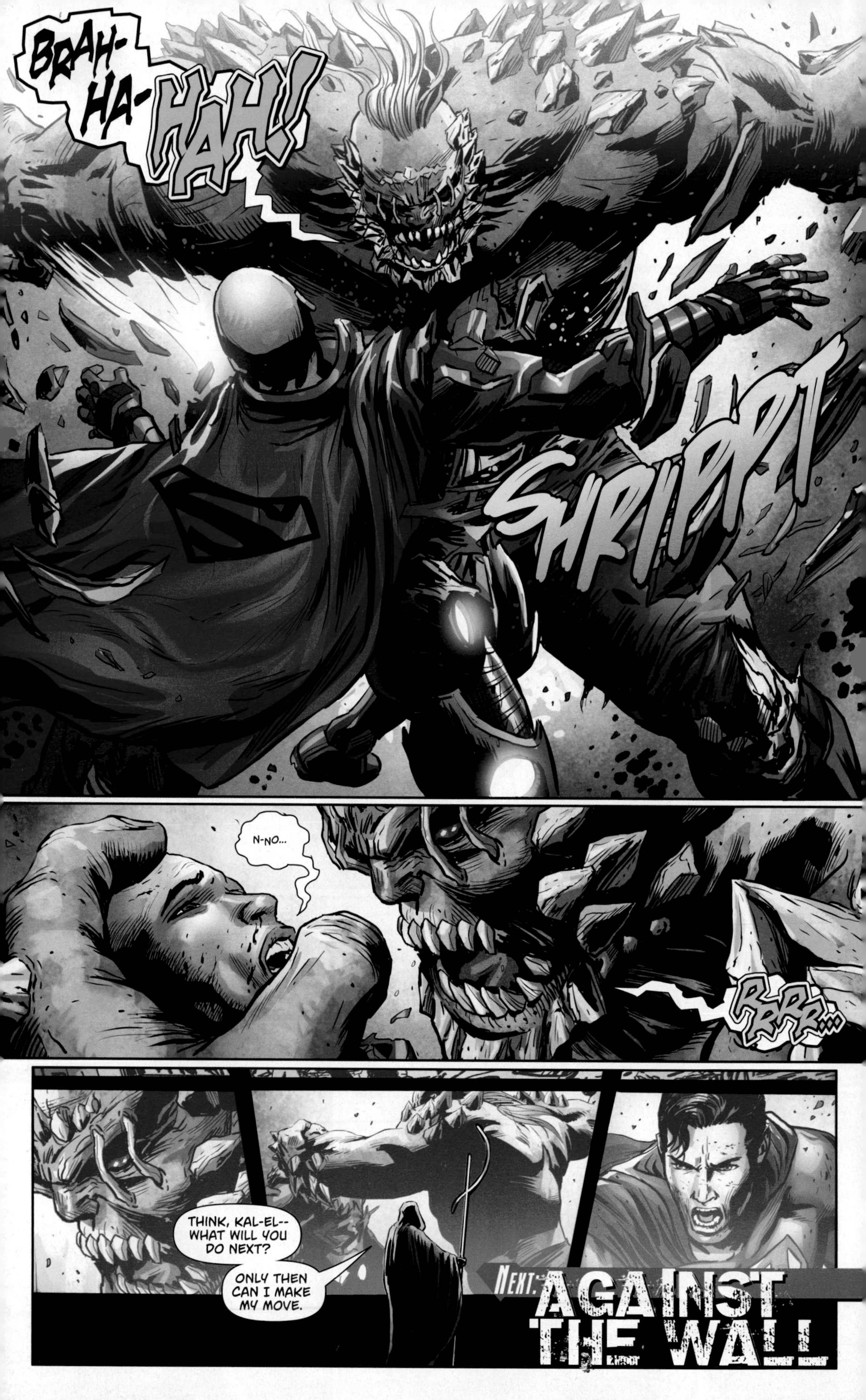
BRAH-HA-HAH!
SHRIPPT
N-NO...
RRRR...
THINK, KAL-EL-- WHAT WILL YOU DO NEXT?
ONLY THEN CAN I MAKE MY MOVE.
NEXT: AGAINST THE WALL

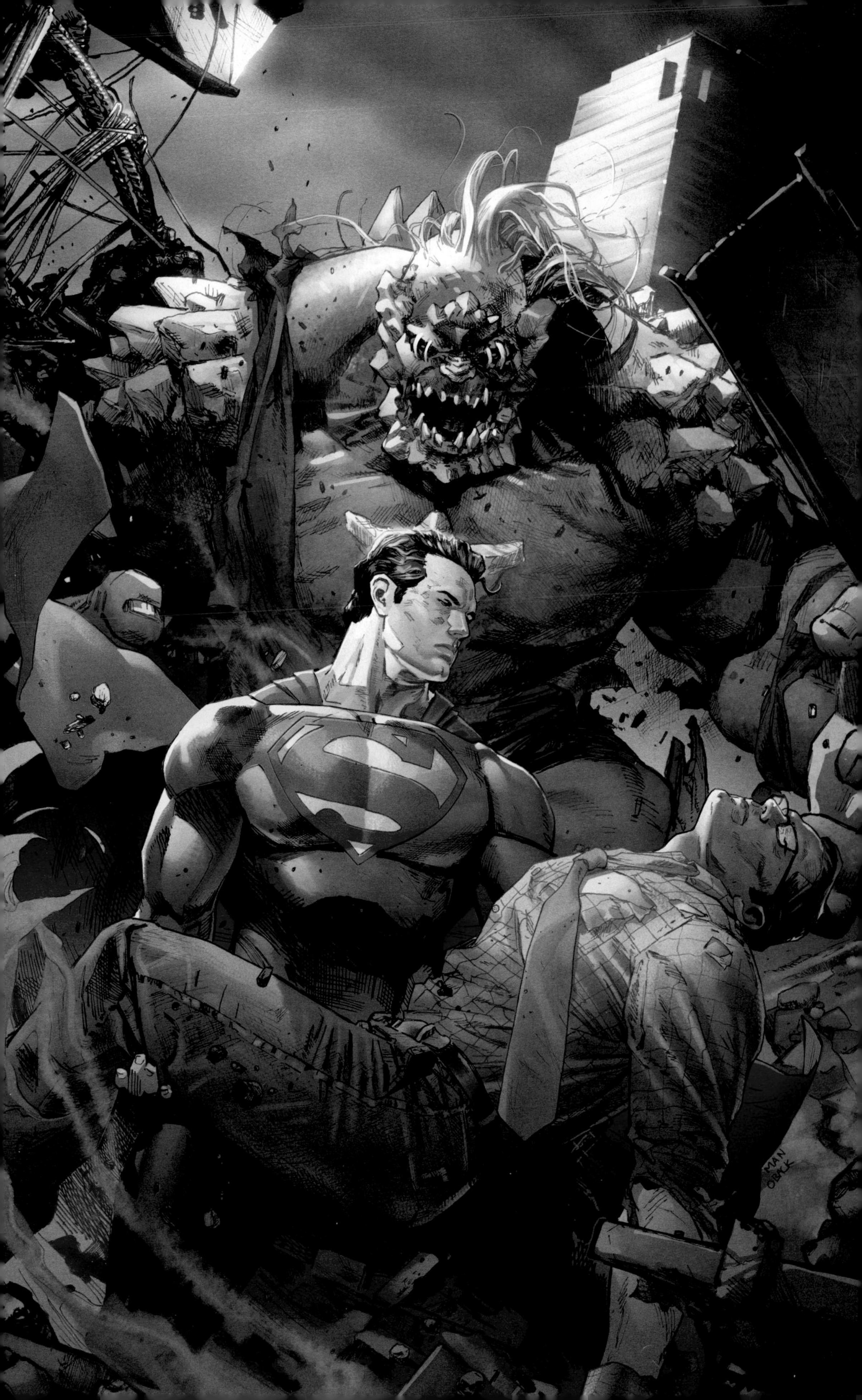

ACTION COMICS #959

CLAY MANN and SONIA OBACK with DAN JURGENS cover artists

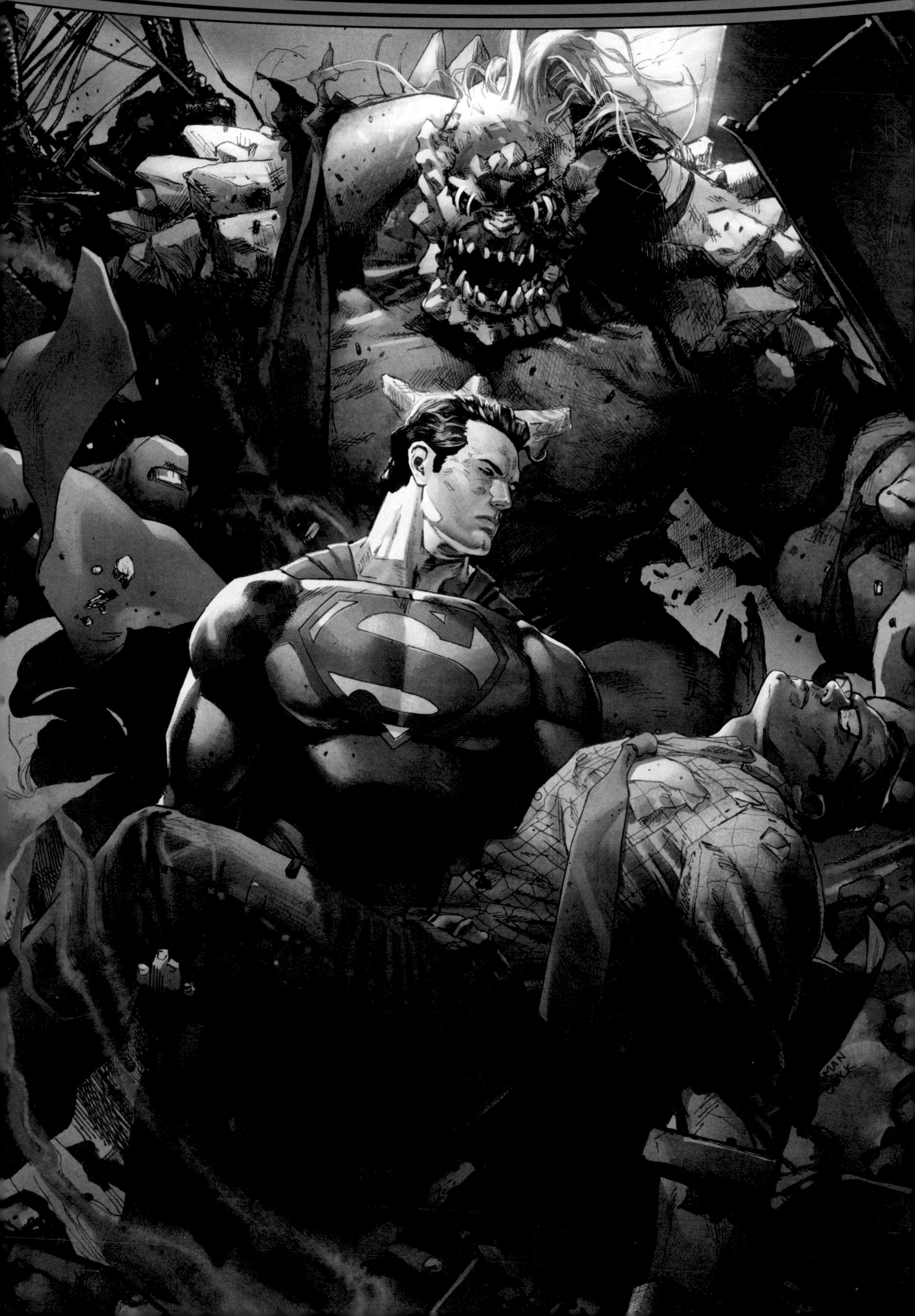

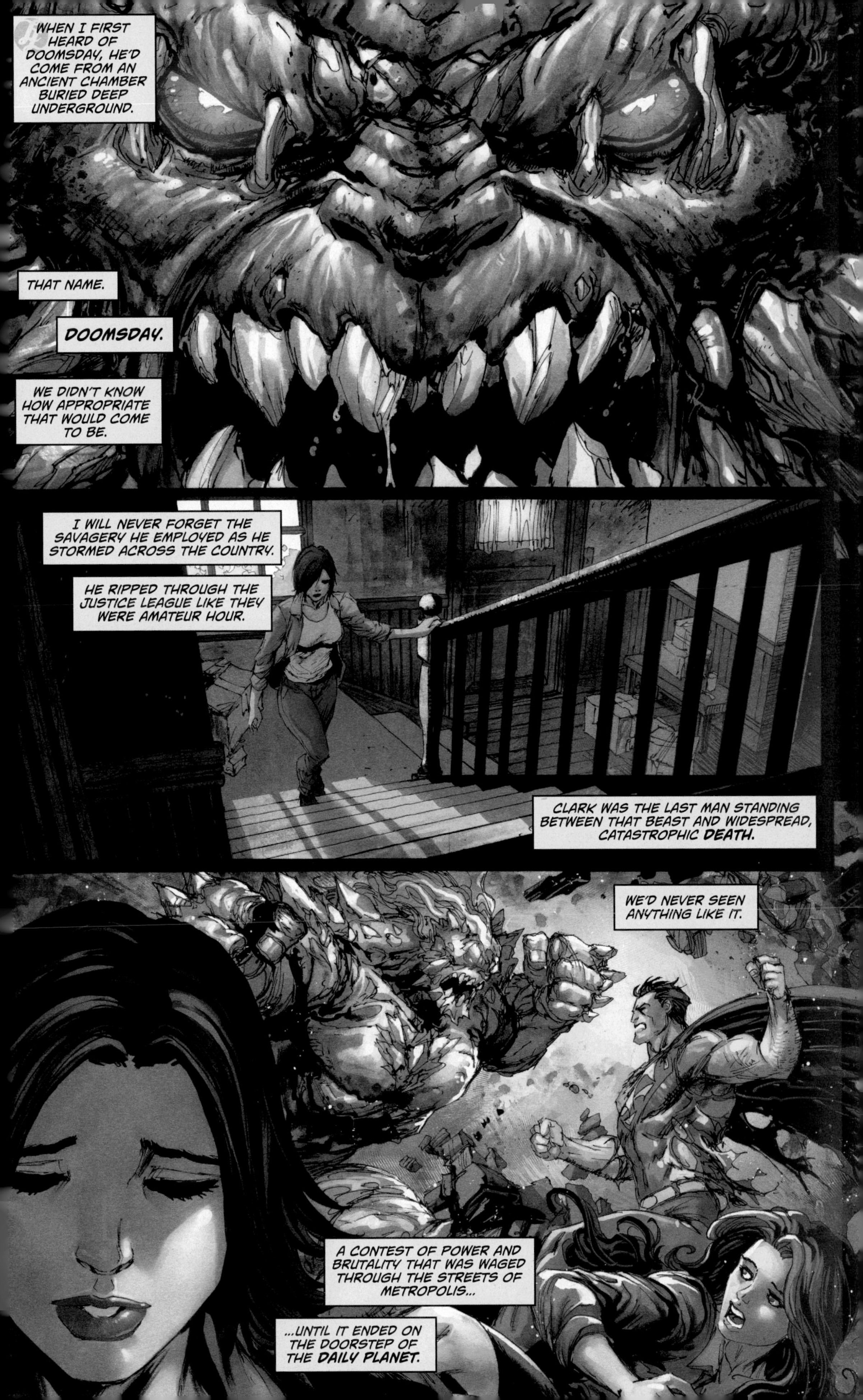
WHEN I FIRST HEARD OF DOOMSDAY, HE'D COME FROM AN ANCIENT CHAMBER BURIED DEEP UNDERGROUND.
THAT NAME.
DOOMSDAY.
WE DIDN'T KNOW HOW APPROPRIATE THAT WOULD COME TO BE.
I WILL NEVER FORGET THE SAVAGERY HE EMPLOYED AS HE STORMED ACROSS THE COUNTRY.
HE RIPPED THROUGH THE JUSTICE LEAGUE LIKE THEY WERE AMATEUR HOUR.
CLARK WAS THE LAST MAN STANDING BETWEEN THAT BEAST AND WIDESPREAD, CATASTROPHIC DEATH.
WE'D NEVER SEEN ANYTHING LIKE IT.
A CONTEST OF POWER AND BRUTALITY THAT WAS WAGED THROUGH THE STREETS OF METROPOLIS...
...UNTIL IT ENDED ON THE DOORSTEP OF THE DAILY PLANET.

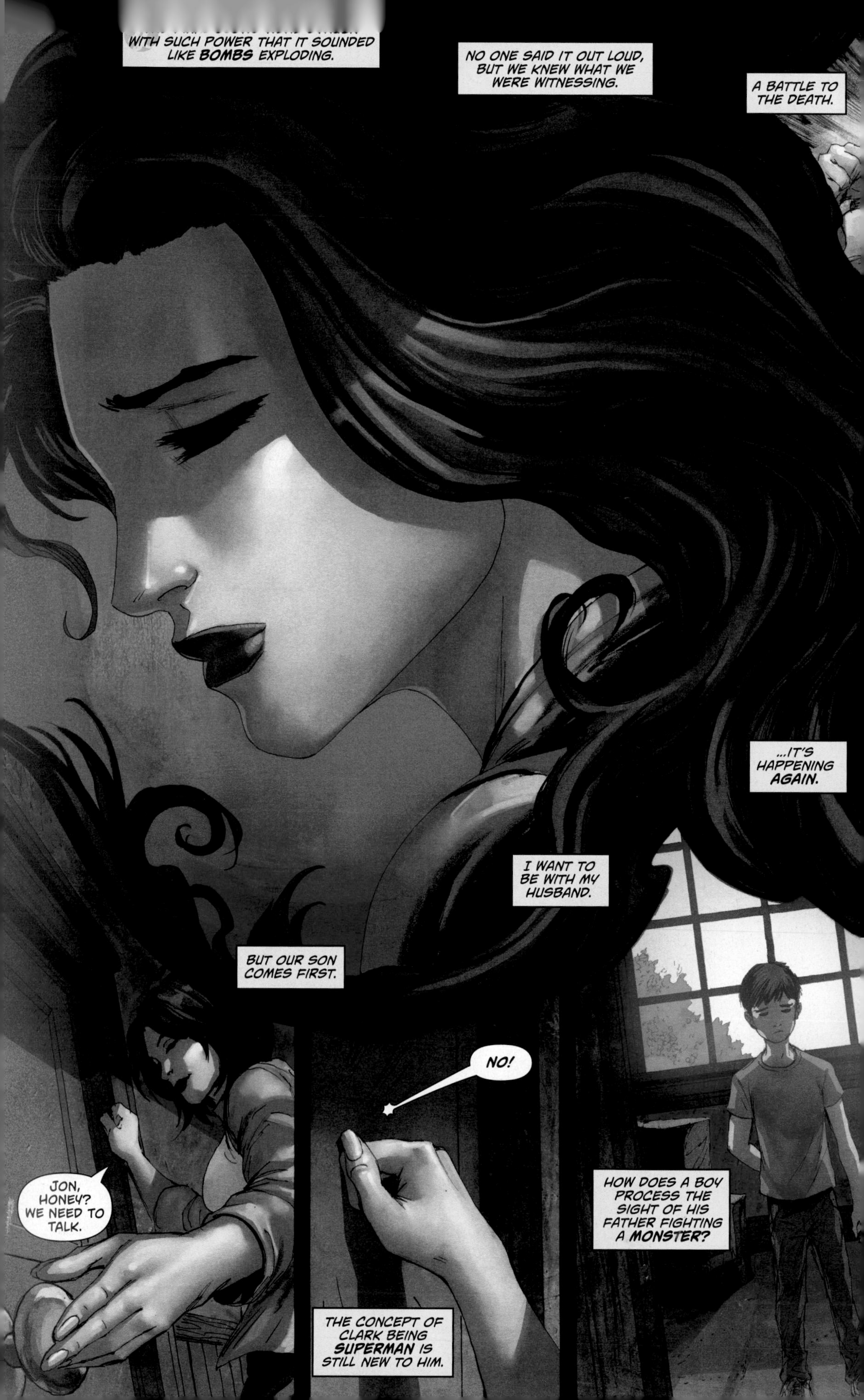
WITH SUCH POWER THAT IT SOUNDED LIKE BOMBS EXPLODING.
NO ONE SAID IT OUT LOUD, BUT WE KNEW WHAT WE WERE WITNESSING.
A BATTLE TO THE DEATH.
...IT'S HAPPENING AGAIN.
I WANT TO BE WITH MY HUSBAND.
BUT OUR SON COMES FIRST.
JON, HONEY? WE NEED TO TALK.
NO!
THE CONCEPT OF CLARK BEING SUPERMAN IS STILL NEW TO HIM.
HOW DOES A BOY PROCESS THE SIGHT OF HIS FATHER FIGHTING A MONSTER?

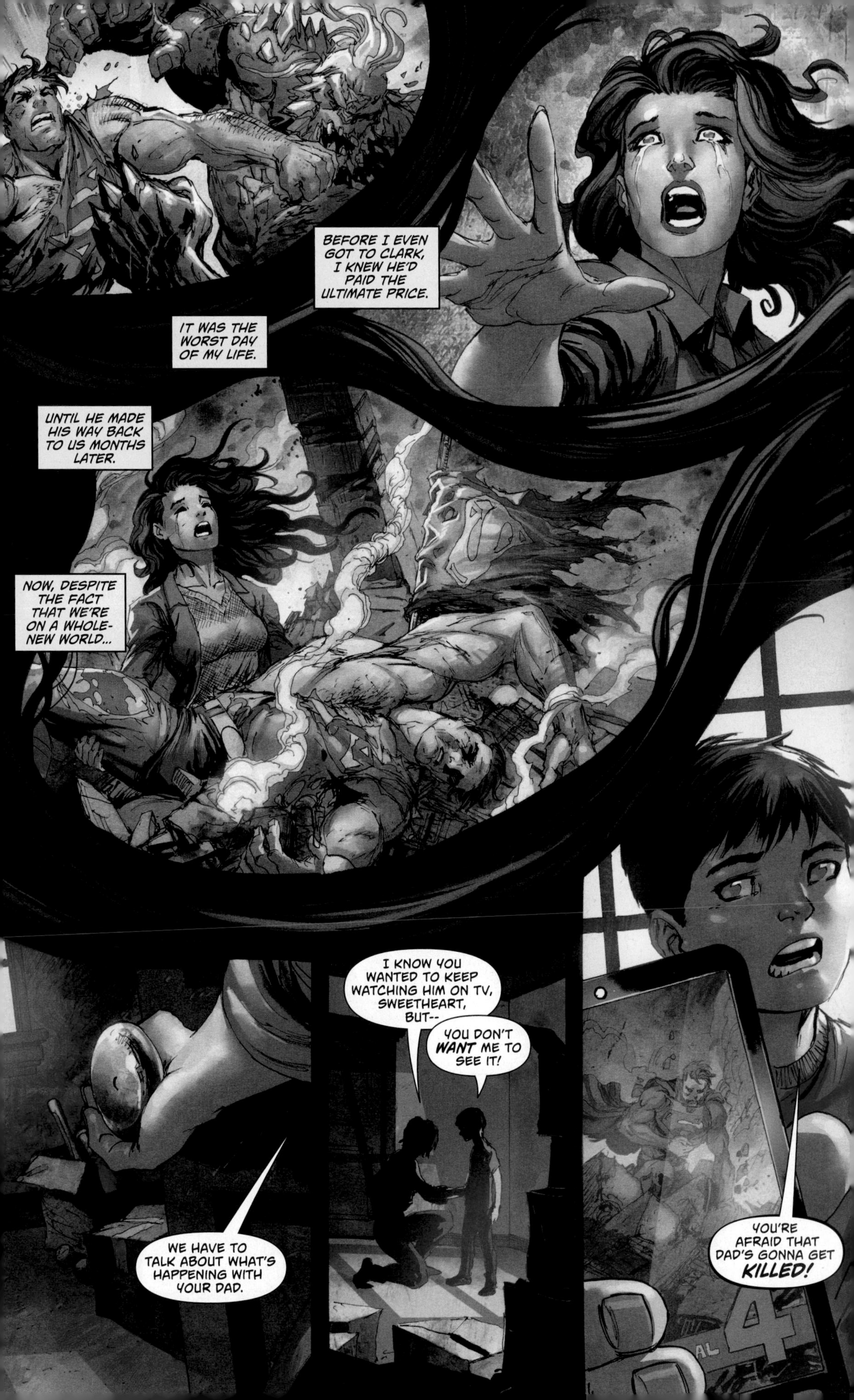
BEFORE I EVEN GOT TO CLARK, I KNEW HE'D PAID THE ULTIMATE PRICE.
IT WAS THE WORST DAY OF MY LIFE.
UNTIL HE MADE HIS WAY BACK TO US MONTHS LATER.
NOW, DESPITE THE FACT THAT WE'RE ON A WHOLE-NEW WORLD...
WE HAVE TO TALK ABOUT WHAT'S HAPPENING WITH YOUR DAD.
I KNOW YOU WANTED TO KEEP WATCHING HIM ON TV, SWEETHEART, BUT--
YOU DON'T WANT ME TO SEE IT!
YOU'RE AFRAID THAT DAD'S GONNA GET KILLED!

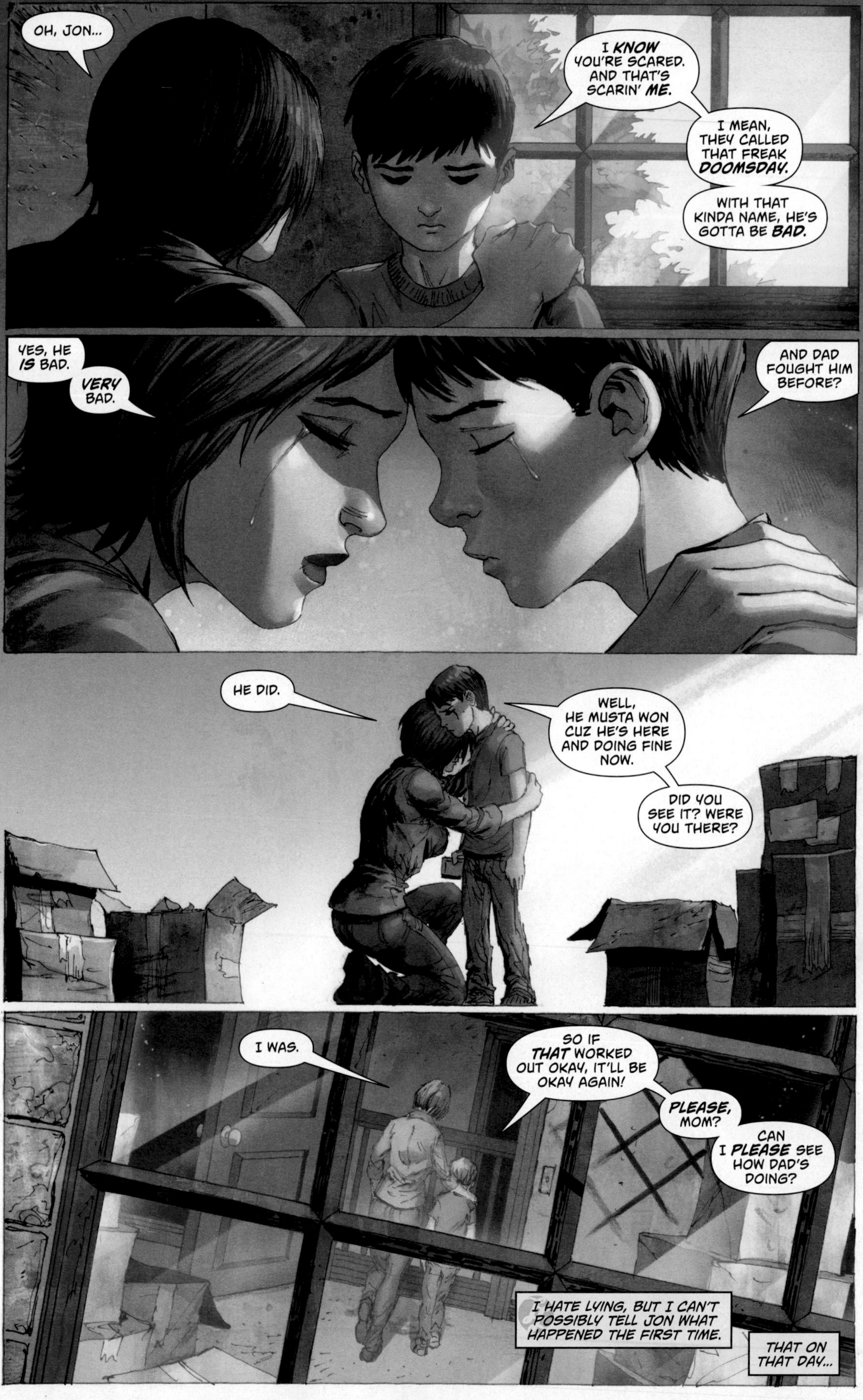
OH, JON...
I KNOW YOU'RE SCARED. AND THAT'S SCARIN' ME.
I MEAN, THEY CALLED THAT FREAK DOOMSDAY.
WITH THAT KINDA NAME, HE'S GOTTA BE BAD.
YES, HE IS BAD.
VERY BAD.
AND DAD FOUGHT HIM BEFORE?
HE DID.
WELL, HE MUSTA WON CUZ HE'S HERE AND DOING FINE NOW.
DID YOU SEE IT? WERE YOU THERE?
I WAS.
SO IF THAT WORKED OUT OKAY, IT'LL BE OKAY AGAIN!
PLEASE, MOM?
CAN I PLEASE SEE HOW DAD'S DOING?
I HATE LYING, BUT I CAN'T POSSIBLY TELL JON WHAT HAPPENED THE FIRST TIME.
THAT ON THAT DAY...

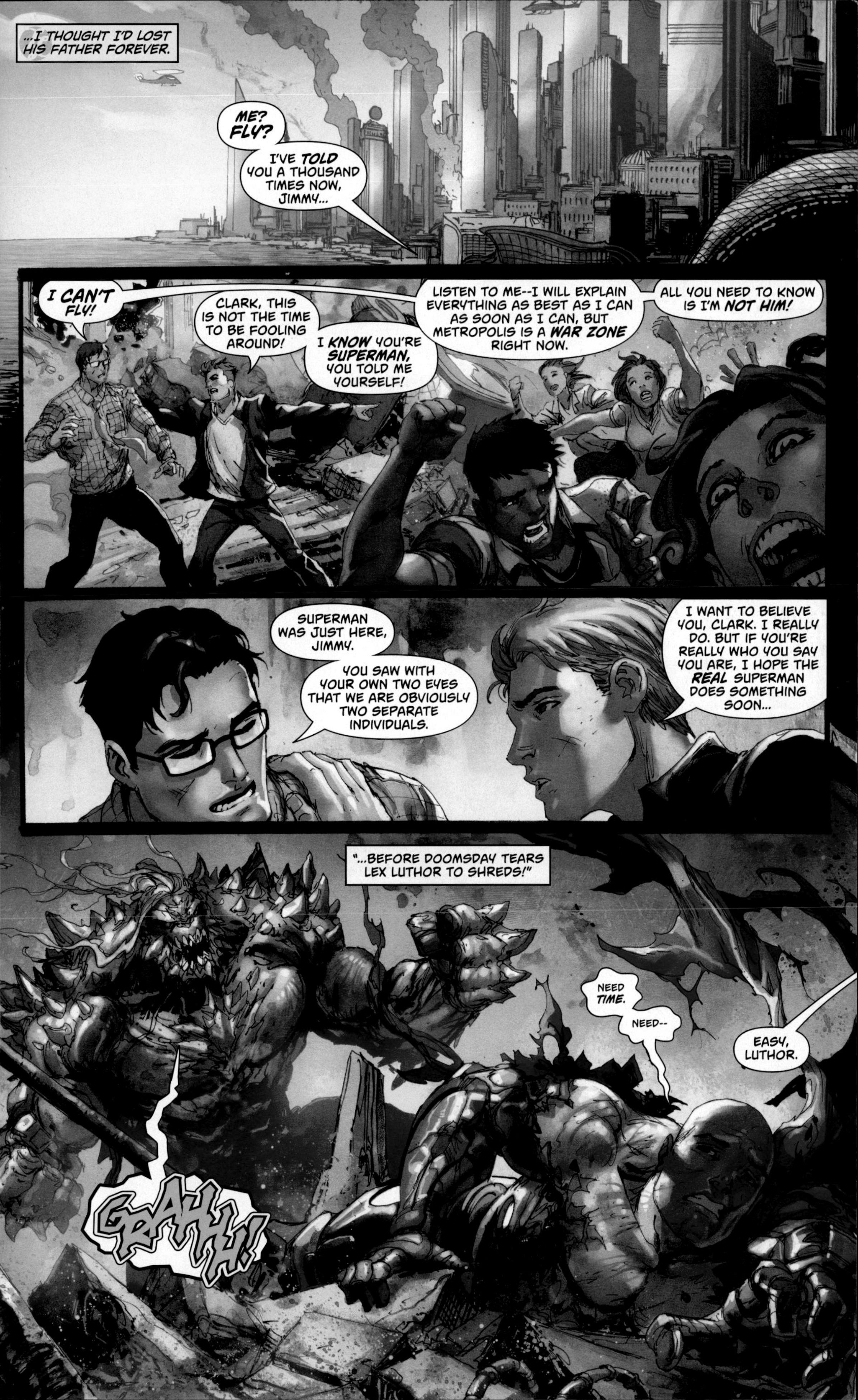
...I THOUGHT I'D LOST HIS FATHER FOREVER.
ME? FLY?
I'VE TOLD YOU A THOUSAND TIMES NOW, JIMMY...
I CAN'T FLY!
CLARK, THIS IS NOT THE TIME TO BE FOOLING AROUND!
I KNOW YOU'RE SUPERMAN, YOU TOLD ME YOURSELF!
LISTEN TO ME--I WILL EXPLAIN EVERYTHING AS BEST AS I CAN AS SOON AS I CAN, BUT METROPOLIS IS A WAR ZONE RIGHT NOW.
ALL YOU NEED TO KNOW IS I'M NOT HIM!
SUPERMAN WAS JUST HERE, JIMMY.
YOU SAW WITH YOUR OWN TWO EYES THAT WE ARE OBVIOUSLY TWO SEPARATE INDIVIDUALS.
I WANT TO BELIEVE YOU, CLARK. I REALLY DO. BUT IF YOU'RE REALLY WHO YOU SAY YOU ARE, I HOPE THE REAL SUPERMAN DOES SOMETHING SOON...
"...BEFORE DOOMSDAY TEARS LEX LUTHOR TO SHREDS!"
NEED TIME.
NEED--
EASY, LUTHOR.
GRAHHH!

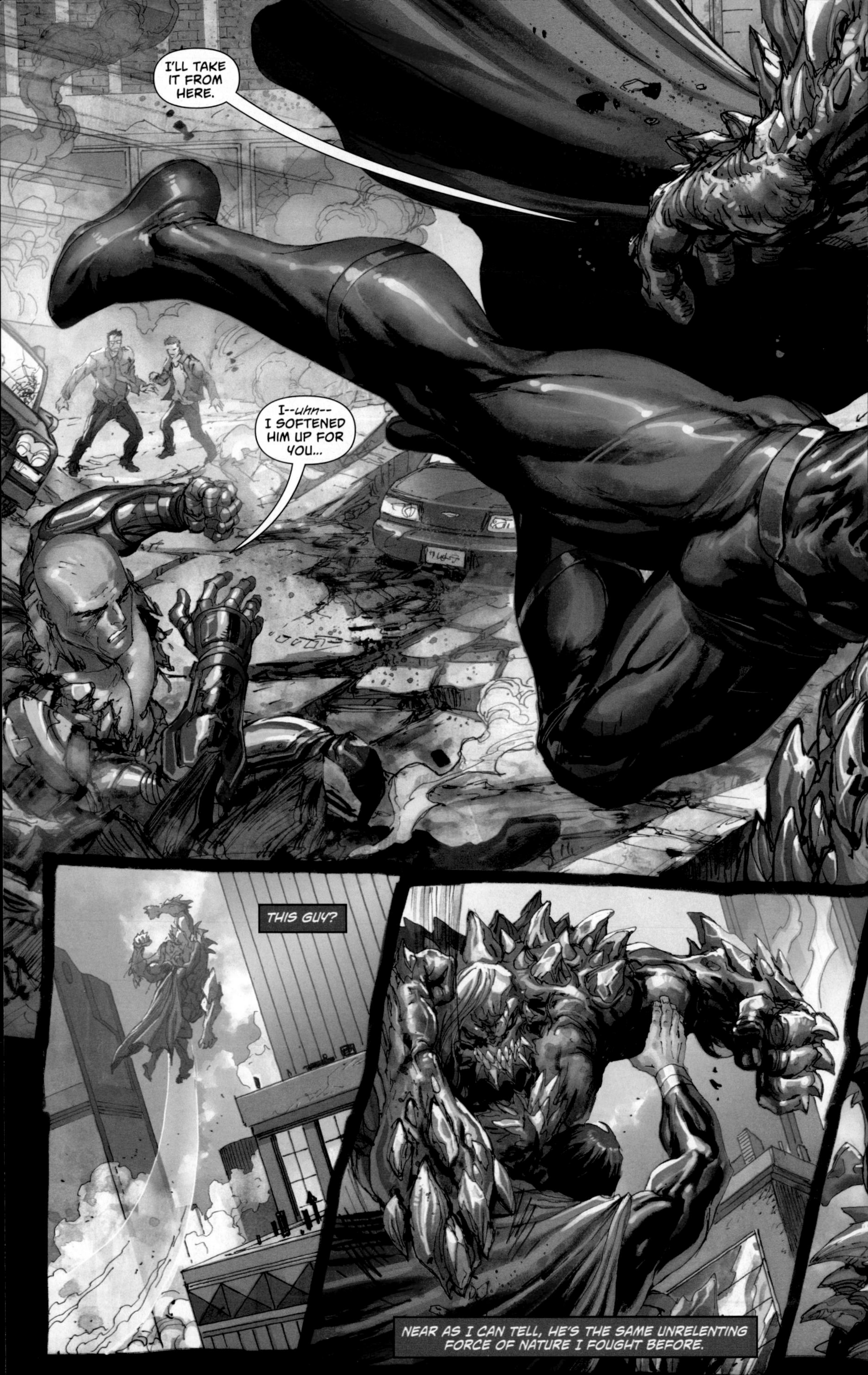

I'LL TAKE IT FROM HERE.
I--uhn-- I SOFTENED HIM UP FOR YOU...
THIS GUY?
NEAR AS I CAN TELL, HE'S THE SAME UNRELENTING FORCE OF NATURE I FOUGHT BEFORE.

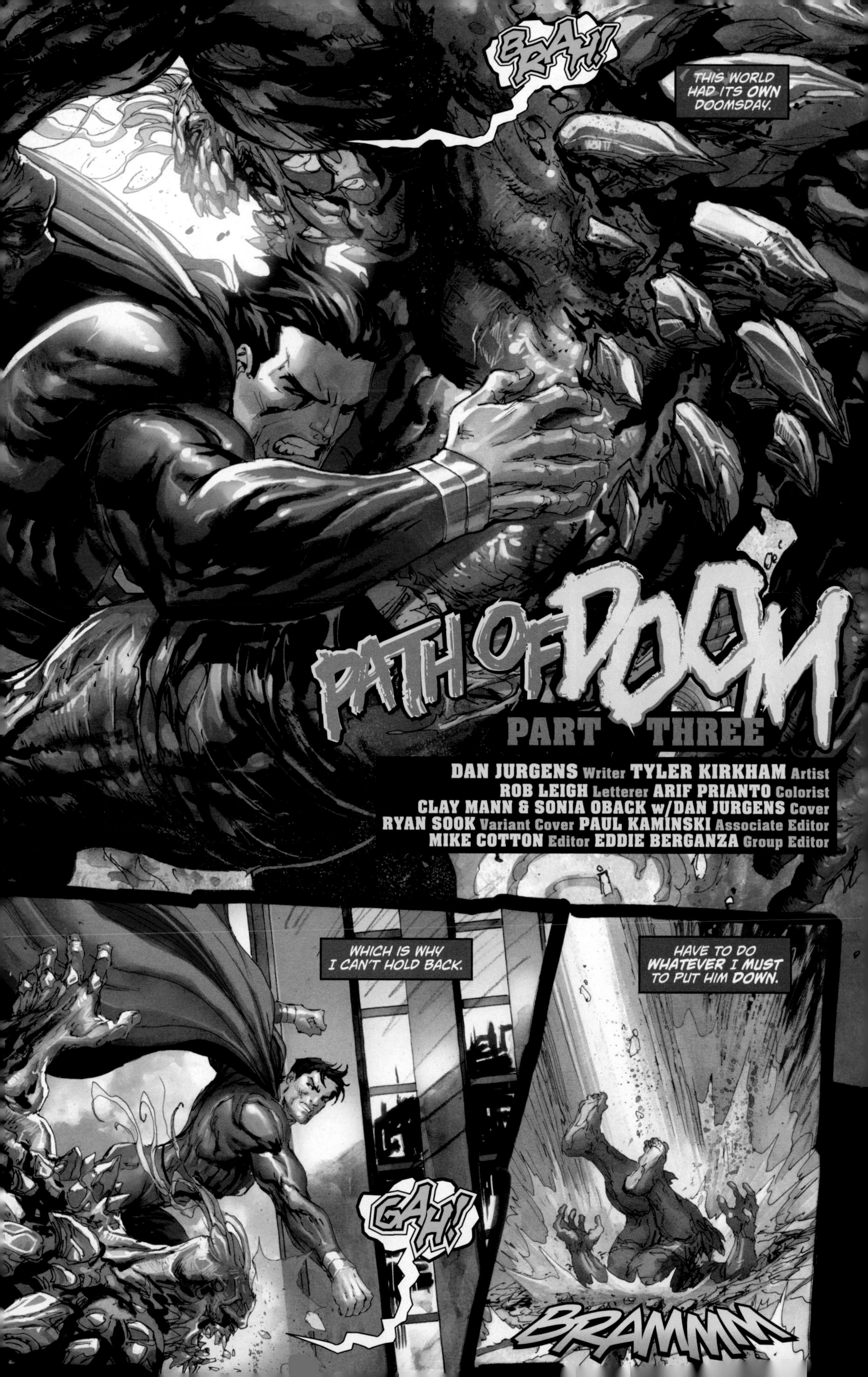
BRAH!
THIS WORLD HAD ITS OWN DOOMSDAY.
PATH OF DOOM
PART THREE
DAN JURGENS Writer TYLER KIRKHAM Artist
ROB LEIGH Letterer ARIF PRIANTO Colorist
CLAY MANN & SONIA OBACK w/DAN JURGENS Cover
RYAN SOOK Variant Cover PAUL KAMINSKI Associate Editor
MIKE COTTON Editor EDDIE BERGANZA Group Editor
WHICH IS WHY I CAN'T HOLD BACK.
GAH!
HAVE TO DO WHATEVER I MUST TO PUT HIM DOWN.
BRAMMM

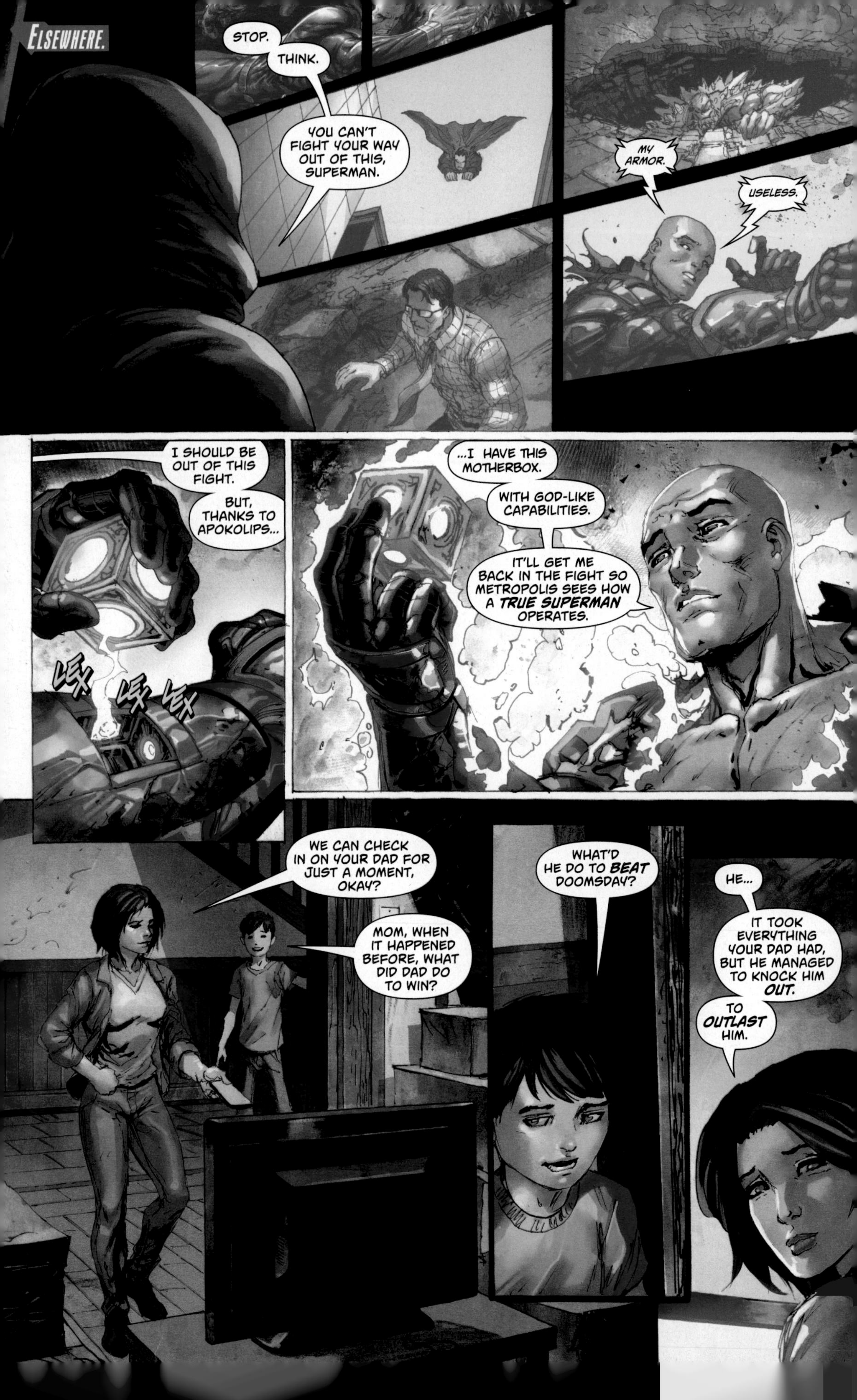
ELSEWHERE.
STOP.
THINK.
YOU CAN'T FIGHT YOUR WAY OUT OF THIS, SUPERMAN.
MY ARMOR.
USELESS.
I SHOULD BE OUT OF THIS FIGHT.
BUT, THANKS TO APOKOLIPS...
LEX LEX LEX
...I HAVE THIS MOTHERBOX.
WITH GOD-LIKE CAPABILITIES.
IT'LL GET ME BACK IN THE FIGHT SO METROPOLIS SEES HOW A TRUE SUPERMAN OPERATES.
WE CAN CHECK IN ON YOUR DAD FOR JUST A MOMENT, OKAY?
MOM, WHEN IT HAPPENED BEFORE, WHAT DID DAD DO TO WIN?
WHAT'D HE DO TO BEAT DOOMSDAY?
HE...
IT TOOK EVERYTHING YOUR DAD HAD, BUT HE MANAGED TO KNOCK HIM OUT.
TO OUTLAST HIM.

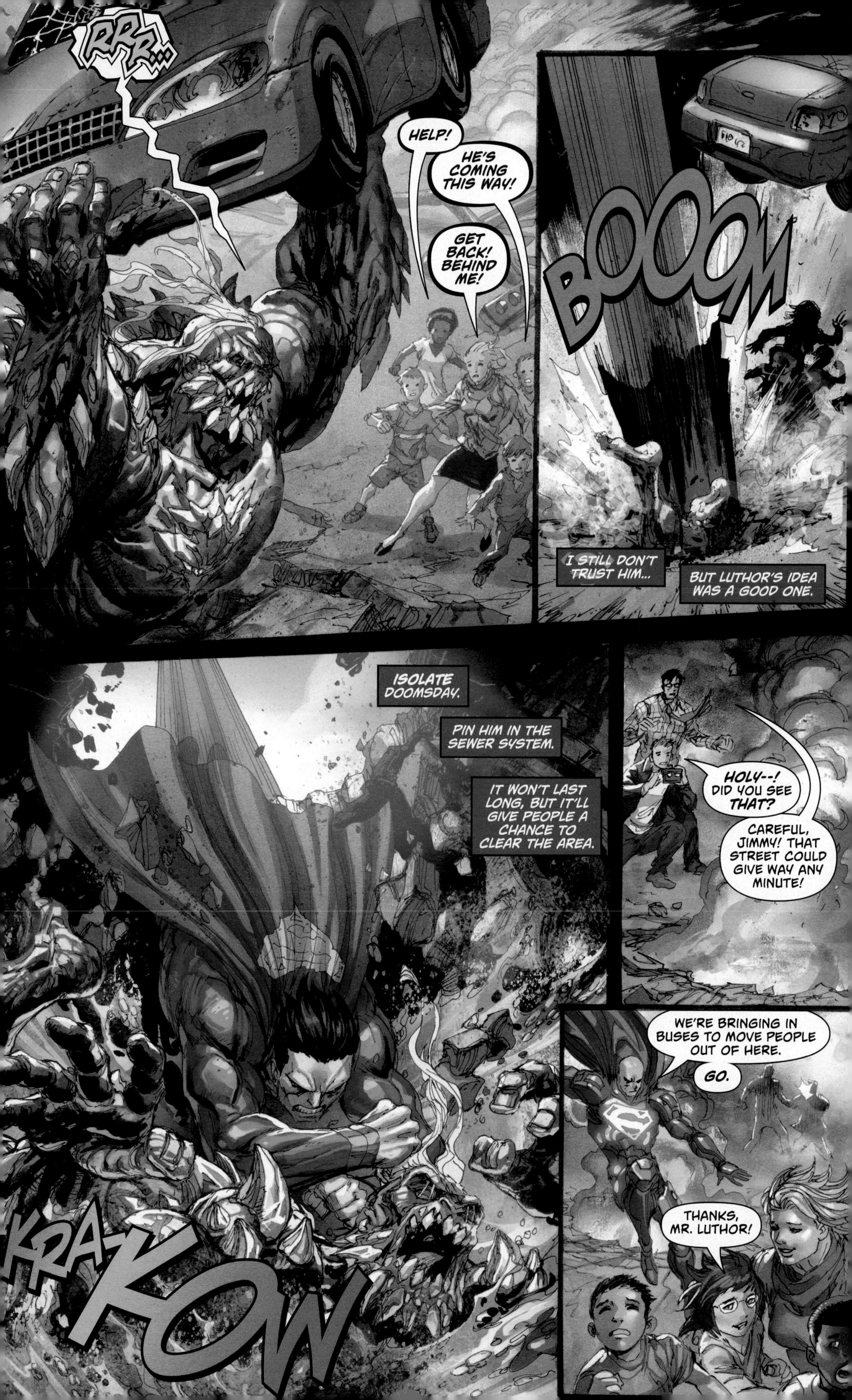
RRR...
HELP!
HE'S COMING THIS WAY!
GET BACK! BEHIND ME!
BOOOOM
I STILL DON'T TRUST HIM...
BUT LUTHOR'S IDEA WAS A GOOD ONE.
ISOLATE DOOMSDAY.
PIN HIM IN THE SEWER SYSTEM.
IT WON'T LAST LONG, BUT IT'LL GIVE PEOPLE A CHANCE TO CLEAR THE AREA.
KRA-KOW
HOLY--! DID YOU SEE THAT?
CAREFUL, JIMMY! THAT STREET COULD GIVE WAY ANY MINUTE!
WE'RE BRINGING IN BUSES TO MOVE PEOPLE OUT OF HERE.
GO.
THANKS, MR. LUTHOR!

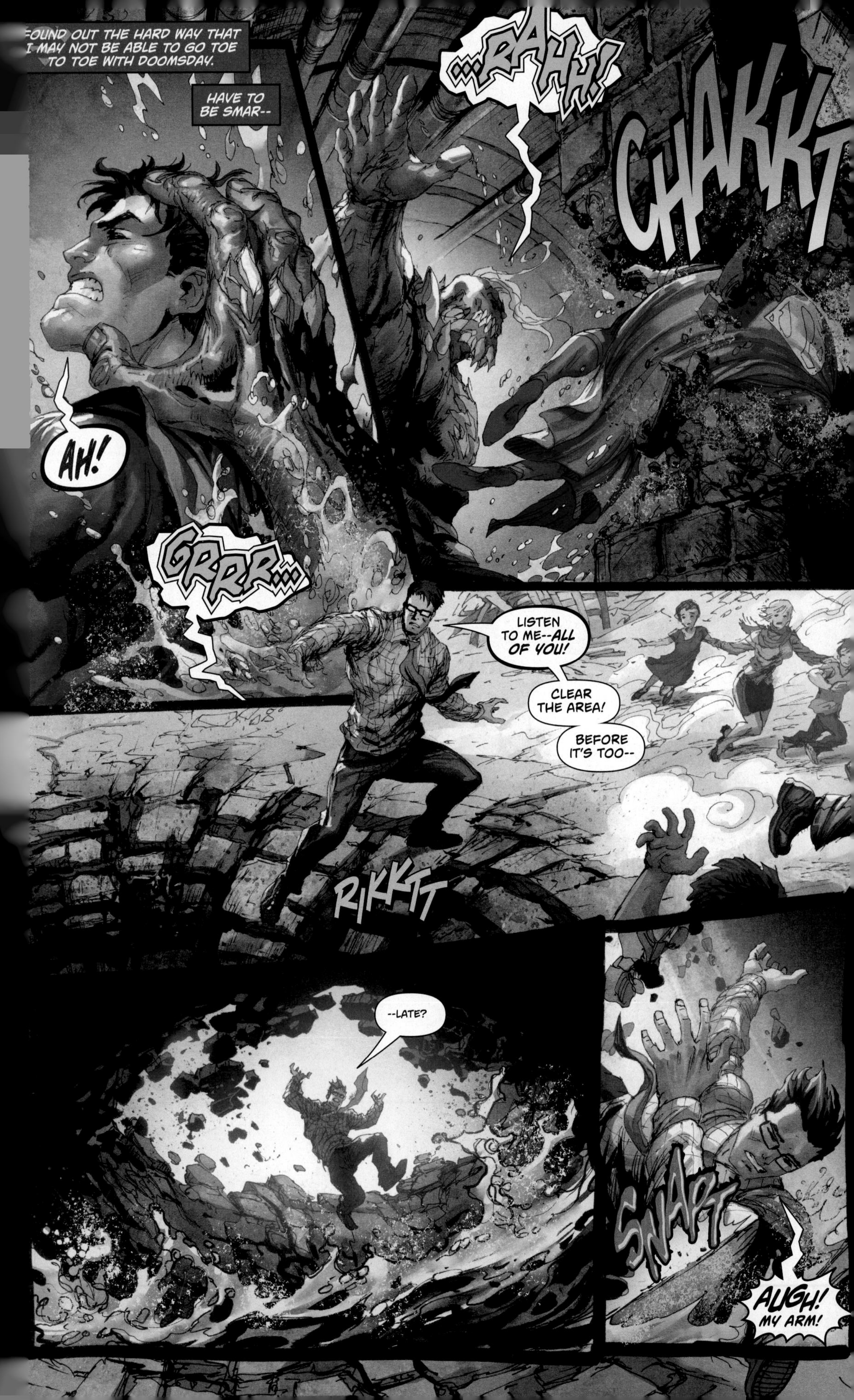
FOUND OUT THE HARD WAY THAT I MAY NOT BE ABLE TO GO TOE TO TOE WITH DOOMSDAY.
HAVE TO BE SMAR--
AH!
GRRR...
...RAHH!
CHAKKT
LISTEN TO ME--ALL OF YOU!
CLEAR THE AREA!
BEFORE IT'S TOO--
RIKKTTT
--LATE?
SNAPT
AUGH! MY ARM!

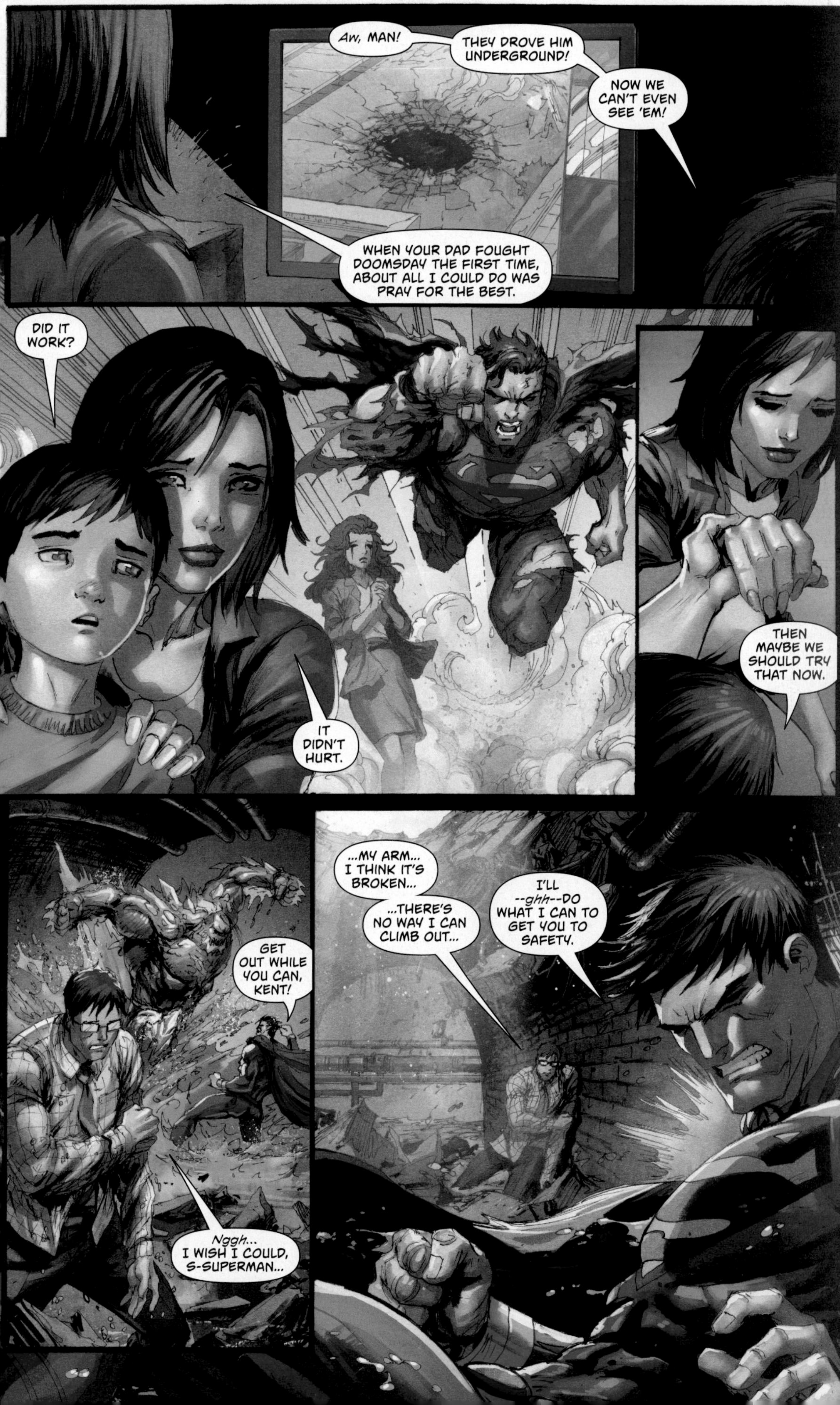

Aw, MAN!
THEY DROVE HIM UNDERGROUND!
NOW WE CAN'T EVEN SEE 'EM!
WHEN YOUR DAD FOUGHT DOOMSDAY THE FIRST TIME, ABOUT ALL I COULD DO WAS PRAY FOR THE BEST.
DID IT WORK?
IT DIDN'T HURT.
THEN MAYBE WE SHOULD TRY THAT NOW.
GET OUT WHILE YOU CAN, KENT!
Nggh... I WISH I COULD, S-SUPERMAN...
...MY ARM... I THINK IT'S BROKEN...
...THERE'S NO WAY I CAN CLIMB OUT...
I'LL --ghh--DO WHAT I CAN TO GET YOU TO SAFETY.

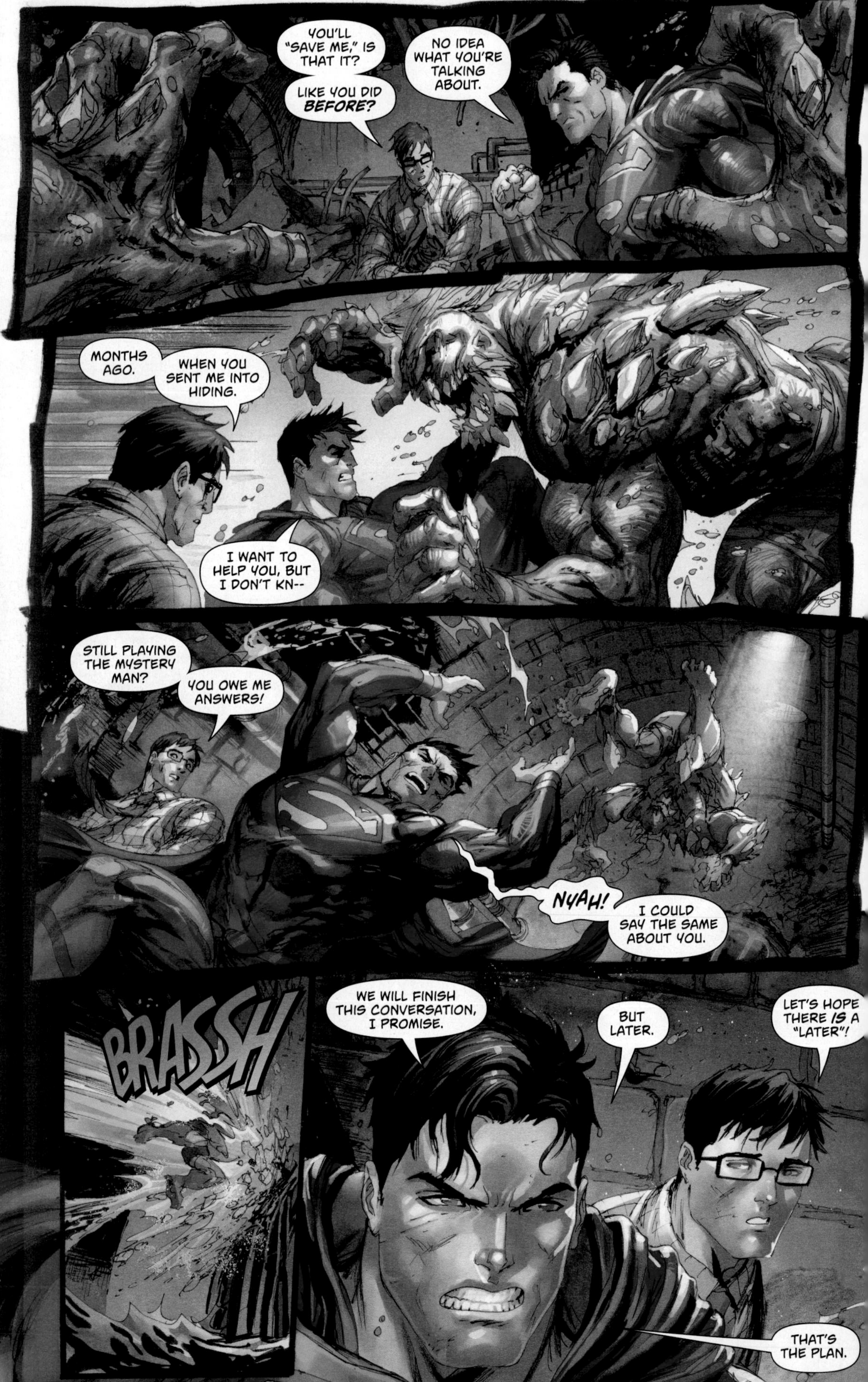
YOU'LL "SAVE ME," IS THAT IT?
LIKE YOU DID *BEFORE?*
NO IDEA WHAT YOU'RE TALKING ABOUT.
MONTHS AGO.
WHEN YOU SENT ME INTO HIDING.
I WANT TO HELP YOU, BUT I DON'T KN--
STILL PLAYING THE MYSTERY MAN?
YOU OWE ME ANSWERS!
NYAH!
I COULD SAY THE SAME ABOUT YOU.
BRASSH
WE WILL FINISH THIS CONVERSATION, I PROMISE.
BUT LATER.
LET'S HOPE THERE *IS* A "LATER"!
THAT'S THE PLAN.

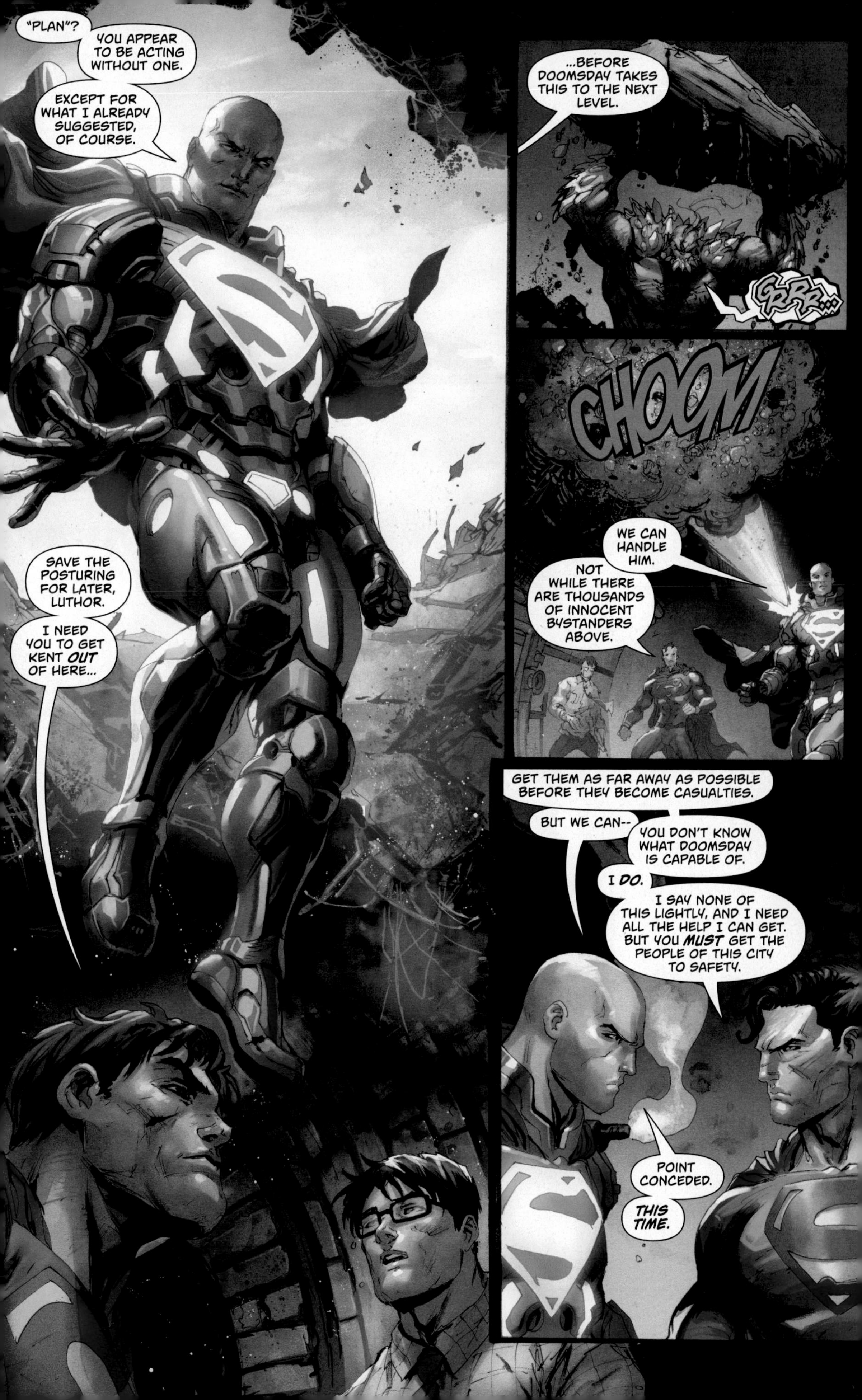
"PLAN"?
YOU APPEAR TO BE ACTING WITHOUT ONE.
EXCEPT FOR WHAT I ALREADY SUGGESTED, OF COURSE.
SAVE THE POSTURING FOR LATER, LUTHOR.
I NEED YOU TO GET KENT *OUT* OF HERE...
...BEFORE DOOMSDAY TAKES THIS TO THE NEXT LEVEL.
GRRR...
CHOOM
WE CAN HANDLE HIM.
NOT WHILE THERE ARE THOUSANDS OF INNOCENT BYSTANDERS ABOVE.
GET THEM AS FAR AWAY AS POSSIBLE BEFORE THEY BECOME CASUALTIES.
BUT WE CAN--
YOU DON'T KNOW WHAT DOOMSDAY IS CAPABLE OF.
I *DO*.
I SAY NONE OF THIS LIGHTLY, AND I NEED ALL THE HELP I CAN GET. BUT YOU *MUST* GET THE PEOPLE OF THIS CITY TO SAFETY.
POINT CONCEDED.
THIS TIME.

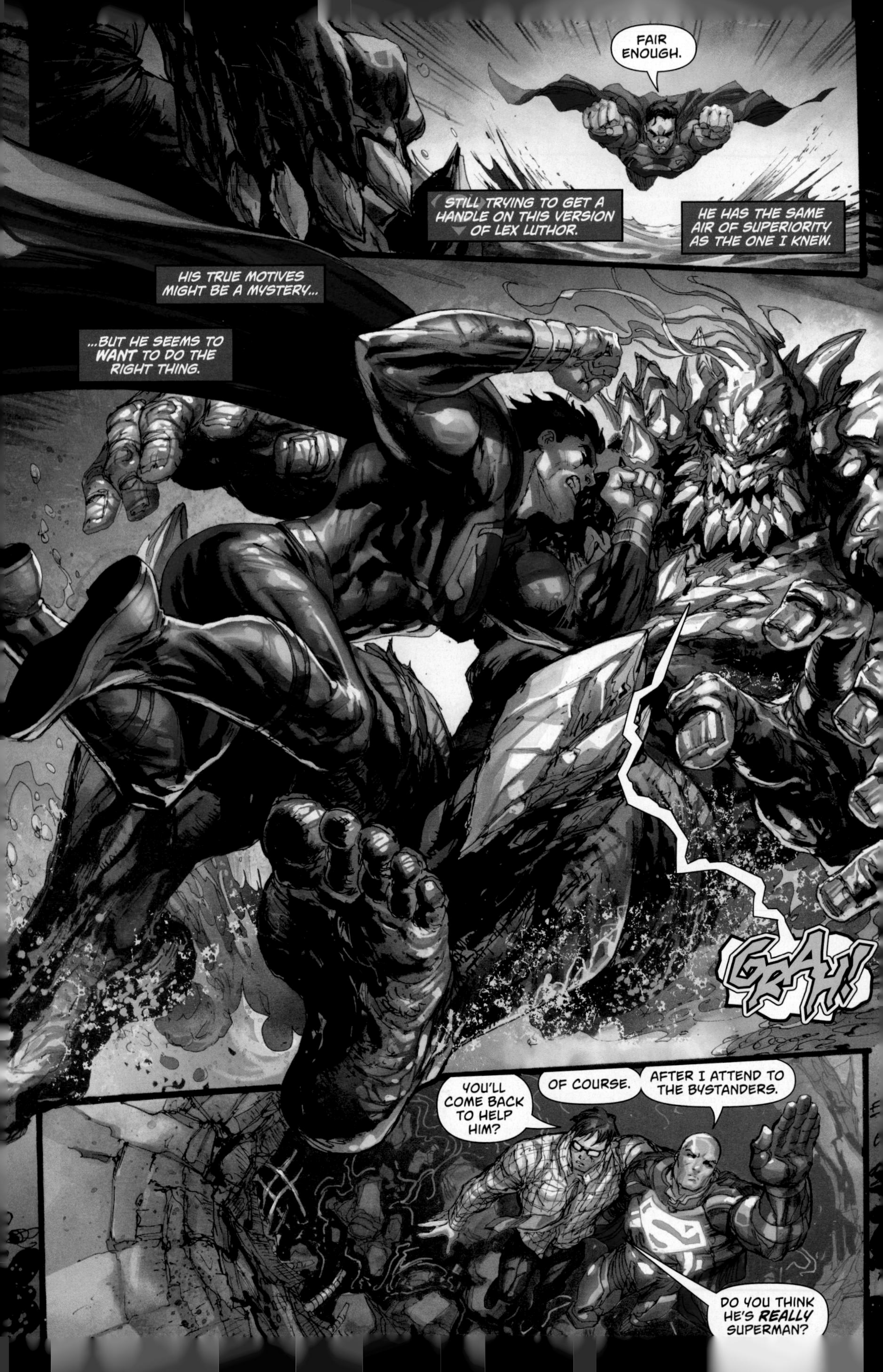
FAIR ENOUGH.
STILL TRYING TO GET A HANDLE ON THIS VERSION OF LEX LUTHOR.
HE HAS THE SAME AIR OF SUPERIORITY AS THE ONE I KNEW.
HIS TRUE MOTIVES MIGHT BE A MYSTERY...
...BUT HE SEEMS TO WANT TO DO THE RIGHT THING.
GRAH!
YOU'LL COME BACK TO HELP HIM?
OF COURSE.
AFTER I ATTEND TO THE BYSTANDERS.
DO YOU THINK HE'S REALLY SUPERMAN?

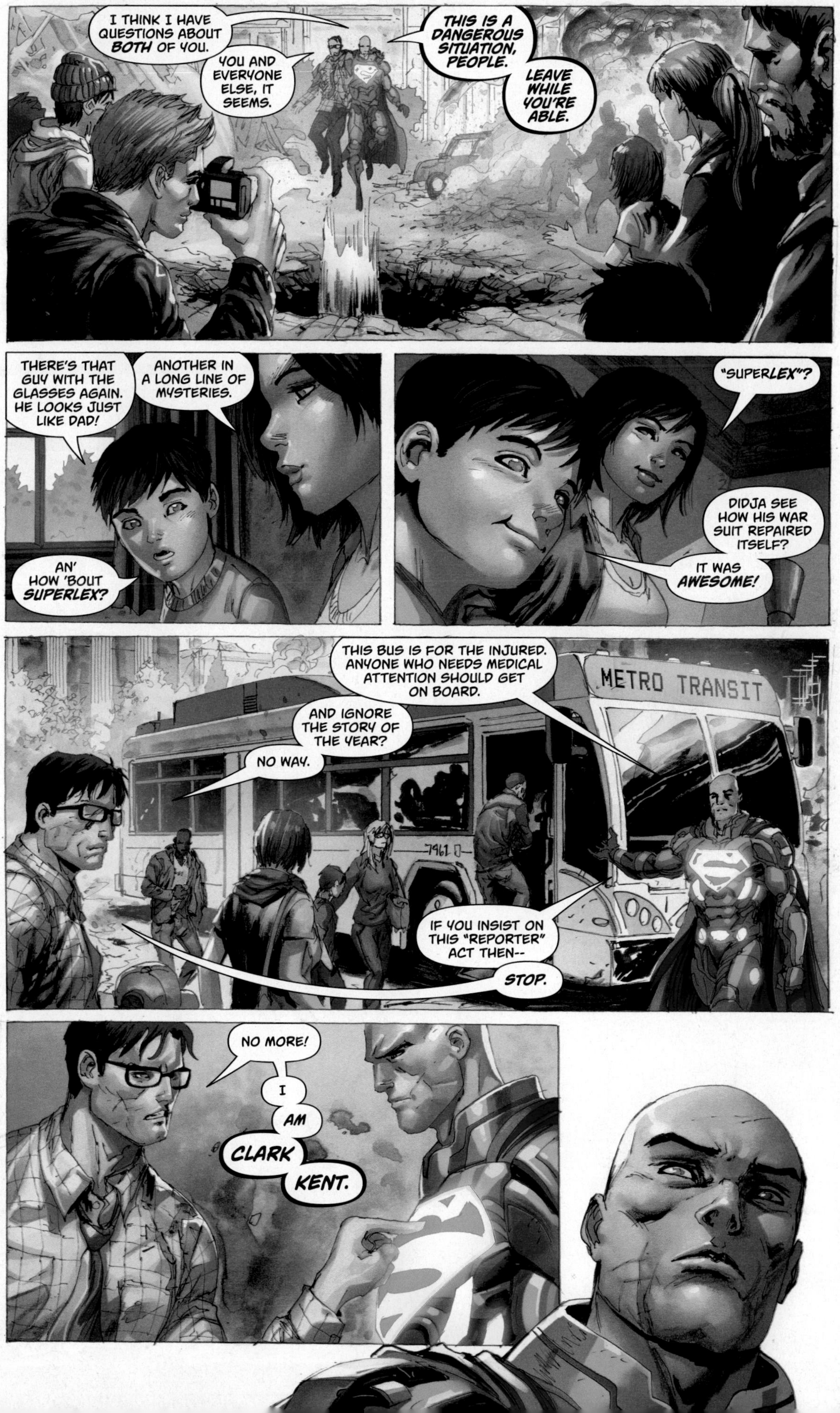
I THINK I HAVE QUESTIONS ABOUT BOTH OF YOU.
YOU AND EVERYONE ELSE, IT SEEMS.
THIS IS A DANGEROUS SITUATION, PEOPLE.
LEAVE WHILE YOU'RE ABLE.
THERE'S THAT GUY WITH THE GLASSES AGAIN. HE LOOKS JUST LIKE DAD!
ANOTHER IN A LONG LINE OF MYSTERIES.
AN' HOW 'BOUT SUPERLEX?
"SUPERLEX"?
DIDJA SEE HOW HIS WAR SUIT REPAIRED ITSELF?
IT WAS AWESOME!
THIS BUS IS FOR THE INJURED. ANYONE WHO NEEDS MEDICAL ATTENTION SHOULD GET ON BOARD.
METRO TRANSIT
AND IGNORE THE STORY OF THE YEAR?
NO WAY.
7962
IF YOU INSIST ON THIS "REPORTER" ACT THEN--
STOP.
NO MORE!
I
AM
CLARK
KENT.

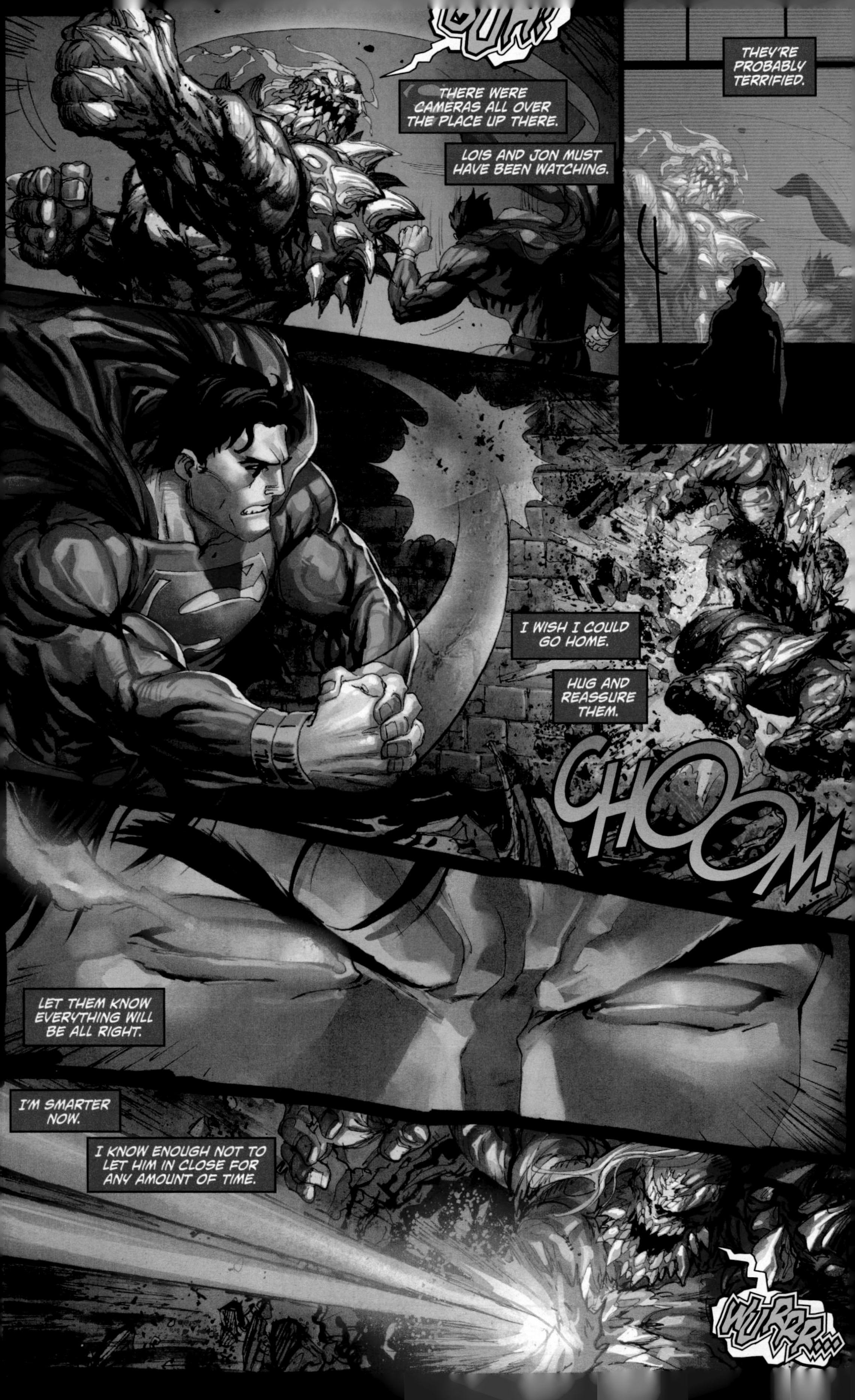
THERE WERE CAMERAS ALL OVER THE PLACE UP THERE.
LOIS AND JON MUST HAVE BEEN WATCHING.
THEY'RE PROBABLY TERRIFIED.
I WISH I COULD GO HOME.
HUG AND REASSURE THEM.
CHOOM
LET THEM KNOW EVERYTHING WILL BE ALL RIGHT.
I'M SMARTER NOW.
I KNOW ENOUGH NOT TO LET HIM IN CLOSE FOR ANY AMOUNT OF TIME.
WURRR...

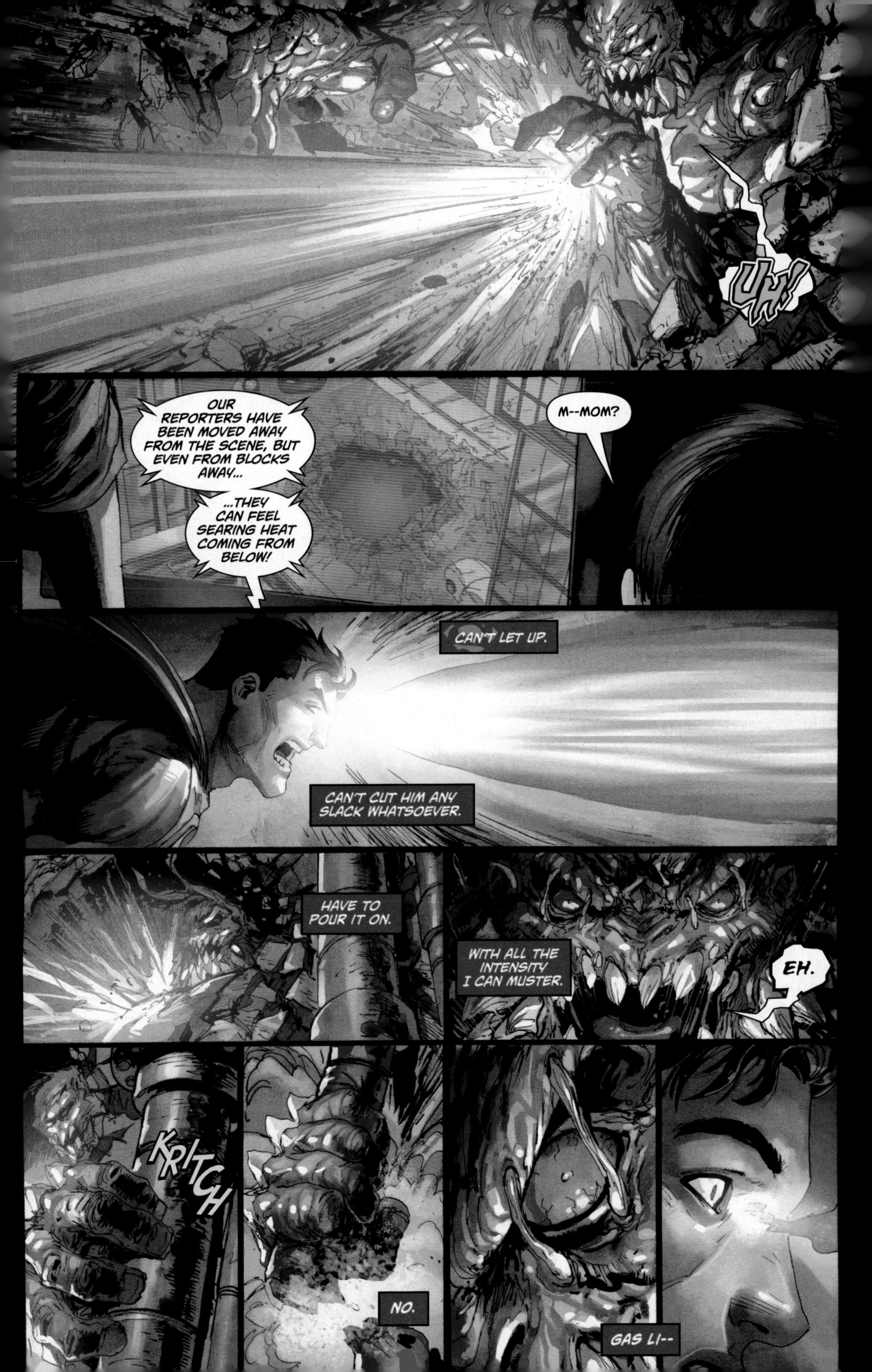

UHN!
OUR REPORTERS HAVE BEEN MOVED AWAY FROM THE SCENE, BUT EVEN FROM BLOCKS AWAY...
...THEY CAN FEEL SEARING HEAT COMING FROM BELOW!
M--MOM?
CAN'T LET UP.
CAN'T CUT HIM ANY SLACK WHATSOEVER.
HAVE TO POUR IT ON.
WITH ALL THE INTENSITY I CAN MUSTER.
EH.
KRITCH
NO.
GAS LI--

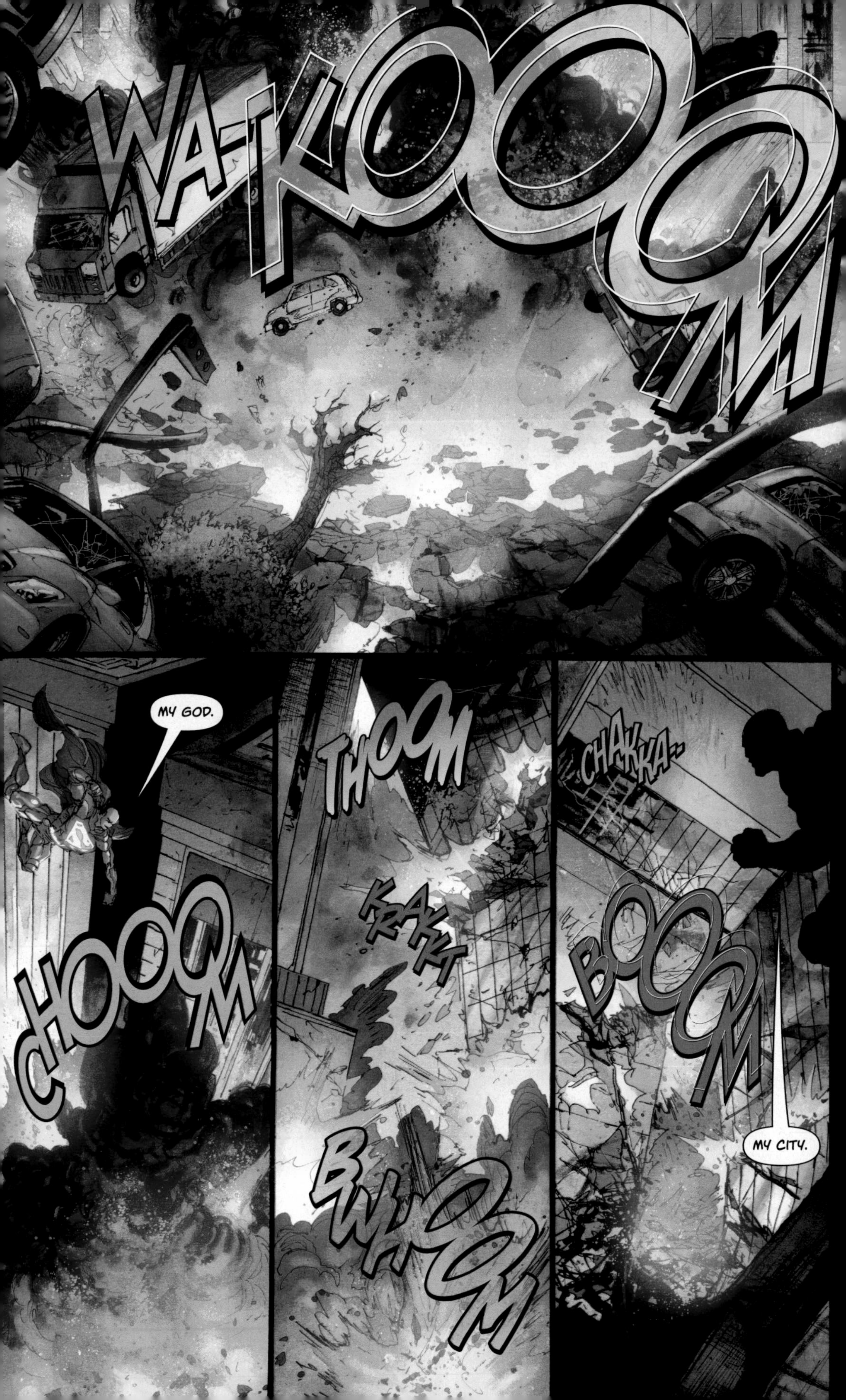
WA-KOOOOM
MY GOD.
CHOOOM
THOOOM
KRAKKT
BWOOOM
CHAKKA-
BOOOM
MY CITY.

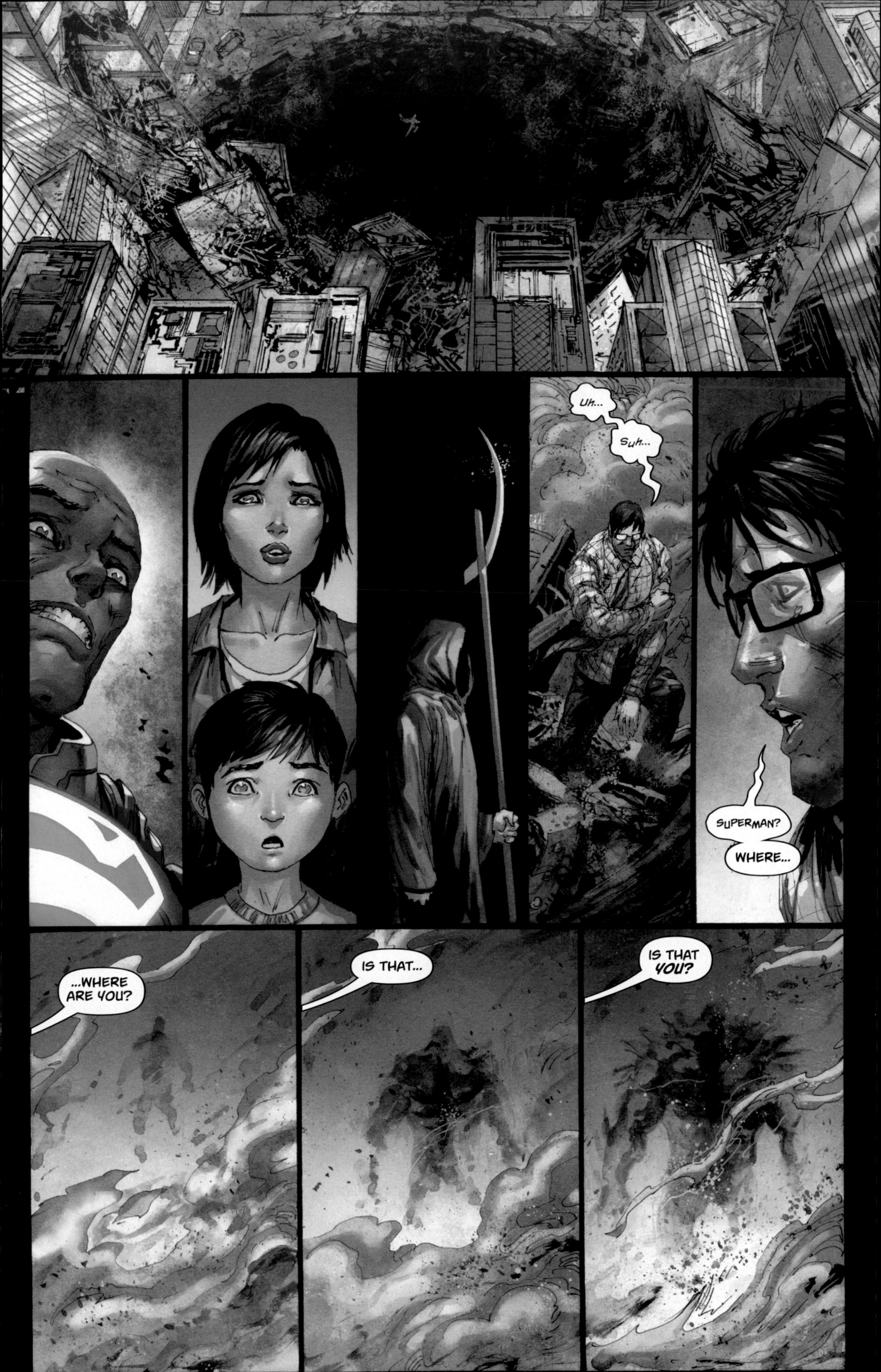
Uh...
Suh...
SUPERMAN?
WHERE...
...WHERE ARE YOU?
IS THAT...
IS THAT *YOU?*

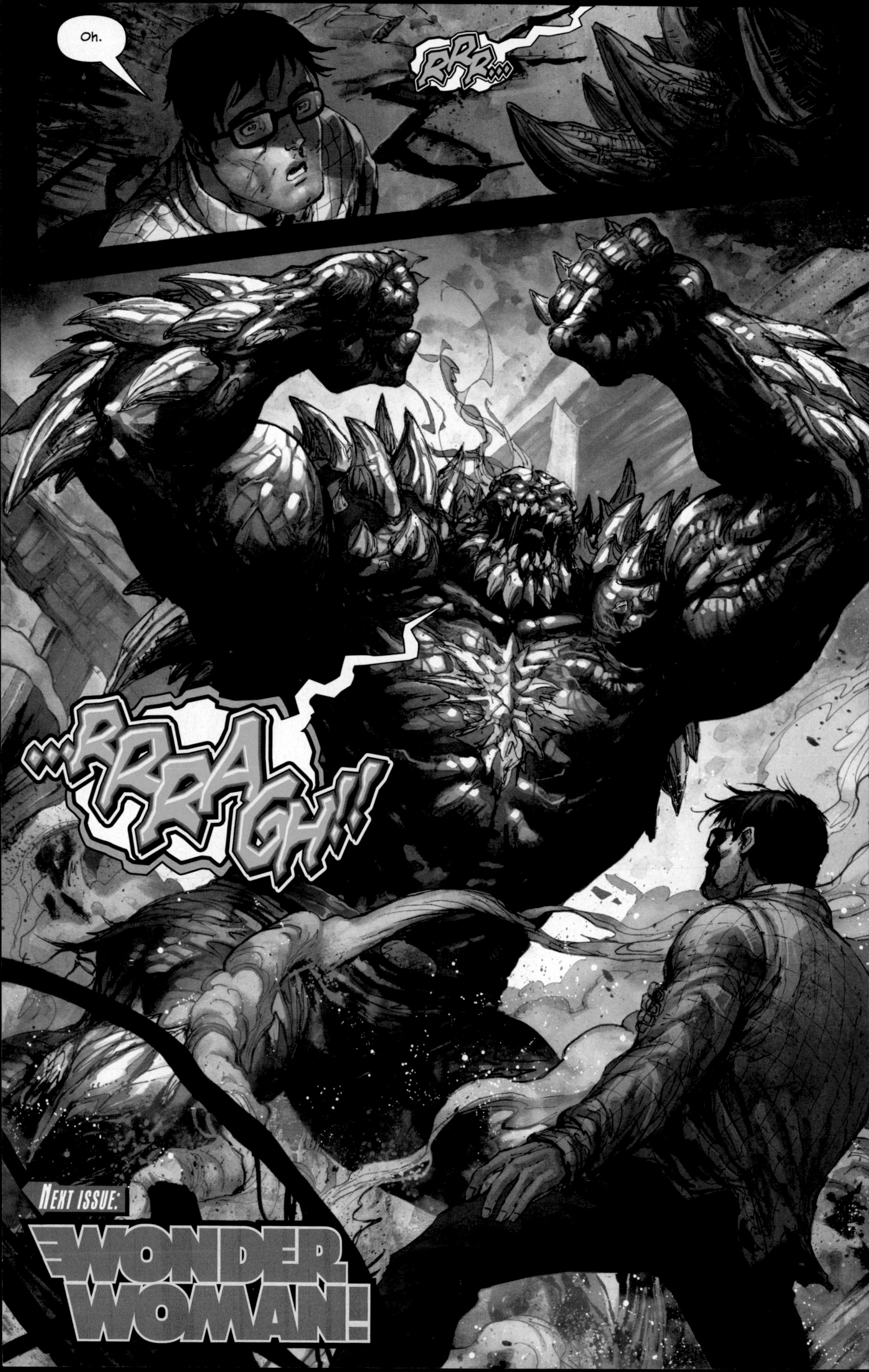
Oh.
RRR...
...RRRAGH!!
NEXT ISSUE:
WONDER WOMAN!

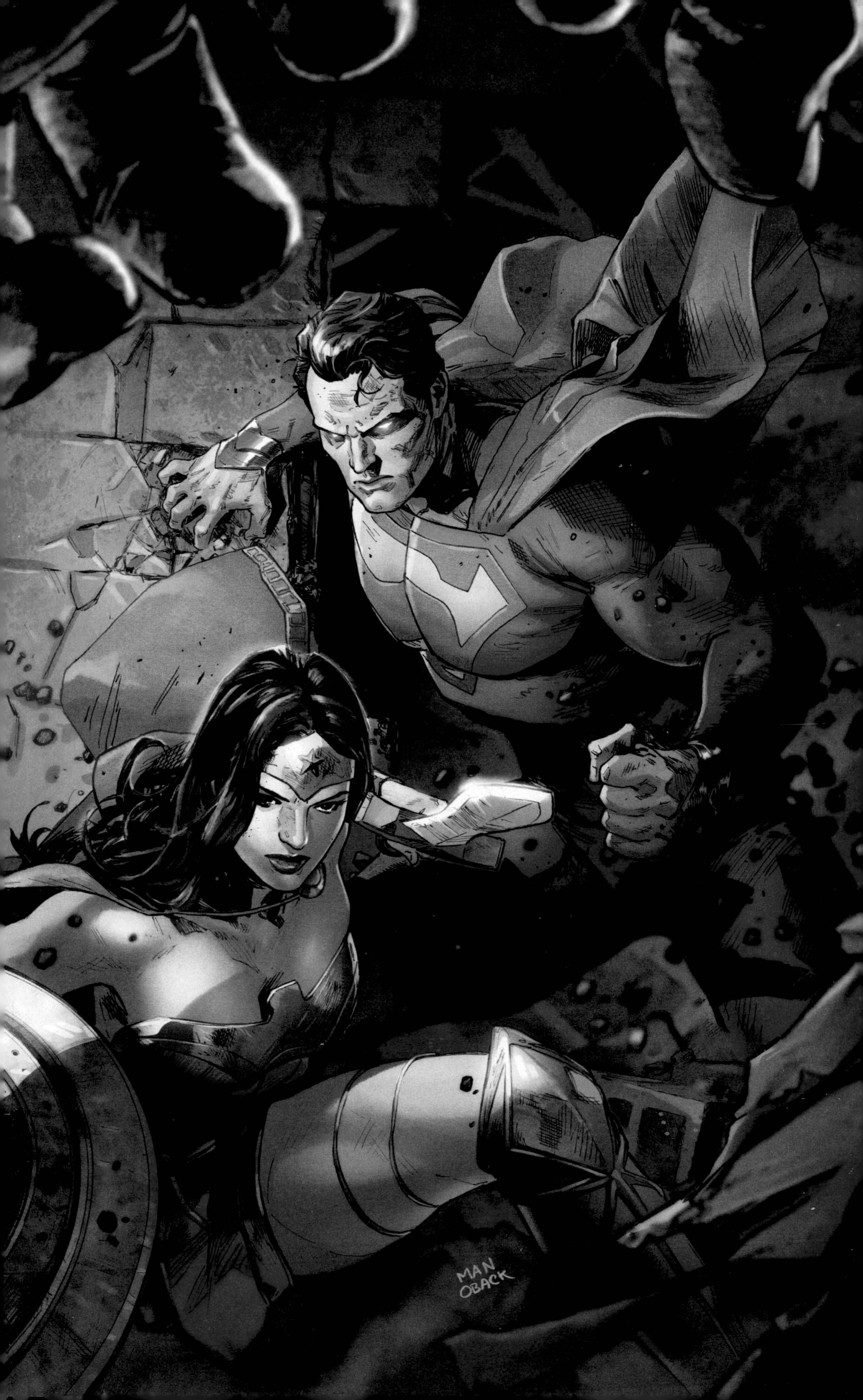
MAN
OBACK

ACTION COMICS #960

CLAY MANN and SONIA OBACK cover artists

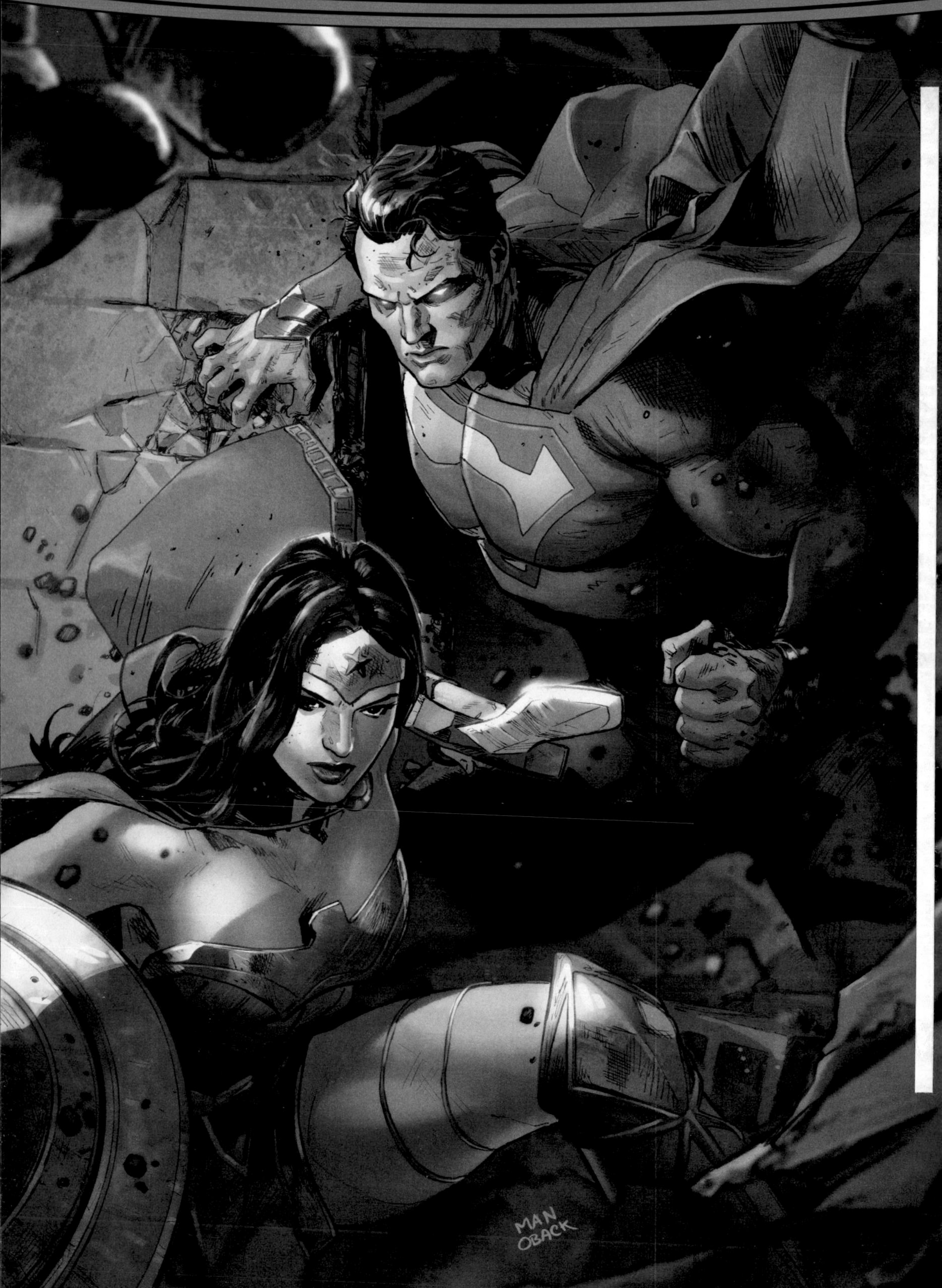
MAN
OBACK

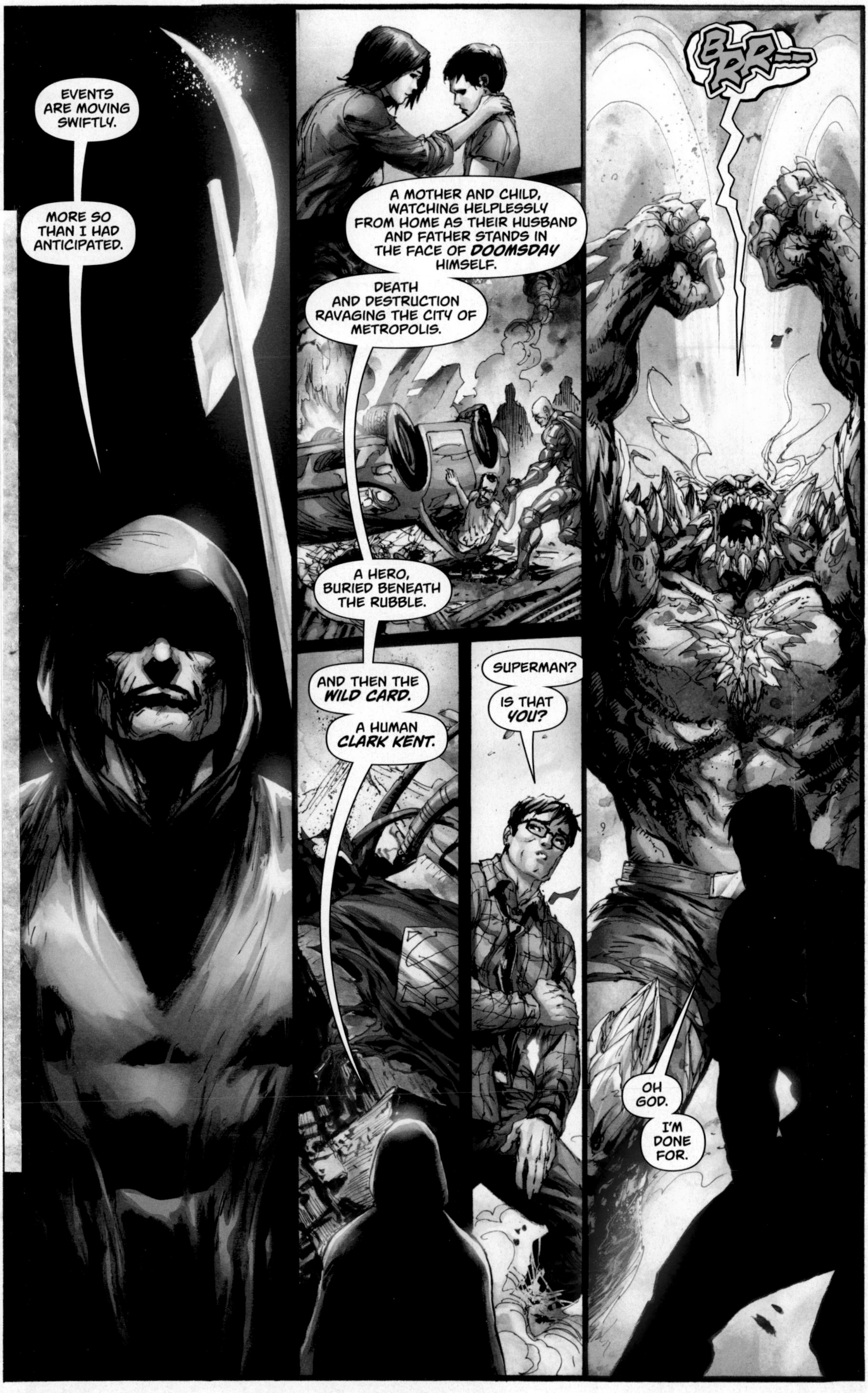
EVENTS ARE MOVING SWIFTLY.
MORE SO THAN I HAD ANTICIPATED.
A MOTHER AND CHILD, WATCHING HELPLESSLY FROM HOME AS THEIR HUSBAND AND FATHER STANDS IN THE FACE OF DOOMSDAY HIMSELF.
DEATH AND DESTRUCTION RAVAGING THE CITY OF METROPOLIS.
A HERO, BURIED BENEATH THE RUBBLE.
AND THEN THE WILD CARD.
A HUMAN CLARK KENT.
SUPERMAN?
IS THAT YOU?
BRR--
OH GOD.
I'M DONE FOR.

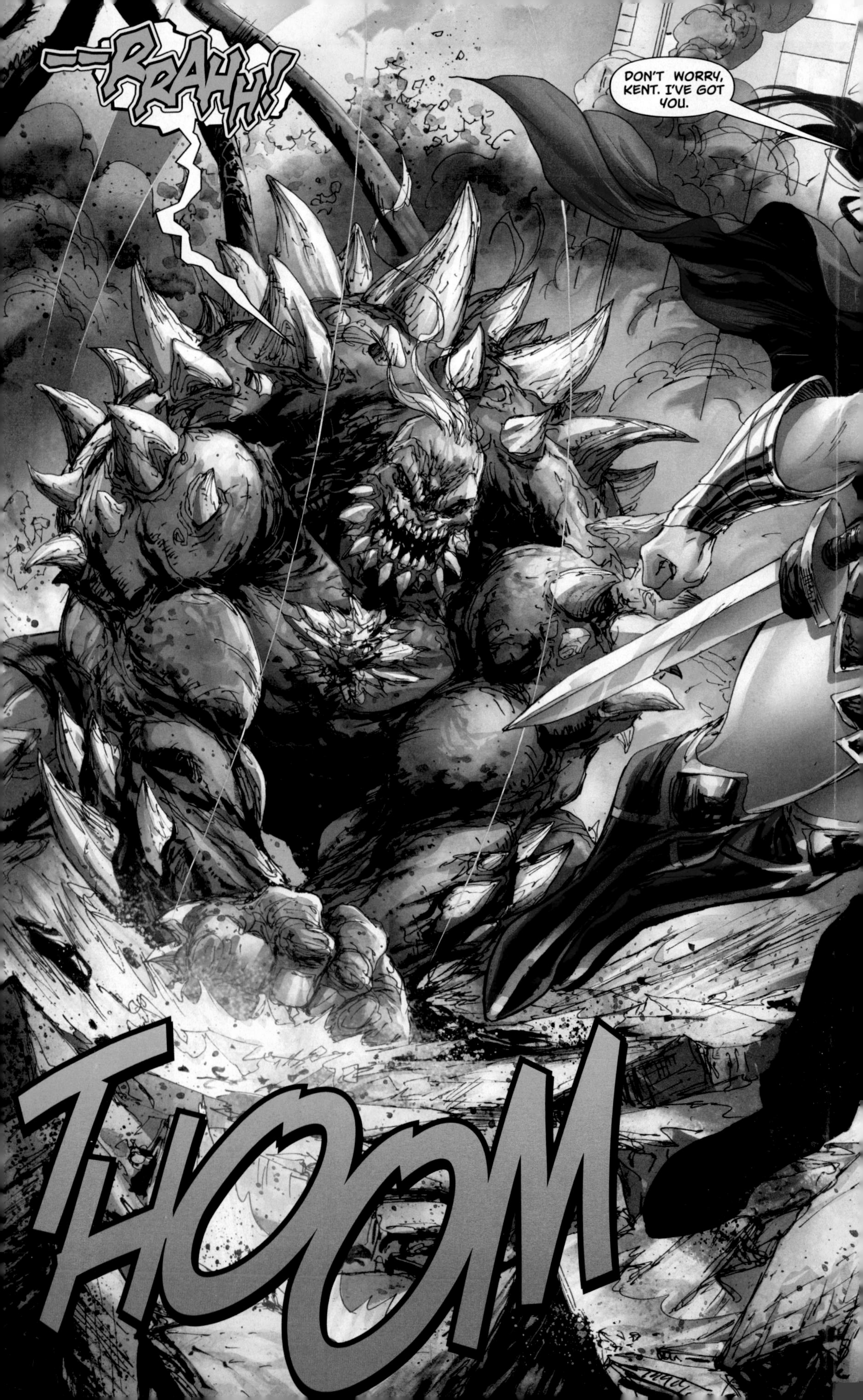

—RRAHH!
DON'T WORRY, KENT. I'VE GOT YOU.
THOOM

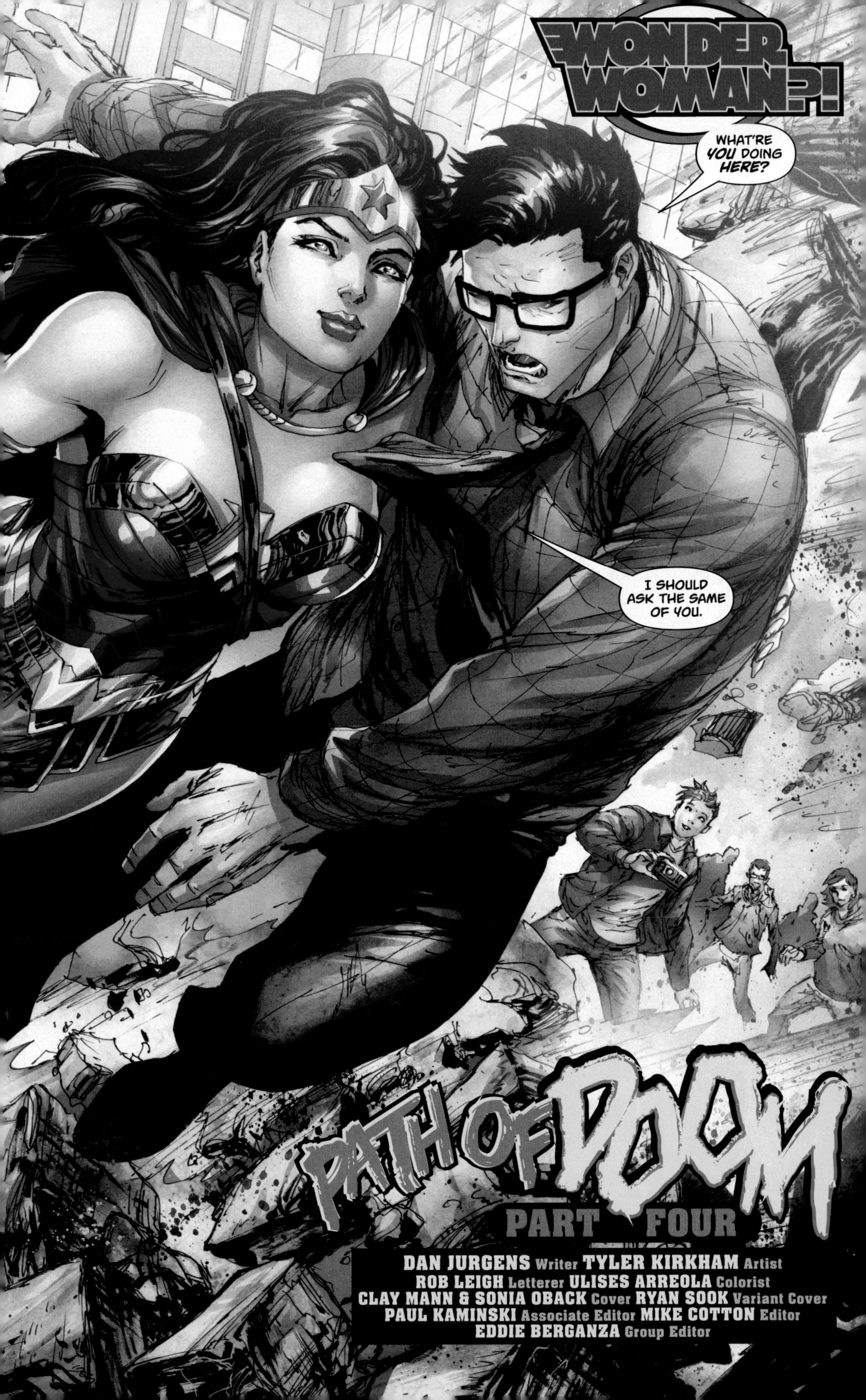
WONDER WOMAN?!
WHAT'RE YOU DOING HERE?
I SHOULD ASK THE SAME OF YOU.
PATH OF DOOM
PART FOUR
DAN JURGENS Writer TYLER KIRKHAM Artist
ROB LEIGH Letterer ULISES ARREOLA Colorist
CLAY MANN & SONIA OBACK Cover RYAN SOOK Variant Cover
PAUL KAMINSKI Associate Editor MIKE COTTON Editor
EDDIE BERGANZA Group Editor

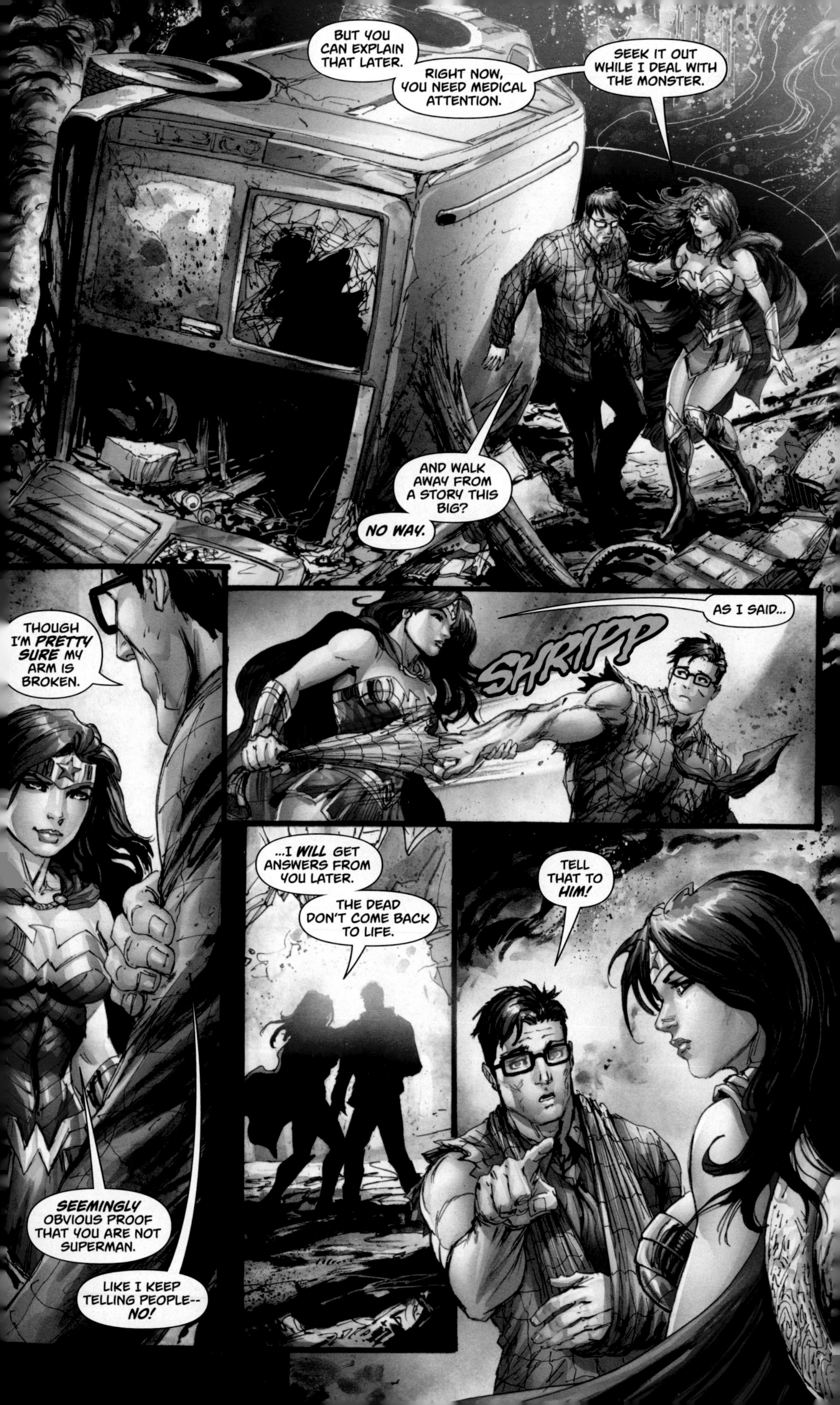
BUT YOU CAN EXPLAIN THAT LATER.
RIGHT NOW, YOU NEED MEDICAL ATTENTION.
SEEK IT OUT WHILE I DEAL WITH THE MONSTER.
AND WALK AWAY FROM A STORY THIS BIG?
NO WAY.
THOUGH I'M PRETTY SURE MY ARM IS BROKEN.
SEEMINGLY OBVIOUS PROOF THAT YOU ARE NOT SUPERMAN.
LIKE I KEEP TELLING PEOPLE-- NO!
AS I SAID...
SHRIPP
...I WILL GET ANSWERS FROM YOU LATER.
THE DEAD DON'T COME BACK TO LIFE.
TELL THAT TO HIM!

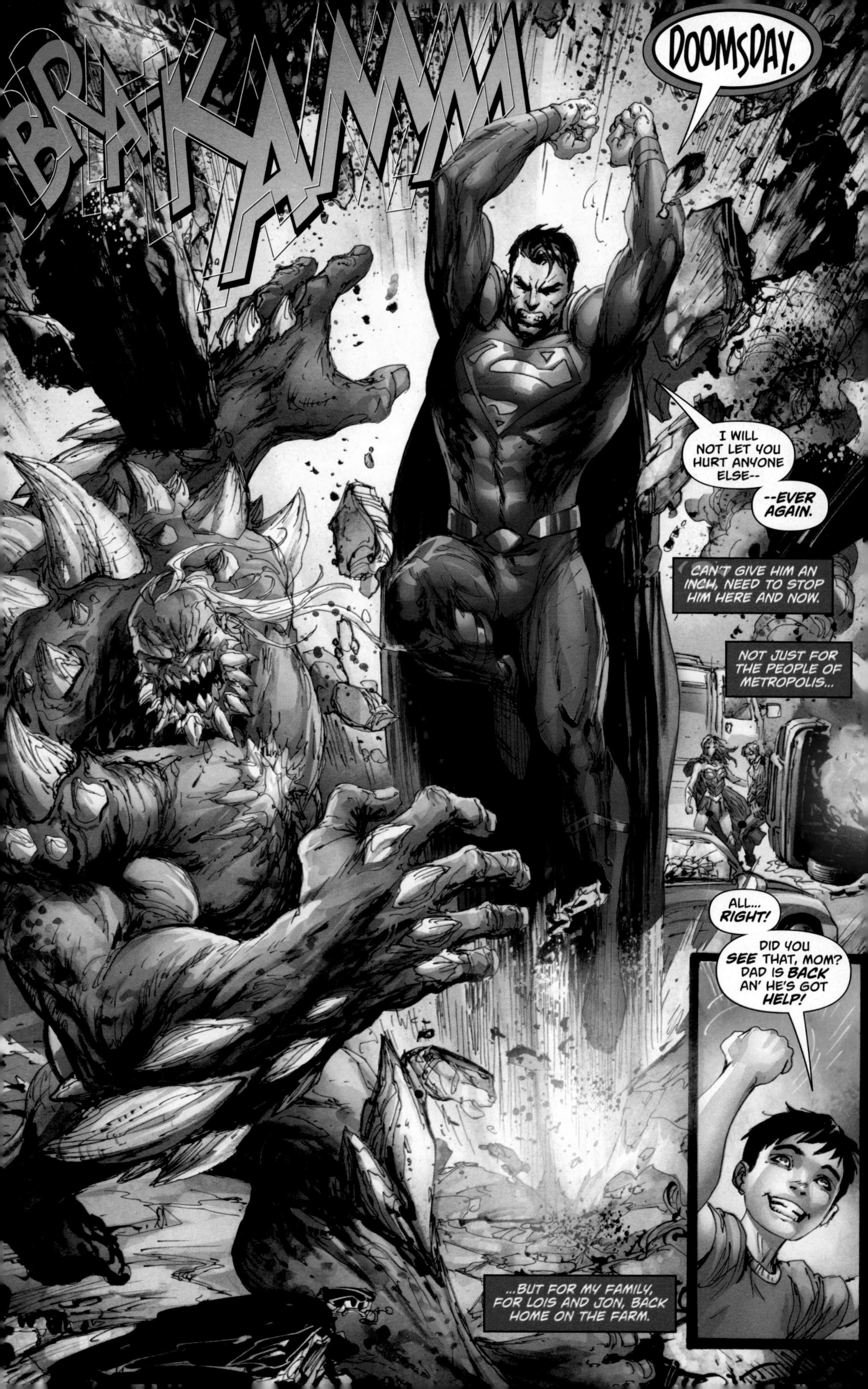
BRAKAMMM
DOOMSDAY.
I WILL NOT LET YOU HURT ANYONE ELSE--
--EVER AGAIN.
CAN'T GIVE HIM AN INCH, NEED TO STOP HIM HERE AND NOW.
NOT JUST FOR THE PEOPLE OF METROPOLIS...
ALL... RIGHT!
DID YOU SEE THAT, MOM? DAD IS BACK AN' HE'S GOT HELP!
...BUT FOR MY FAMILY, FOR LOIS AND JON, BACK HOME ON THE FARM.

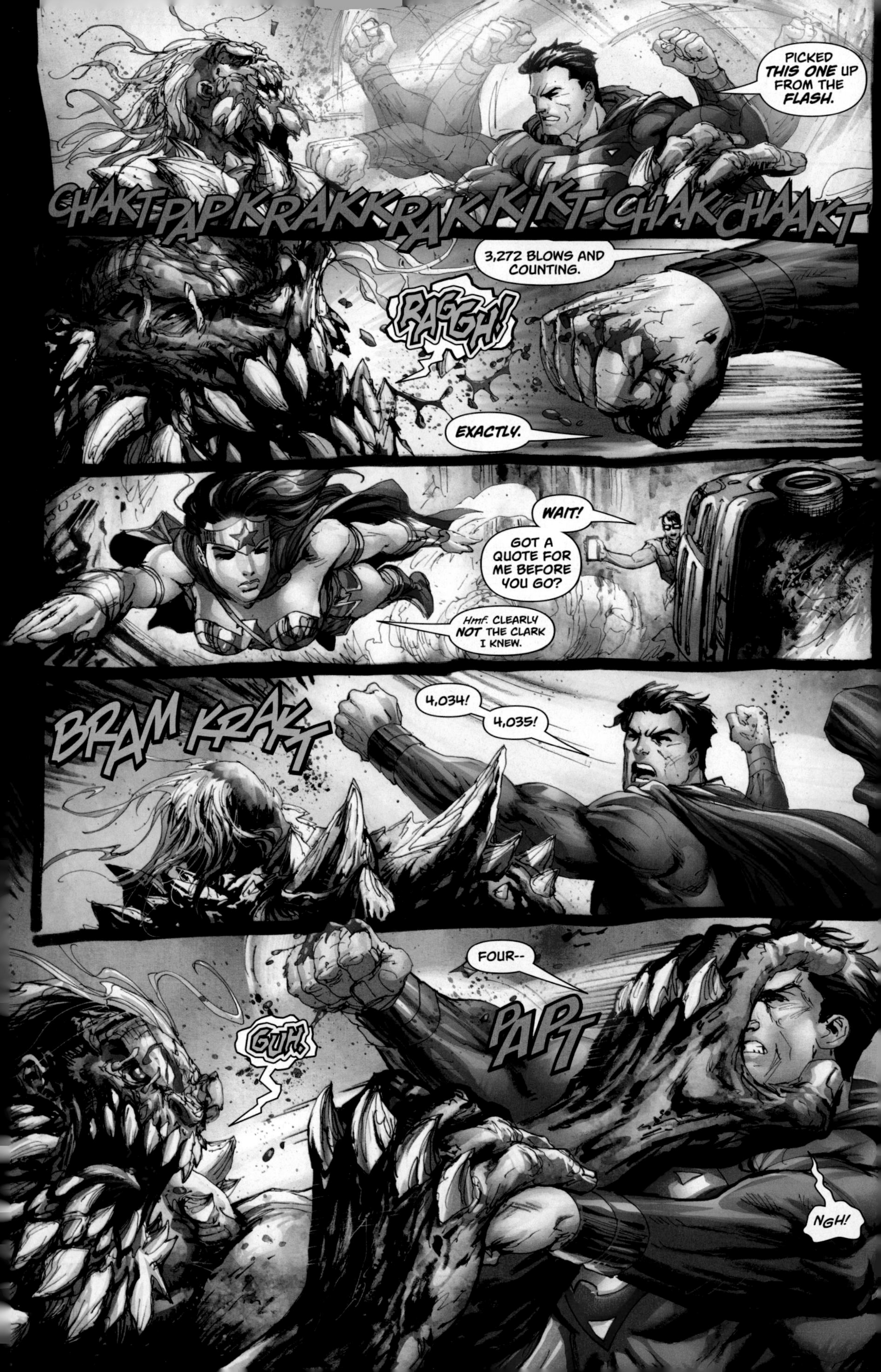
PICKED THIS ONE UP FROM THE FLASH.
CHAKT PAP KRAKK RAKK KIKT CHAK CHAAKT
3,272 BLOWS AND COUNTING.
RAGGH!
EXACTLY.
WAIT!
GOT A QUOTE FOR ME BEFORE YOU GO?
Hmf. CLEARLY NOT THE CLARK I KNEW.
BRAM KRAKK
4,034!
4,035!
FOUR--
PAPT
GUH.
NGH!

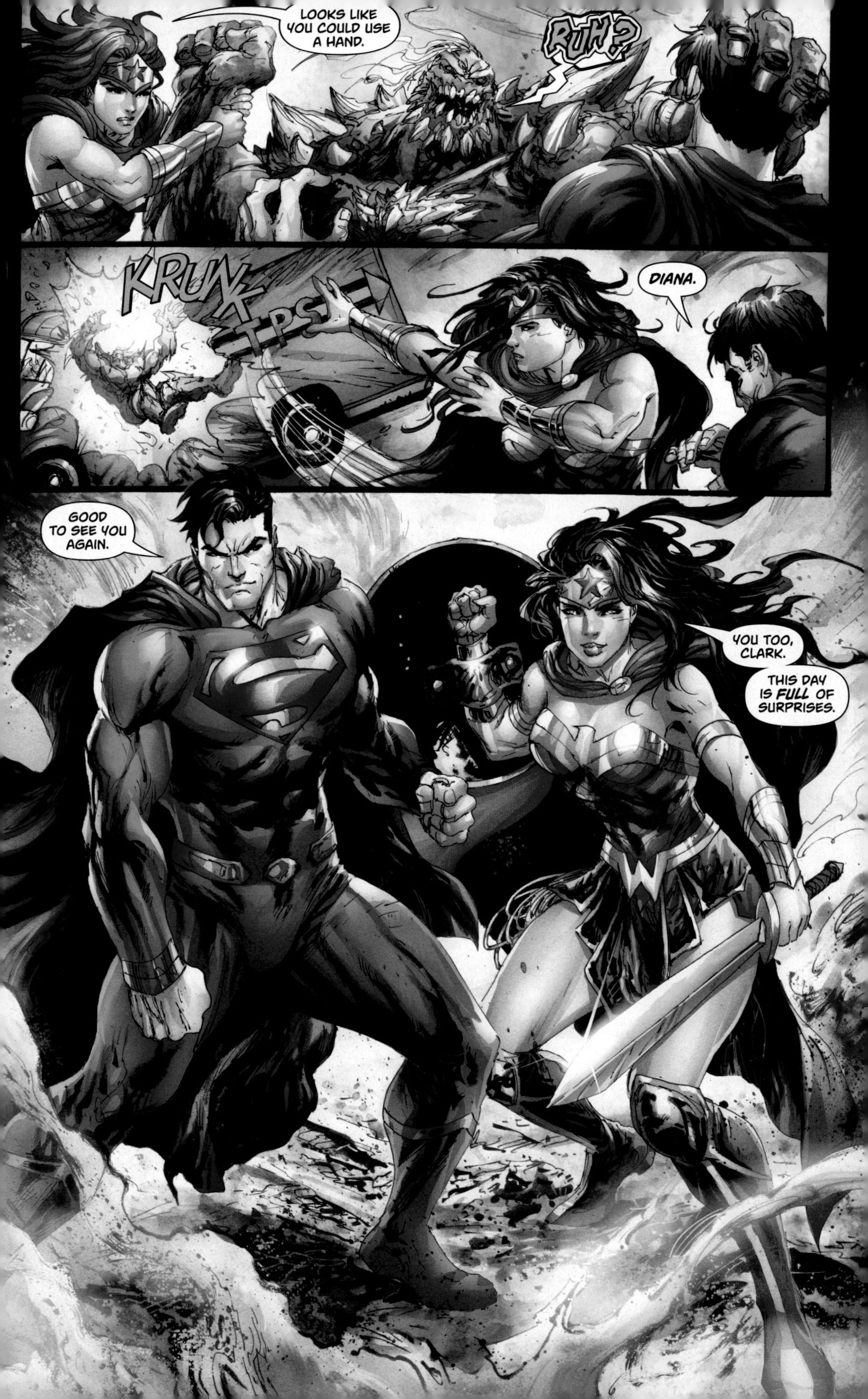
LOOKS LIKE YOU COULD USE A HAND.
RUH?
KRUNK
TPSS
DIANA.
GOOD TO SEE YOU AGAIN.
YOU TOO, CLARK.
THIS DAY IS FULL OF SURPRISES.

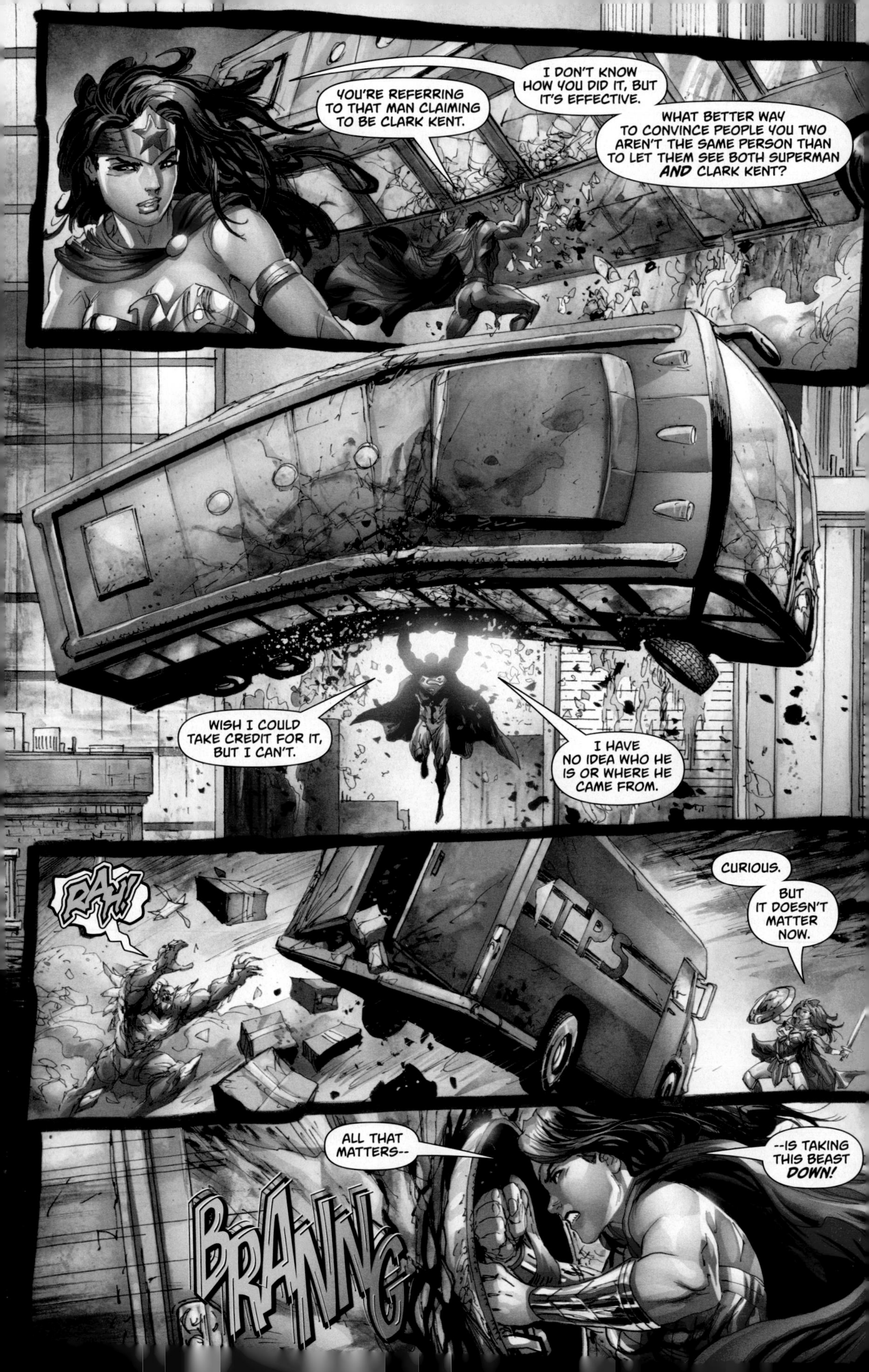
YOU'RE REFERRING TO THAT MAN CLAIMING TO BE CLARK KENT.
I DON'T KNOW HOW YOU DID IT, BUT IT'S EFFECTIVE.
WHAT BETTER WAY TO CONVINCE PEOPLE YOU TWO AREN'T THE SAME PERSON THAN TO LET THEM SEE BOTH SUPERMAN AND CLARK KENT?
WISH I COULD TAKE CREDIT FOR IT, BUT I CAN'T.
I HAVE NO IDEA WHO HE IS OR WHERE HE CAME FROM.
RAH!
CURIOUS.
BUT IT DOESN'T MATTER NOW.
ALL THAT MATTERS--
--IS TAKING THIS BEAST DOWN!
BRANNG

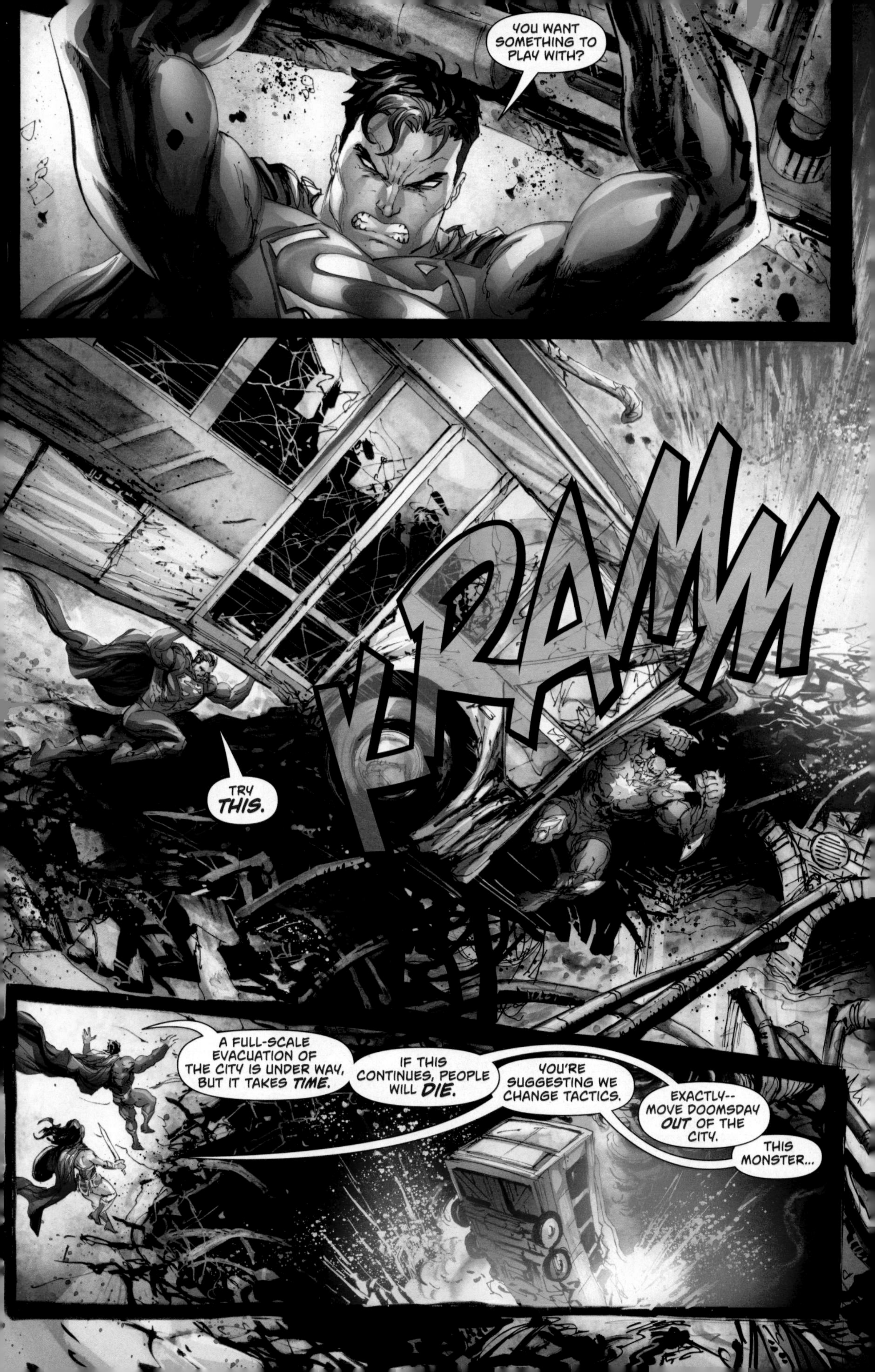
YOU WANT SOMETHING TO PLAY WITH?
KRAMM
TRY THIS.
A FULL-SCALE EVACUATION OF THE CITY IS UNDER WAY, BUT IT TAKES TIME.
IF THIS CONTINUES, PEOPLE WILL DIE.
YOU'RE SUGGESTING WE CHANGE TACTICS.
EXACTLY-- MOVE DOOMSDAY OUT OF THE CITY.
THIS MONSTER...

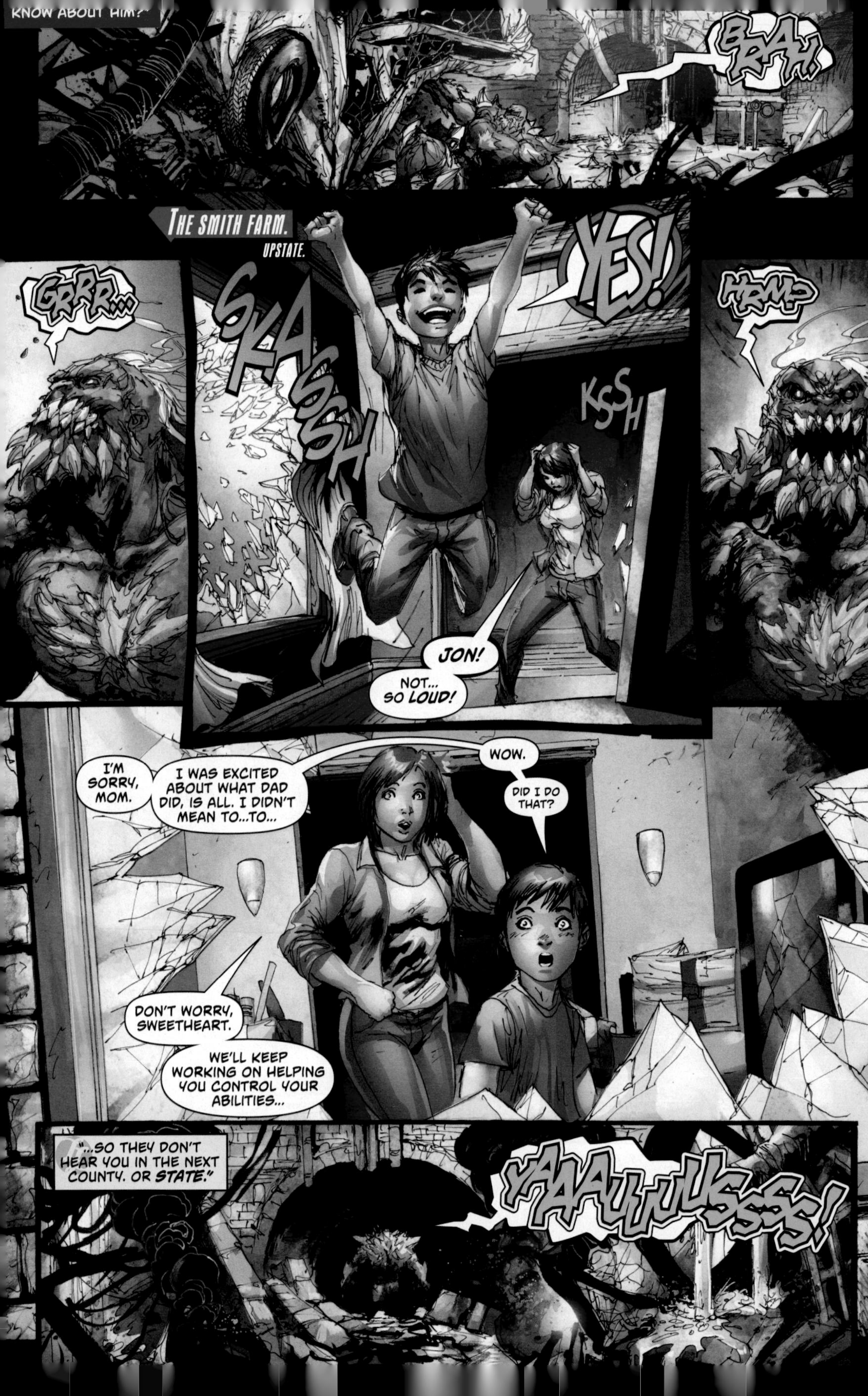
KNOW ABOUT HIM?"
BRAH.
THE SMITH FARM.
UPSTATE.
GRRR...
SKASSH
YES!
HRMP
KSSH
JON!
NOT... SO LOUD!
I'M SORRY, MOM.
I WAS EXCITED ABOUT WHAT DAD DID, IS ALL. I DIDN'T MEAN TO...TO...
WOW.
DID I DO THAT?
DON'T WORRY, SWEETHEART.
WE'LL KEEP WORKING ON HELPING YOU CONTROL YOUR ABILITIES...
"...SO THEY DON'T HEAR YOU IN THE NEXT COUNTY. OR STATE."
YAAUUUSSSS!

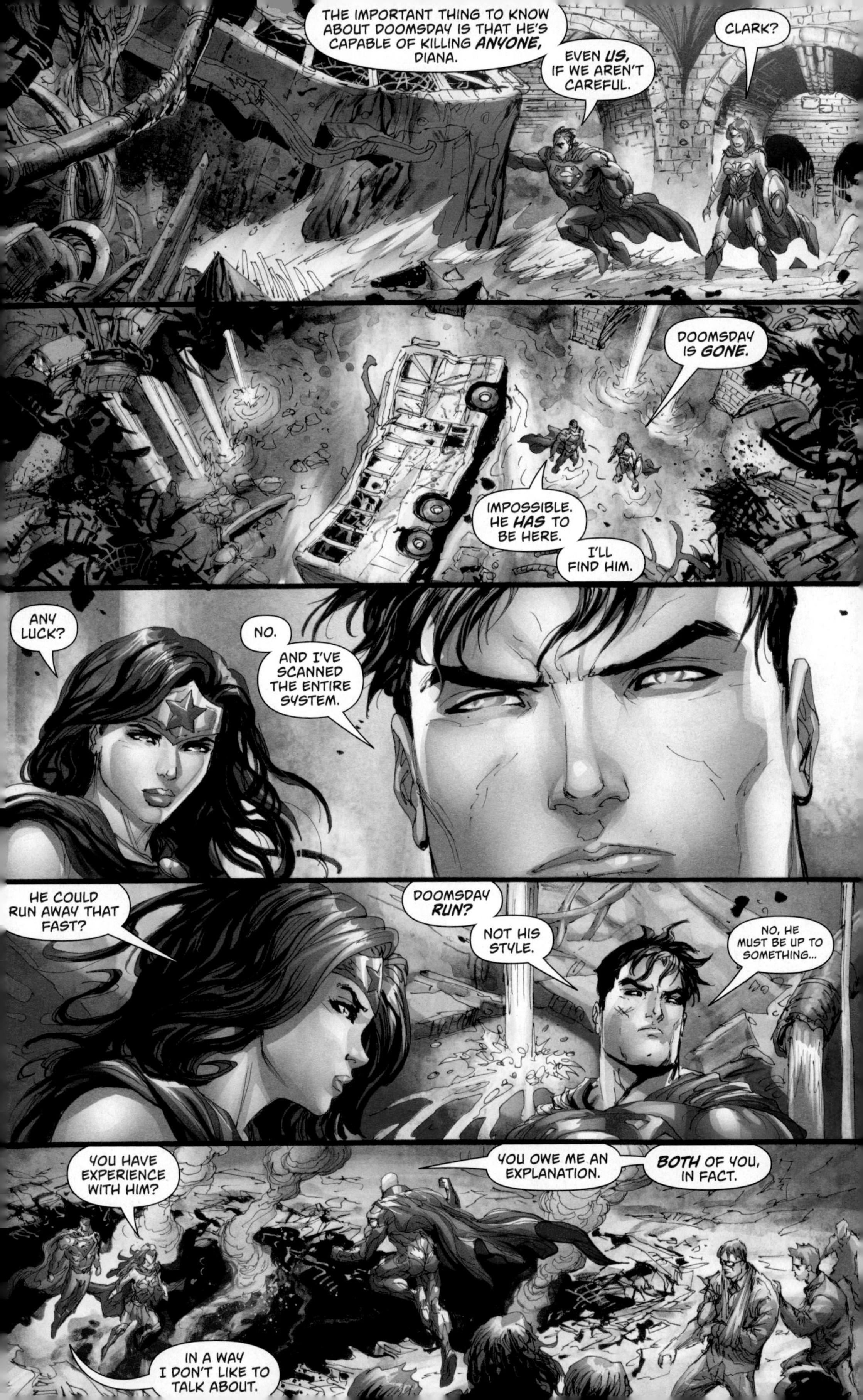
THE IMPORTANT THING TO KNOW ABOUT DOOMSDAY IS THAT HE'S CAPABLE OF KILLING ANYONE, DIANA.
EVEN US, IF WE AREN'T CAREFUL.
CLARK?
DOOMSDAY IS GONE.
IMPOSSIBLE. HE HAS TO BE HERE.
I'LL FIND HIM.
ANY LUCK?
NO.
AND I'VE SCANNED THE ENTIRE SYSTEM.
HE COULD RUN AWAY THAT FAST?
DOOMSDAY RUN?
NOT HIS STYLE.
NO, HE MUST BE UP TO SOMETHING...
YOU HAVE EXPERIENCE WITH HIM?
YOU OWE ME AN EXPLANATION.
BOTH OF YOU, IN FACT.
IN A WAY I DON'T LIKE TO TALK ABOUT.

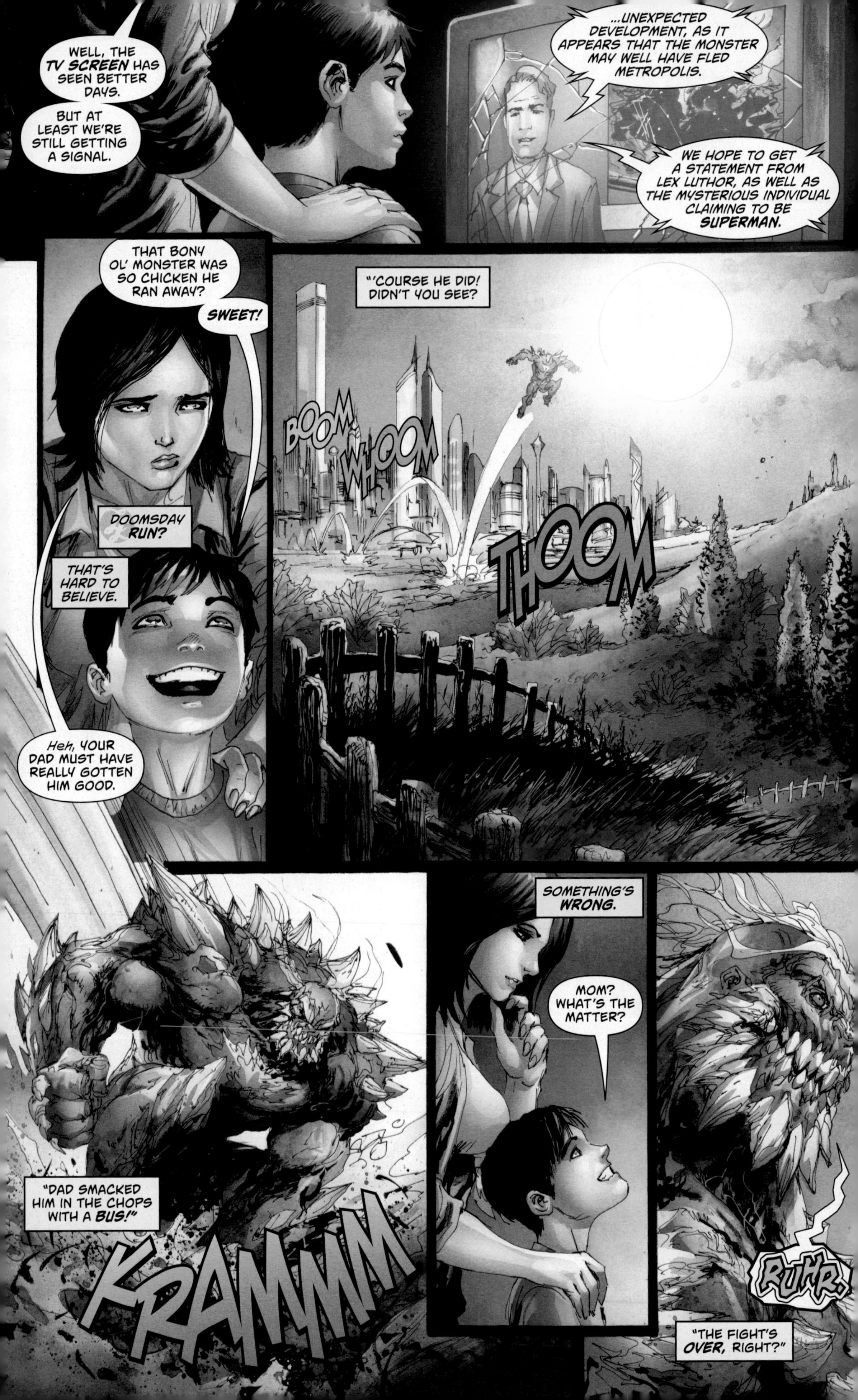
WELL, THE TV SCREEN HAS SEEN BETTER DAYS.
BUT AT LEAST WE'RE STILL GETTING A SIGNAL.
...UNEXPECTED DEVELOPMENT, AS IT APPEARS THAT THE MONSTER MAY WELL HAVE FLED METROPOLIS.
WE HOPE TO GET A STATEMENT FROM LEX LUTHOR, AS WELL AS THE MYSTERIOUS INDIVIDUAL CLAIMING TO BE SUPERMAN.
THAT BONY OL' MONSTER WAS SO CHICKEN HE RAN AWAY?
SWEET!
DOOMSDAY RUN?
THAT'S HARD TO BELIEVE.
Heh, YOUR DAD MUST HAVE REALLY GOTTEN HIM GOOD.
"'COURSE HE DID! DIDN'T YOU SEE?
BOOM
WHOOM
THOOM
"DAD SMACKED HIM IN THE CHOPS WITH A BUS!"
KRAMMM
SOMETHING'S WRONG.
MOM? WHAT'S THE MATTER?
RUHR.
"THE FIGHT'S OVER, RIGHT?"

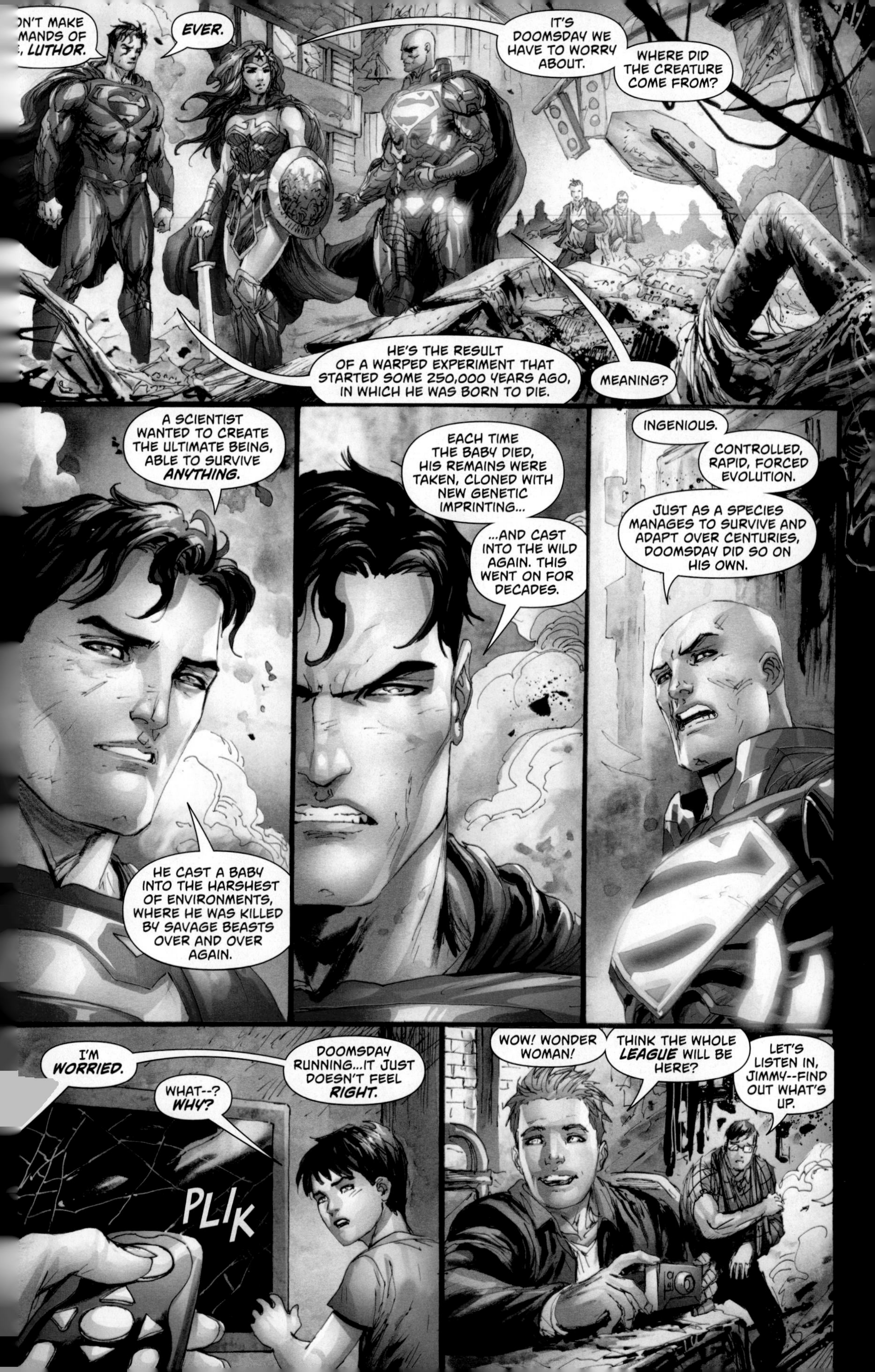

N'T MAKE
MANDS OF
, LUTHOR.
EVER.
IT'S DOOMSDAY WE HAVE TO WORRY ABOUT.
WHERE DID THE CREATURE COME FROM?
HE'S THE RESULT OF A WARPED EXPERIMENT THAT STARTED SOME 250,000 YEARS AGO, IN WHICH HE WAS BORN TO DIE.
MEANING?
A SCIENTIST WANTED TO CREATE THE ULTIMATE BEING, ABLE TO SURVIVE ANYTHING.
HE CAST A BABY INTO THE HARSHEST OF ENVIRONMENTS, WHERE HE WAS KILLED BY SAVAGE BEASTS OVER AND OVER AGAIN.
EACH TIME THE BABY DIED, HIS REMAINS WERE TAKEN, CLONED WITH NEW GENETIC IMPRINTING...
...AND CAST INTO THE WILD AGAIN. THIS WENT ON FOR DECADES.
INGENIOUS.
CONTROLLED, RAPID, FORCED EVOLUTION.
JUST AS A SPECIES MANAGES TO SURVIVE AND ADAPT OVER CENTURIES, DOOMSDAY DID SO ON HIS OWN.
I'M WORRIED.
DOOMSDAY RUNNING...IT JUST DOESN'T FEEL RIGHT.
WHAT--? WHY?
PLIK
WOW! WONDER WOMAN!
THINK THE WHOLE LEAGUE WILL BE HERE?
LET'S LISTEN IN, JIMMY--FIND OUT WHAT'S UP.

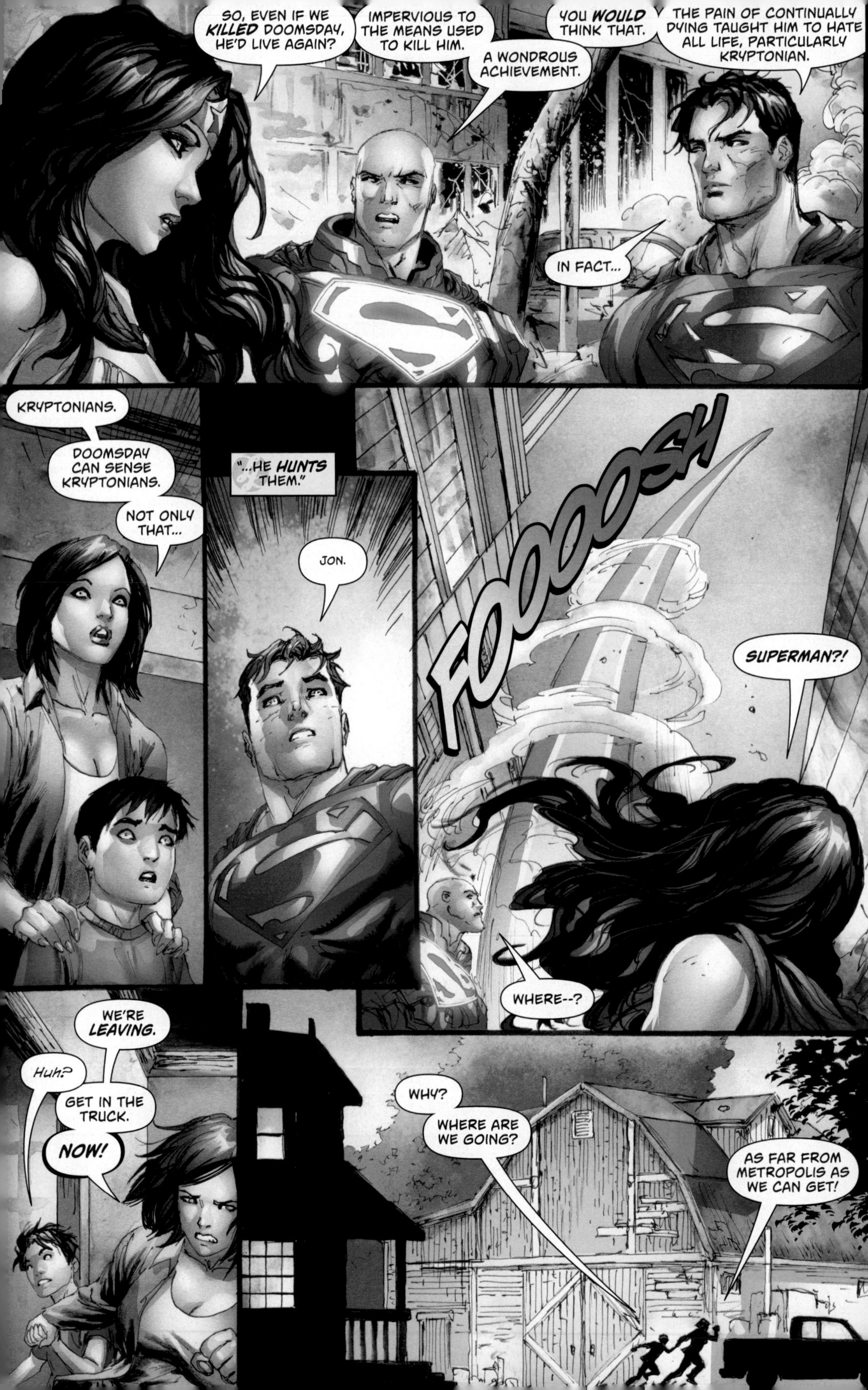
SO, EVEN IF WE KILLED DOOMSDAY, HE'D LIVE AGAIN?
IMPERVIOUS TO THE MEANS USED TO KILL HIM.
A WONDROUS ACHIEVEMENT.
YOU WOULD THINK THAT.
THE PAIN OF CONTINUALLY DYING TAUGHT HIM TO HATE ALL LIFE, PARTICULARLY KRYPTONIAN.
IN FACT...
KRYPTONIANS.
DOOMSDAY CAN SENSE KRYPTONIANS.
NOT ONLY THAT...
"...HE HUNTS THEM."
JON.
FOOOOOSH
SUPERMAN?!
WHERE--?
WE'RE LEAVING.
Huh?
GET IN THE TRUCK.
NOW!
WHY?
WHERE ARE WE GOING?
AS FAR FROM METROPOLIS AS WE CAN GET!

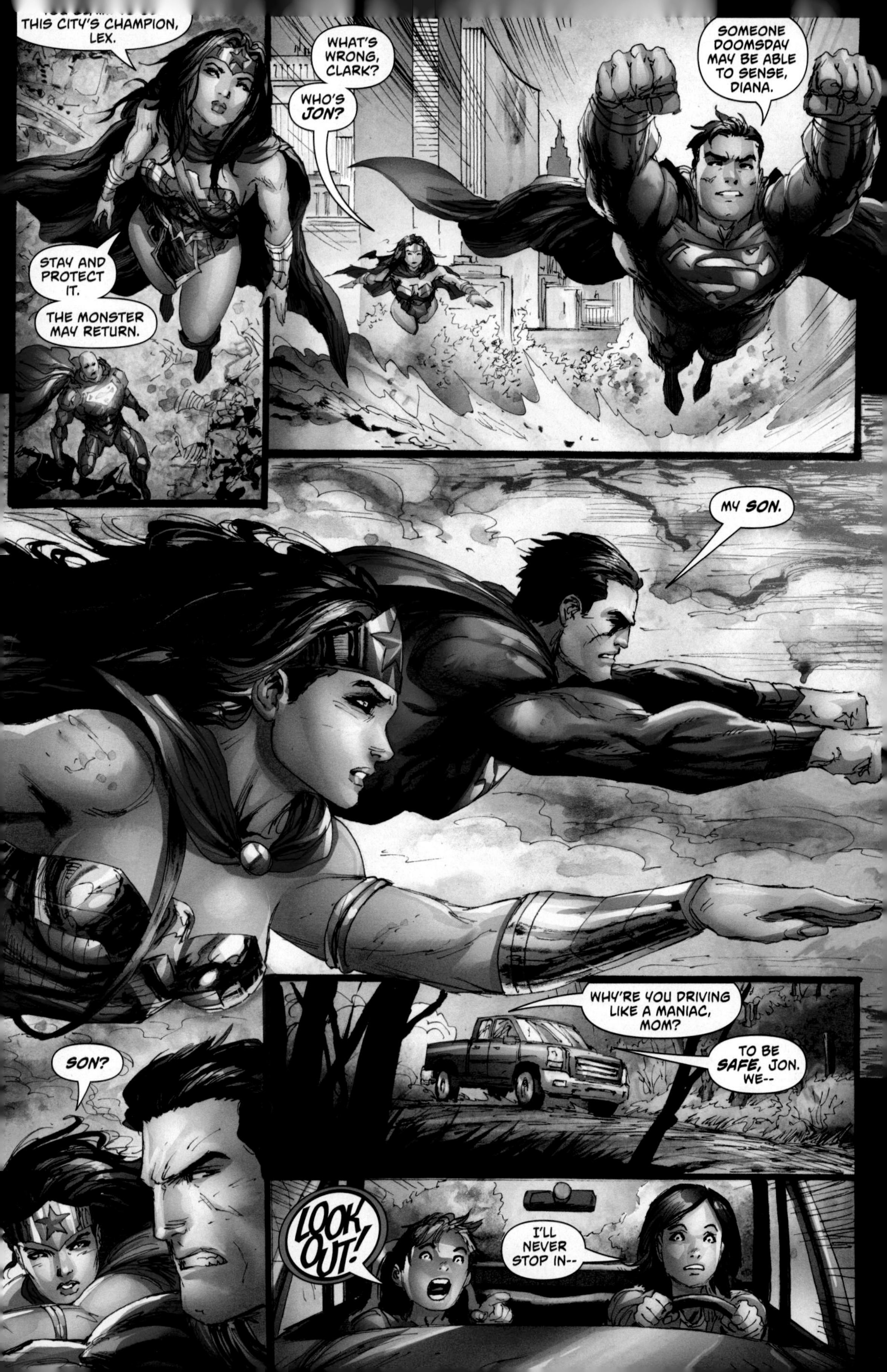
THIS CITY'S CHAMPION, LEX.
STAY AND PROTECT IT.
THE MONSTER MAY RETURN.
WHAT'S WRONG, CLARK?
WHO'S JON?
SOMEONE DOOMSDAY MAY BE ABLE TO SENSE, DIANA.
MY SON.
SON?
WHY'RE YOU DRIVING LIKE A MANIAC, MOM?
TO BE SAFE, JON. WE--
I'LL NEVER STOP IN--
LOOK OUT!

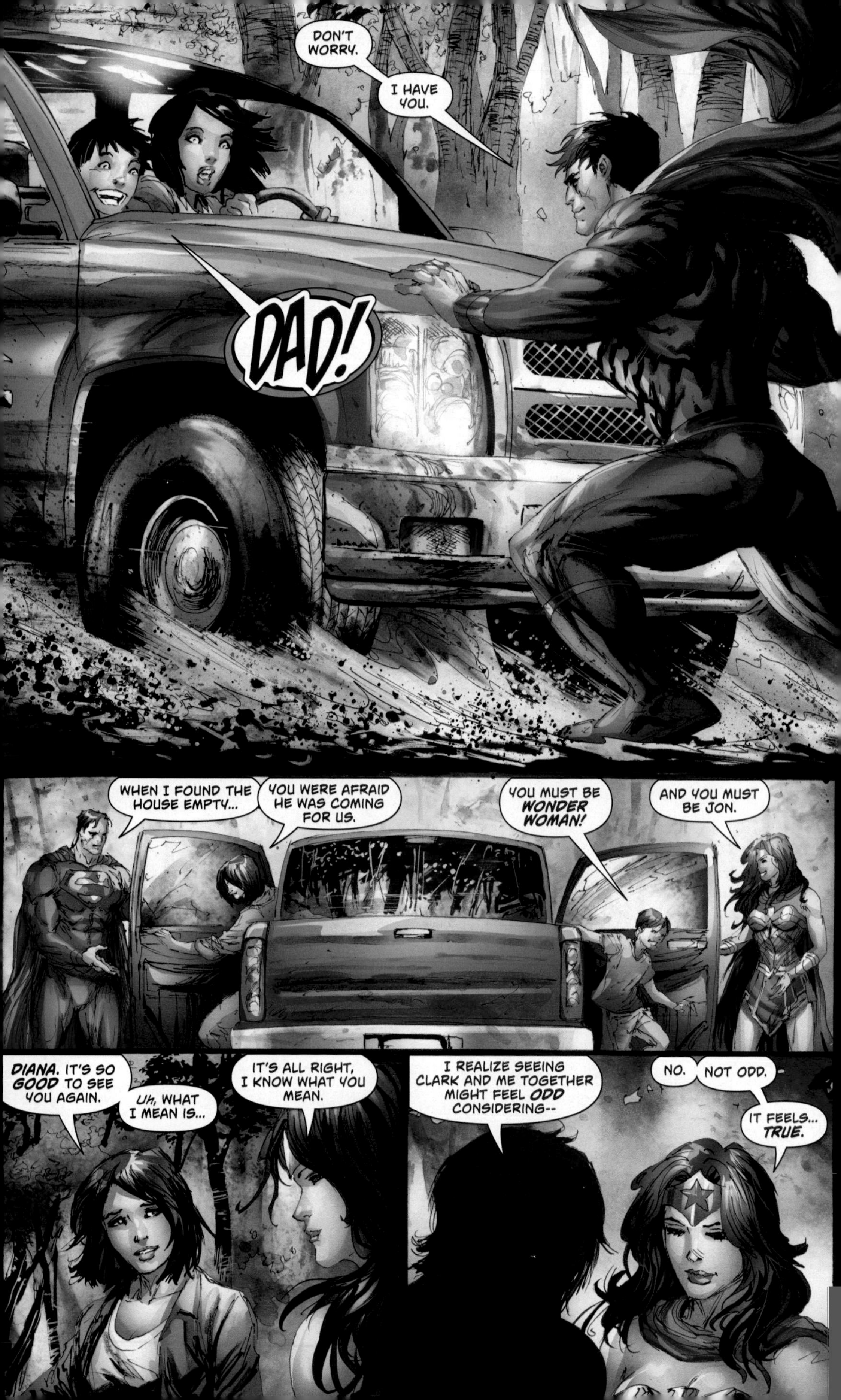
DON'T WORRY.
I HAVE YOU.
DAD!
WHEN I FOUND THE HOUSE EMPTY...
YOU WERE AFRAID HE WAS COMING FOR US.
YOU MUST BE *WONDER WOMAN!*
AND YOU MUST BE JON.
DIANA. IT'S SO *GOOD* TO SEE YOU AGAIN.
Uh, WHAT I MEAN IS...
IT'S ALL RIGHT, I KNOW WHAT YOU MEAN.
I REALIZE SEEING CLARK AND ME TOGETHER MIGHT FEEL *ODD* CONSIDERING--
NO.
NOT ODD.
IT FEELS... *TRUE.*

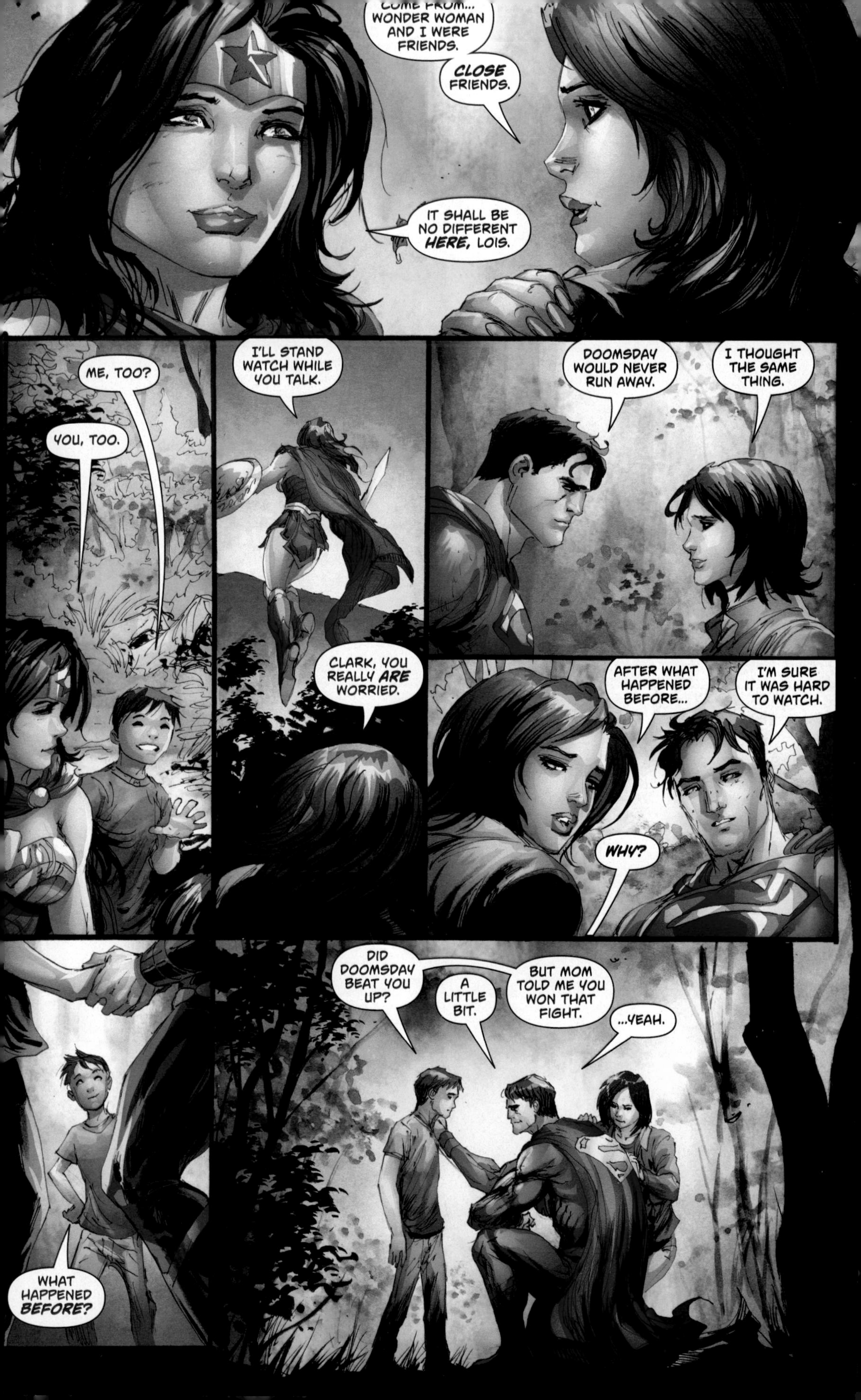
COME FROM... WONDER WOMAN AND I WERE FRIENDS.
CLOSE FRIENDS.
IT SHALL BE NO DIFFERENT HERE, LOIS.
ME, TOO?
YOU, TOO.
I'LL STAND WATCH WHILE YOU TALK.
CLARK, YOU REALLY ARE WORRIED.
DOOMSDAY WOULD NEVER RUN AWAY.
I THOUGHT THE SAME THING.
AFTER WHAT HAPPENED BEFORE...
I'M SURE IT WAS HARD TO WATCH.
WHY?
WHAT HAPPENED BEFORE?
DID DOOMSDAY BEAT YOU UP?
A LITTLE BIT.
BUT MOM TOLD ME YOU WON THAT FIGHT.
...YEAH.

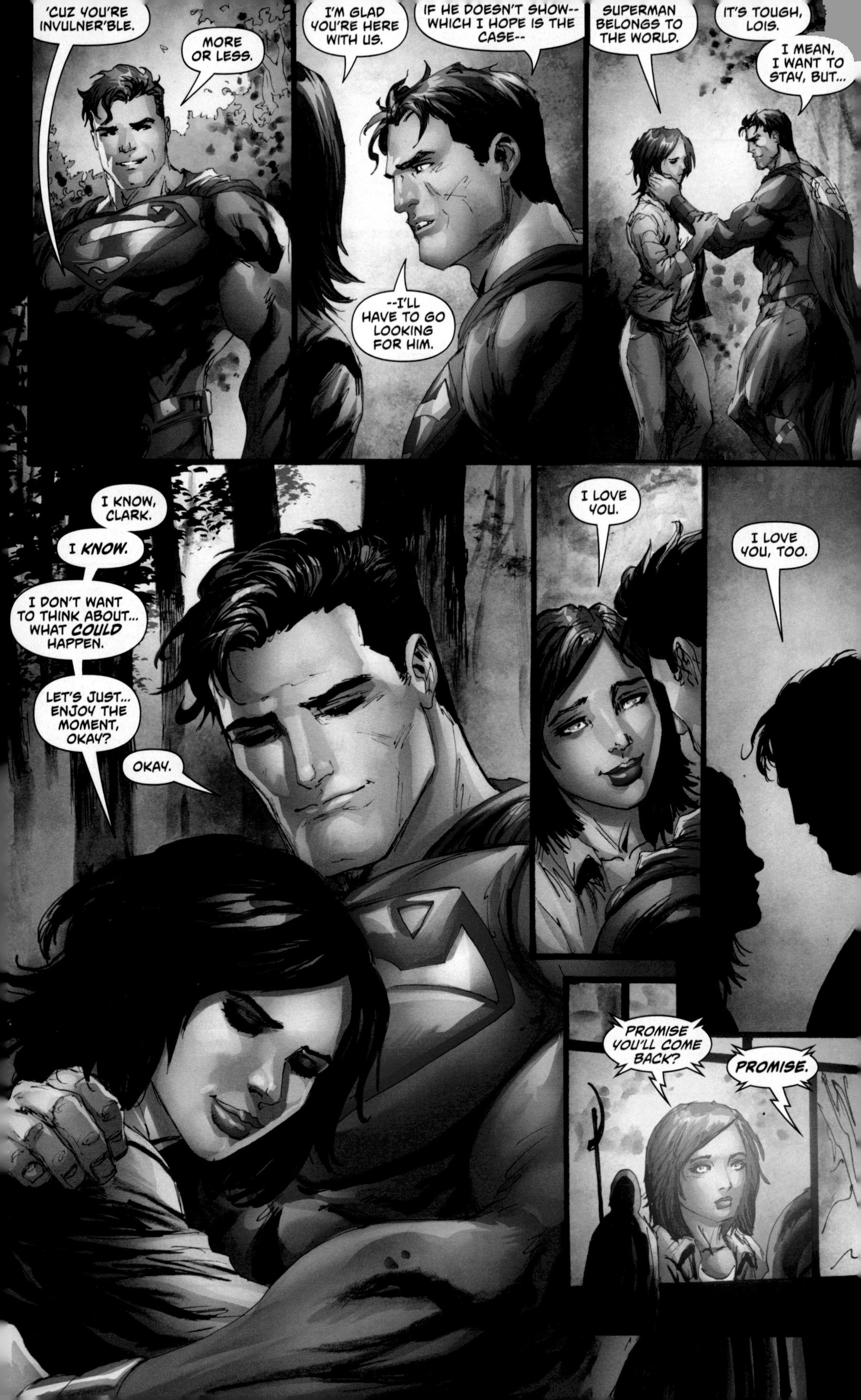
'CUZ YOU'RE INVULNER'BLE.
MORE OR LESS.
I'M GLAD YOU'RE HERE WITH US.
IF HE DOESN'T SHOW-- WHICH I HOPE IS THE CASE--
--I'LL HAVE TO GO LOOKING FOR HIM.
SUPERMAN BELONGS TO THE WORLD.
IT'S TOUGH, LOIS.
I MEAN, I WANT TO STAY, BUT...
I KNOW, CLARK.
I ***KNOW.***
I DON'T WANT TO THINK ABOUT... WHAT ***COULD*** HAPPEN.
LET'S JUST... ENJOY THE MOMENT, OKAY?
OKAY.
I LOVE YOU.
I LOVE YOU, TOO.
PROMISE YOU'LL COME BACK?
PROMISE.

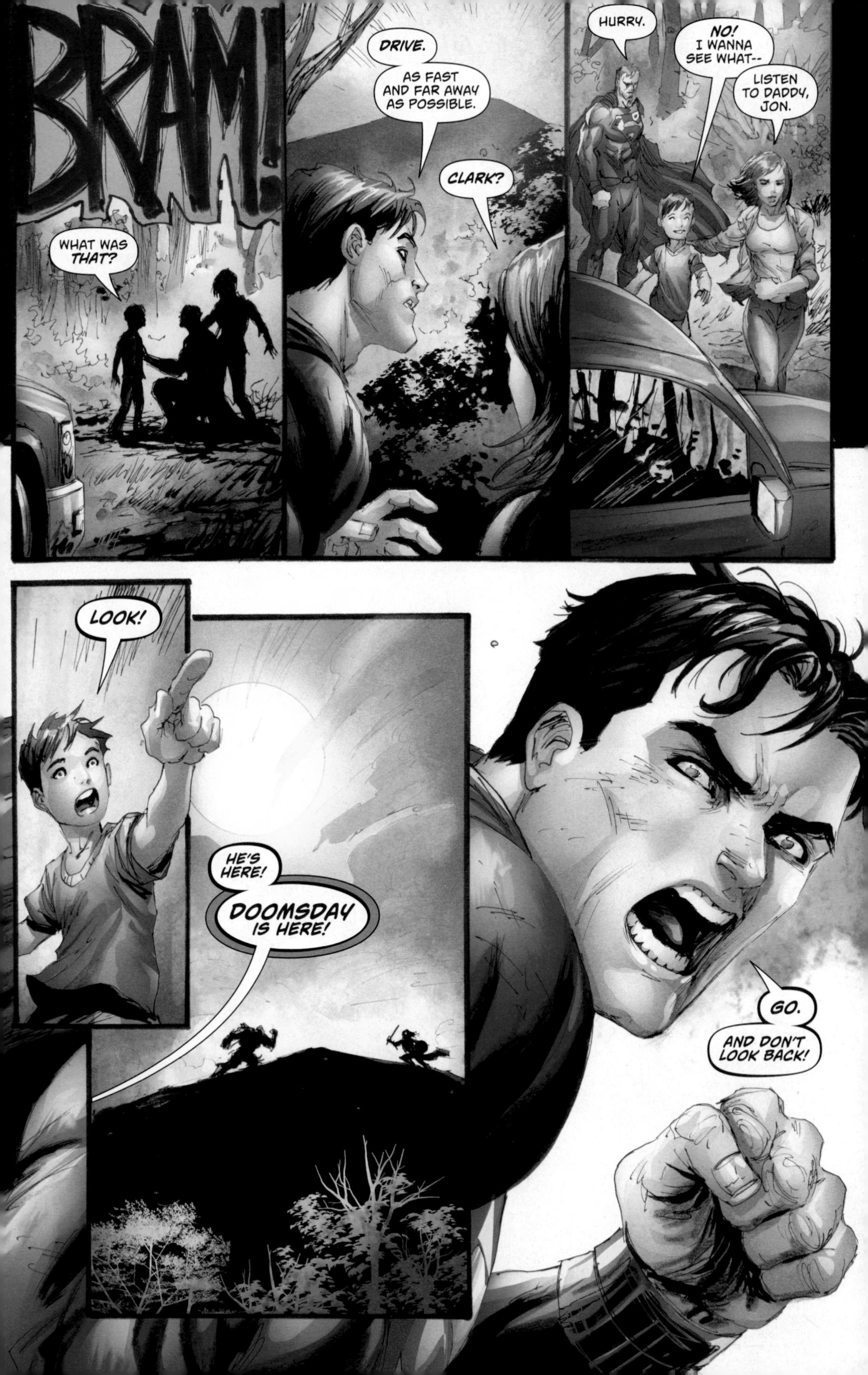
BRAM!
WHAT WAS THAT?
DRIVE.
AS FAST AND FAR AWAY AS POSSIBLE.
CLARK?
HURRY.
NO! I WANNA SEE WHAT--
LISTEN TO DADDY, JON.
LOOK!
HE'S HERE!
DOOMSDAY IS HERE!
GO.
AND DON'T LOOK BACK!

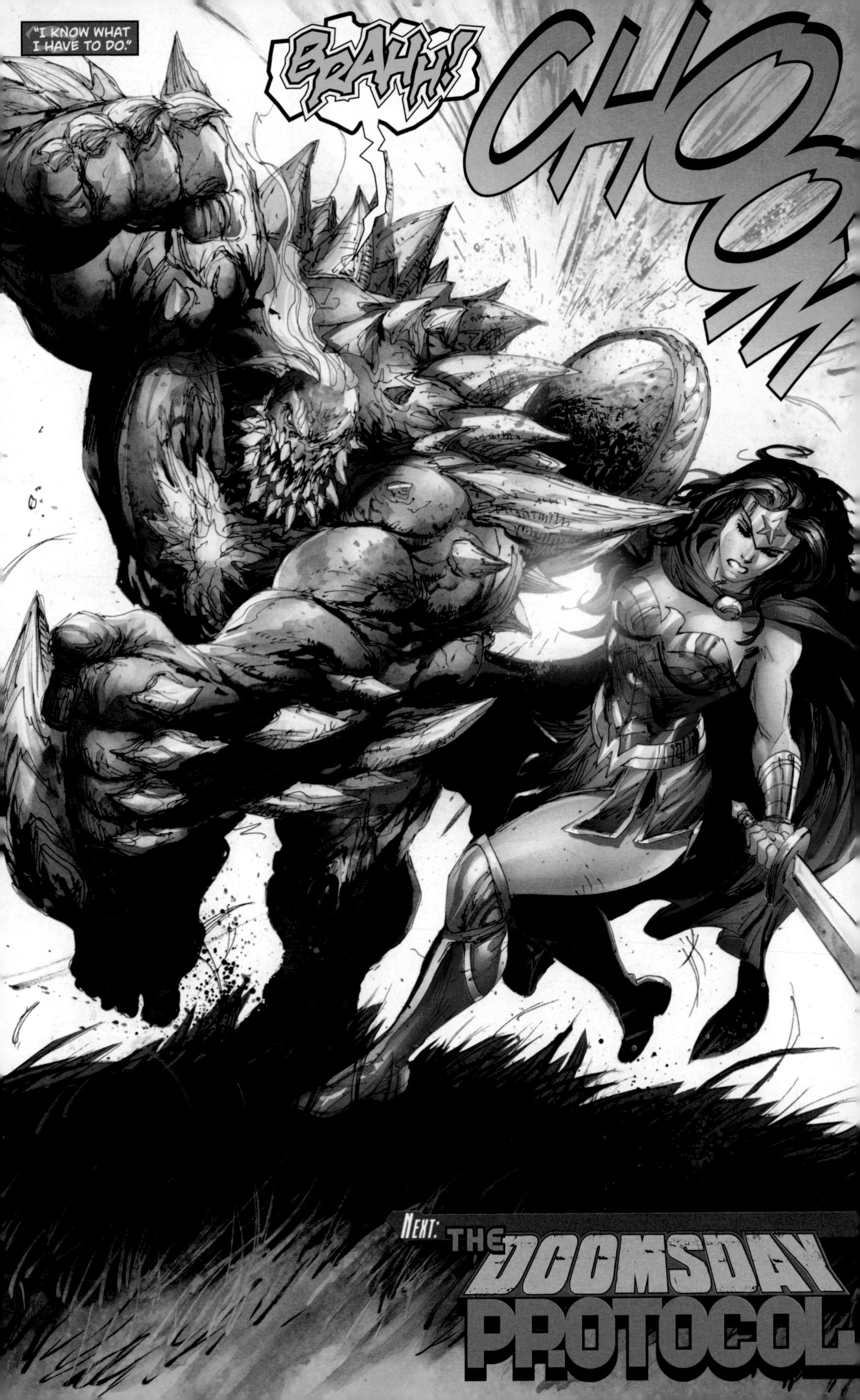
"I KNOW WHAT I HAVE TO DO."
BRAHH!
CHOOM
NEXT: THE DOOMSDAY PROTOCOL

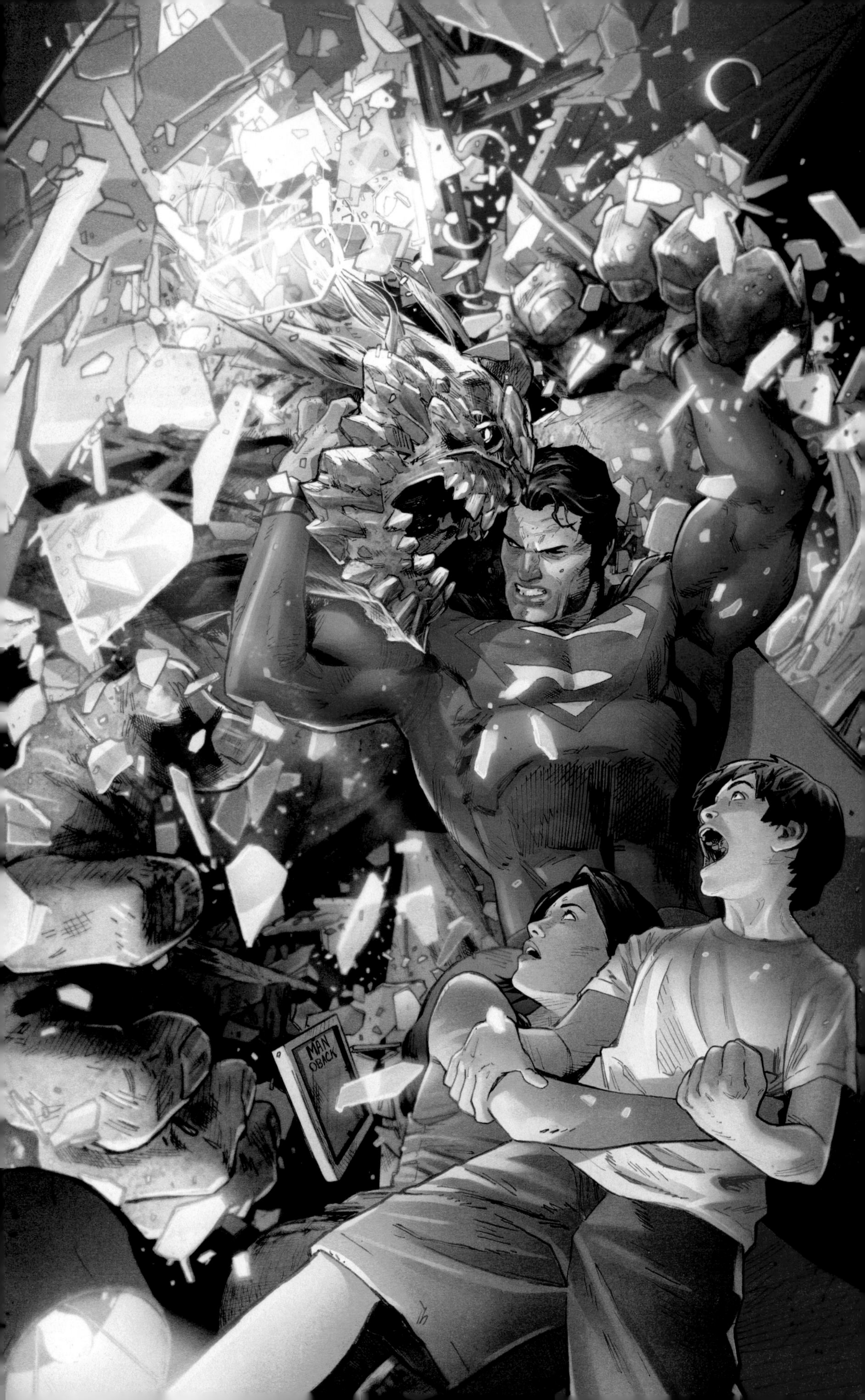
MAN
OBACK

ACTION COMICS #961

CLAY MANN and SONIA OBACK with DAN JURGENS cover artists

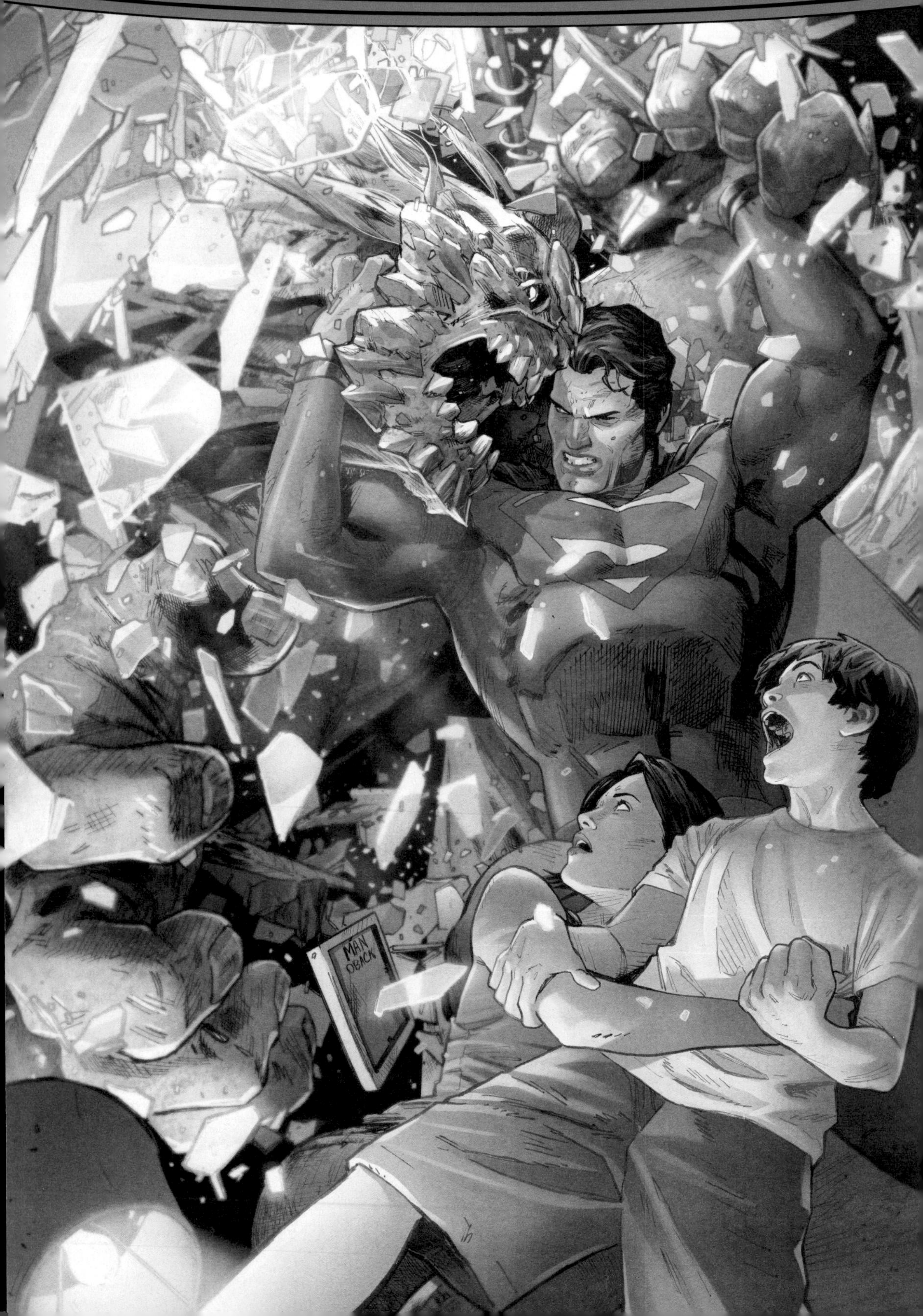
MAN
OBACK

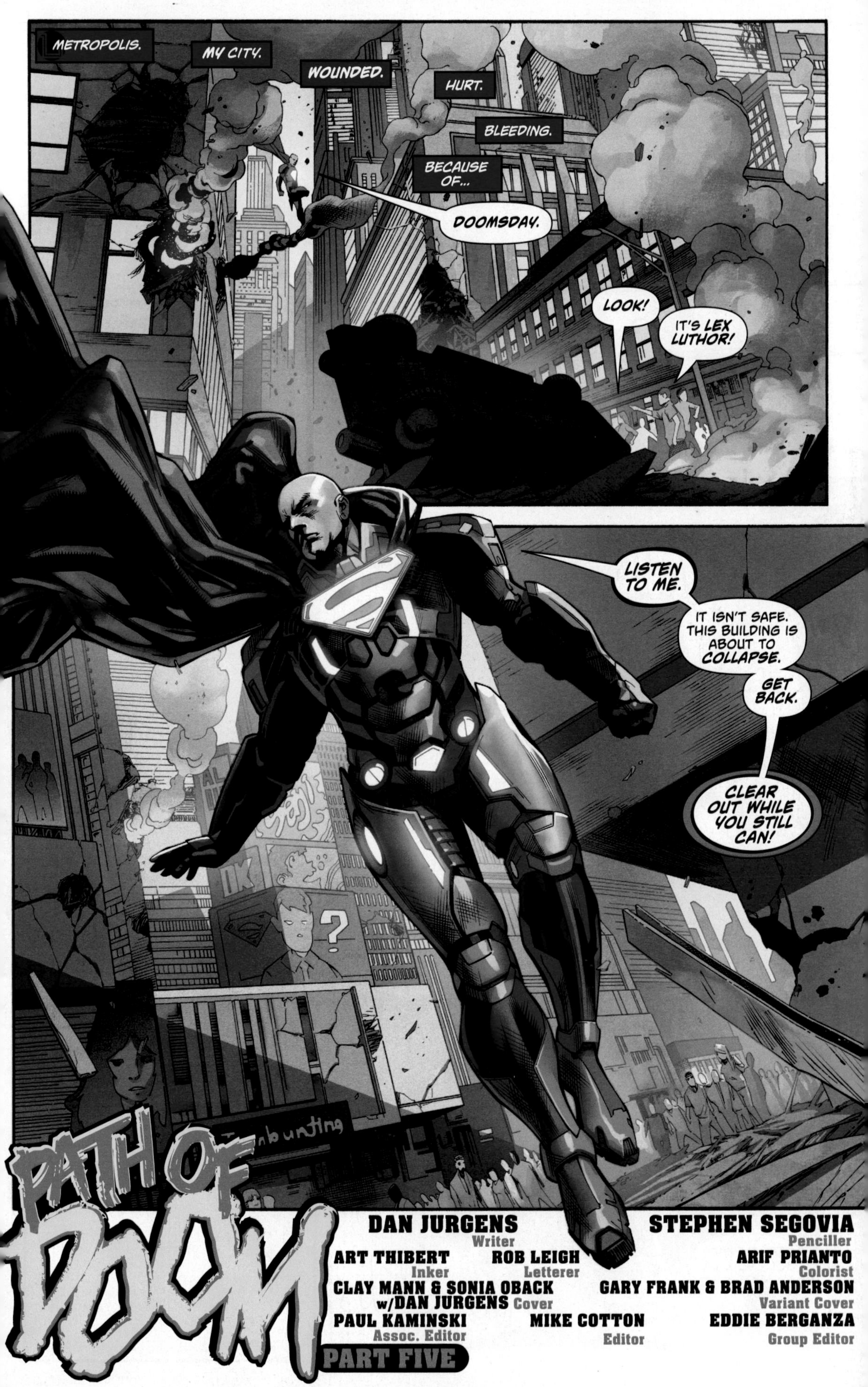
METROPOLIS.
MY CITY.
WOUNDED.
HURT.
BLEEDING.
BECAUSE OF...
DOOMSDAY.
LOOK!
IT'S LEX LUTHOR!
LISTEN TO ME.
IT ISN'T SAFE. THIS BUILDING IS ABOUT TO COLLAPSE.
GET BACK.
CLEAR OUT WHILE YOU STILL CAN!
PATH OF DOOM
PART FIVE
DAN JURGENS Writer
STEPHEN SEGOVIA Penciller
ART THIBERT Inker
ROB LEIGH Letterer
ARIF PRIANTO Colorist
CLAY MANN & SONIA OBACK w/DAN JURGENS Cover
GARY FRANK & BRAD ANDERSON Variant Cover
PAUL KAMINSKI Assoc. Editor
MIKE COTTON Editor
EDDIE BERGANZA Group Editor

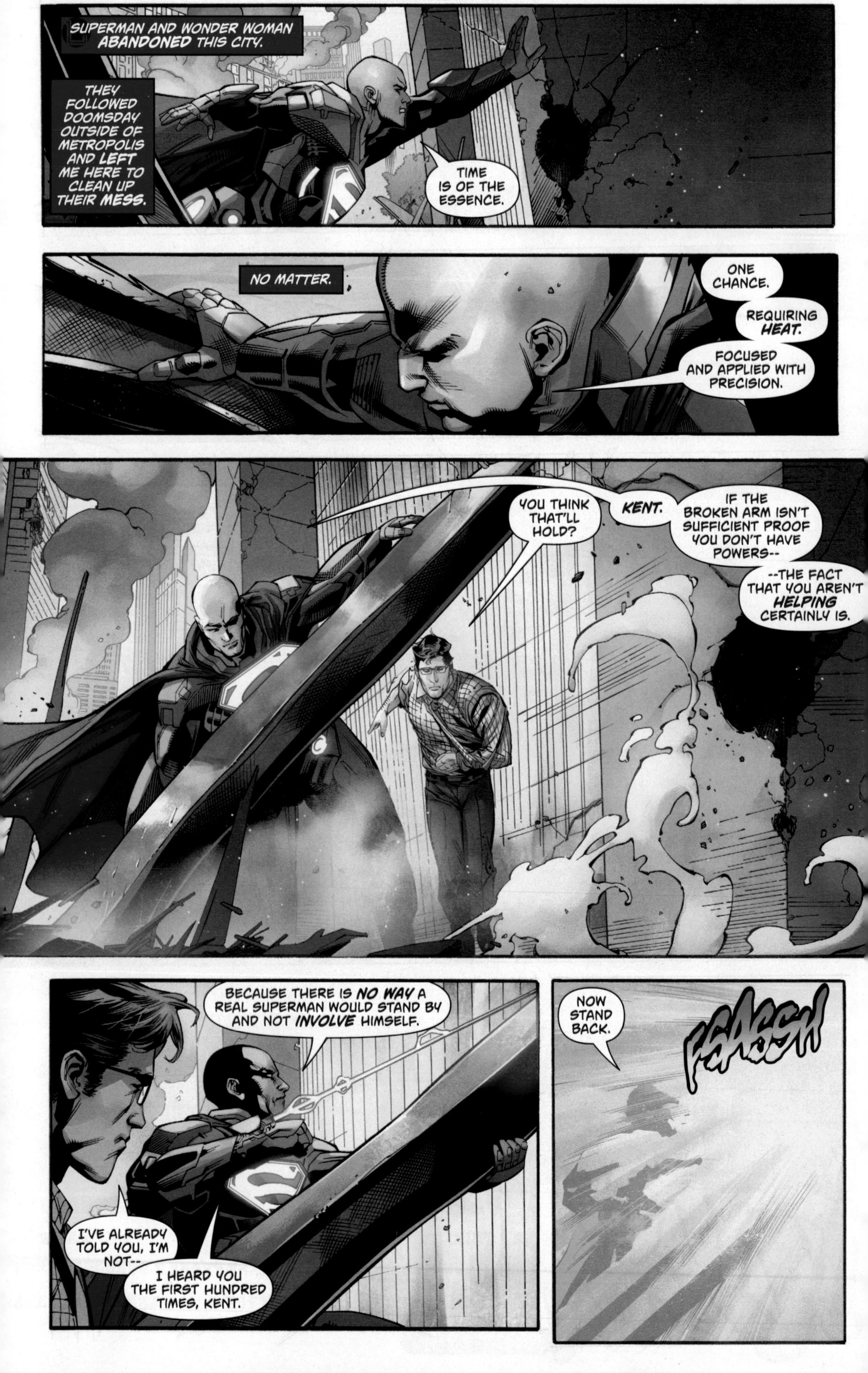
SUPERMAN AND WONDER WOMAN ABANDONED THIS CITY.
THEY FOLLOWED DOOMSDAY OUTSIDE OF METROPOLIS AND LEFT ME HERE TO CLEAN UP THEIR MESS.
TIME IS OF THE ESSENCE.
NO MATTER.
ONE CHANCE.
REQUIRING HEAT.
FOCUSED AND APPLIED WITH PRECISION.
YOU THINK THAT'LL HOLD?
KENT.
IF THE BROKEN ARM ISN'T SUFFICIENT PROOF YOU DON'T HAVE POWERS--
--THE FACT THAT YOU AREN'T HELPING CERTAINLY IS.
BECAUSE THERE IS NO WAY A REAL SUPERMAN WOULD STAND BY AND NOT INVOLVE HIMSELF.
I'VE ALREADY TOLD YOU, I'M NOT--
I HEARD YOU THE FIRST HUNDRED TIMES, KENT.
NOW STAND BACK.
FSSSH

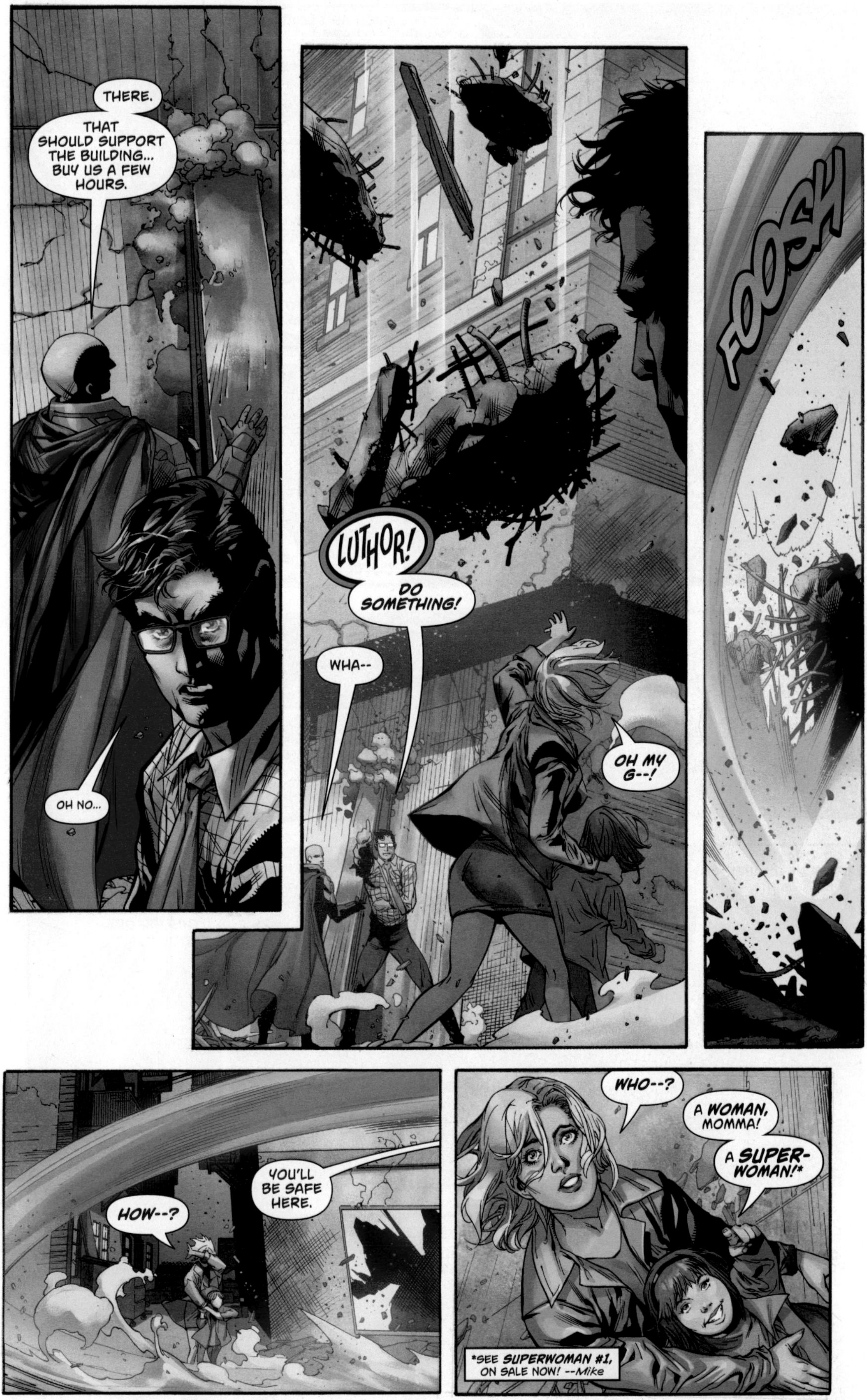
THERE.
THAT SHOULD SUPPORT THE BUILDING... BUY US A FEW HOURS.
OH NO...
LUTHOR!
DO SOMETHING!
WHA--
OH MY G--!
FOOSH
HOW--?
YOU'LL BE SAFE HERE.
WHO--?
A WOMAN, MOMMA!
A SUPER-WOMAN!*
*SEE SUPERWOMAN #1, ON SALE NOW! --Mike

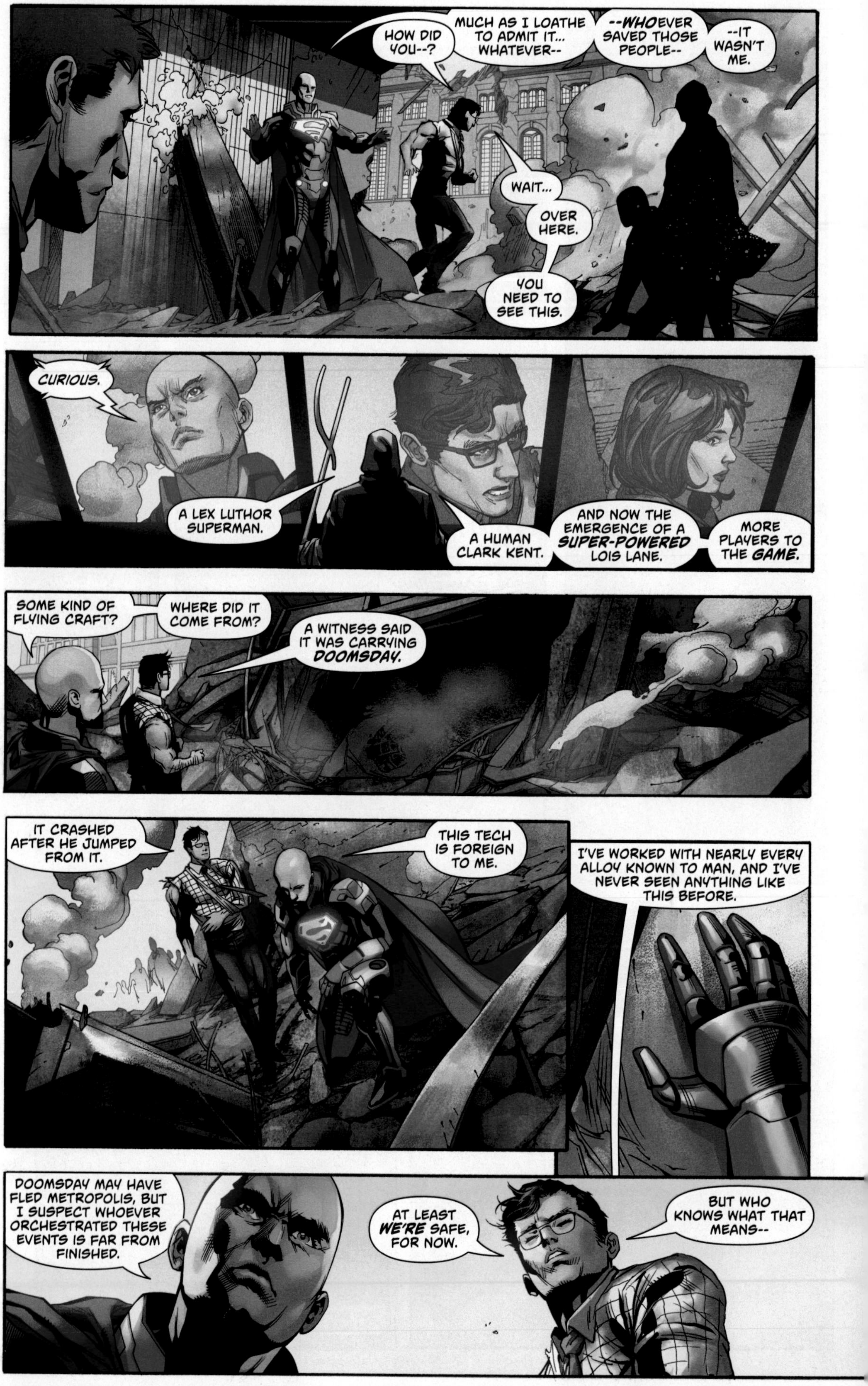
HOW DID YOU--?
MUCH AS I LOATHE TO ADMIT IT... WHATEVER--
--WHOEVER SAVED THOSE PEOPLE--
--IT WASN'T ME.
WAIT...
OVER HERE.
YOU NEED TO SEE THIS.
CURIOUS.
A LEX LUTHOR SUPERMAN.
A HUMAN CLARK KENT.
AND NOW THE EMERGENCE OF A SUPER-POWERED LOIS LANE.
MORE PLAYERS TO THE GAME.
SOME KIND OF FLYING CRAFT?
WHERE DID IT COME FROM?
A WITNESS SAID IT WAS CARRYING DOOMSDAY.
IT CRASHED AFTER HE JUMPED FROM IT.
THIS TECH IS FOREIGN TO ME.
I'VE WORKED WITH NEARLY EVERY ALLOY KNOWN TO MAN, AND I'VE NEVER SEEN ANYTHING LIKE THIS BEFORE.
DOOMSDAY MAY HAVE FLED METROPOLIS, BUT I SUSPECT WHOEVER ORCHESTRATED THESE EVENTS IS FAR FROM FINISHED.
AT LEAST WE'RE SAFE, FOR NOW.
BUT WHO KNOWS WHAT THAT MEANS--

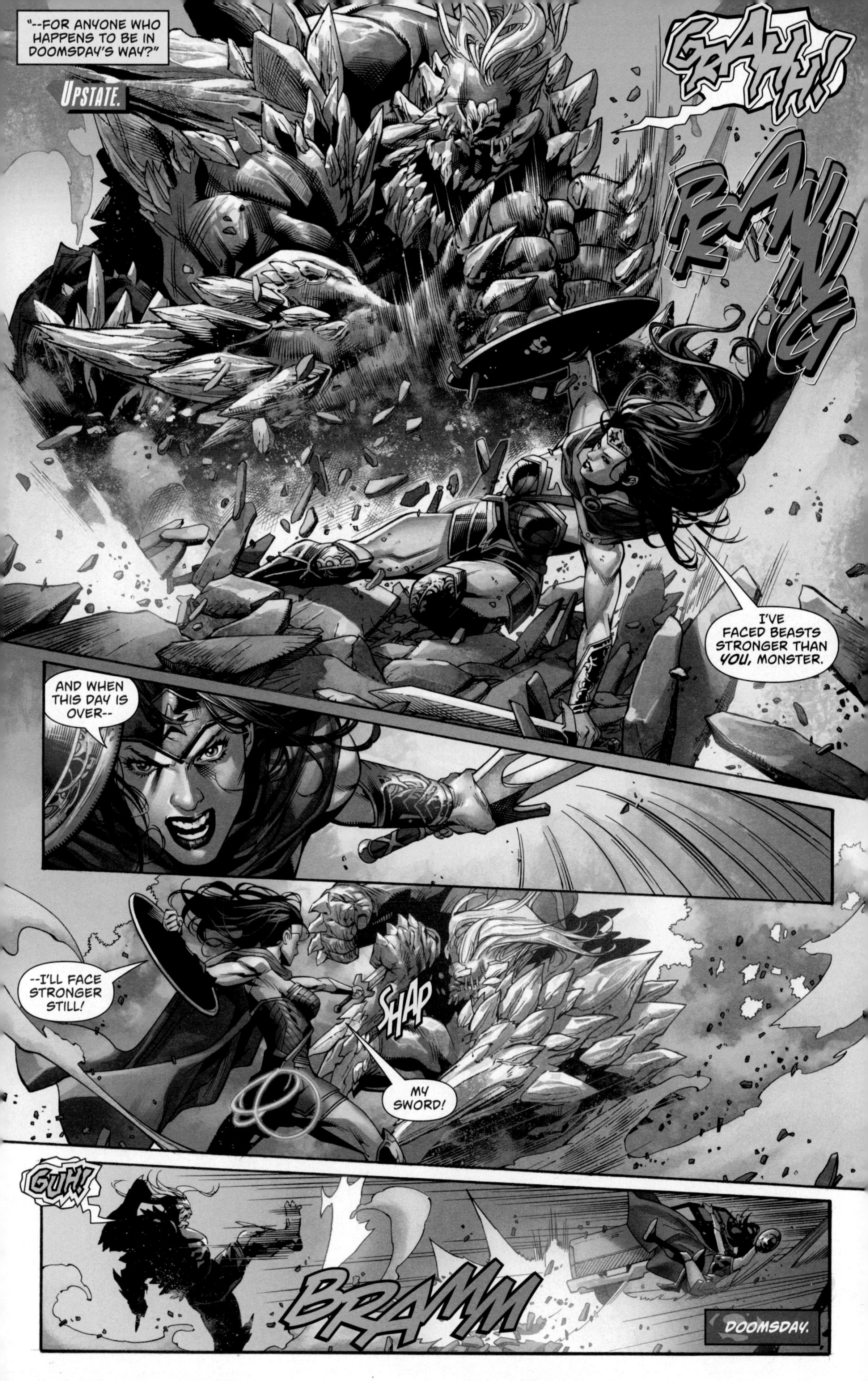
"--FOR ANYONE WHO HAPPENS TO BE IN DOOMSDAY'S WAY?"
UPSTATE.
GRAHH!
BRANNG
I'VE FACED BEASTS STRONGER THAN *YOU*, MONSTER.
AND WHEN THIS DAY IS OVER--
--I'LL FACE STRONGER STILL!
SHAP
MY SWORD!
GUH!
BRAMM
DOOMSDAY.

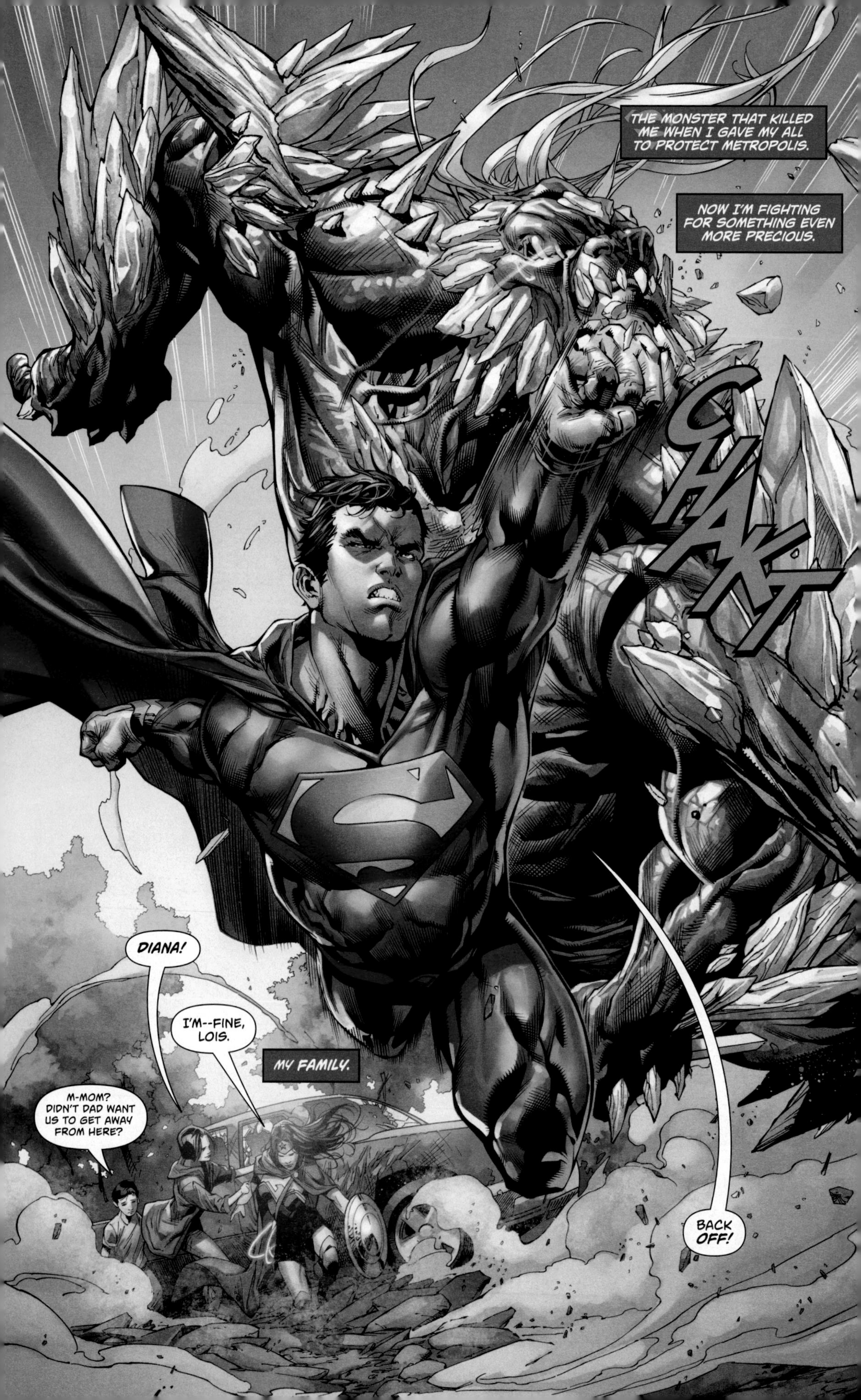
THE MONSTER THAT KILLED ME WHEN I GAVE MY ALL TO PROTECT METROPOLIS.
NOW I'M FIGHTING FOR SOMETHING EVEN MORE PRECIOUS.
CHAKT
DIANA!
I'M--FINE, LOIS.
MY FAMILY.
M-MOM? DIDN'T DAD WANT US TO GET AWAY FROM HERE?
BACK OFF!

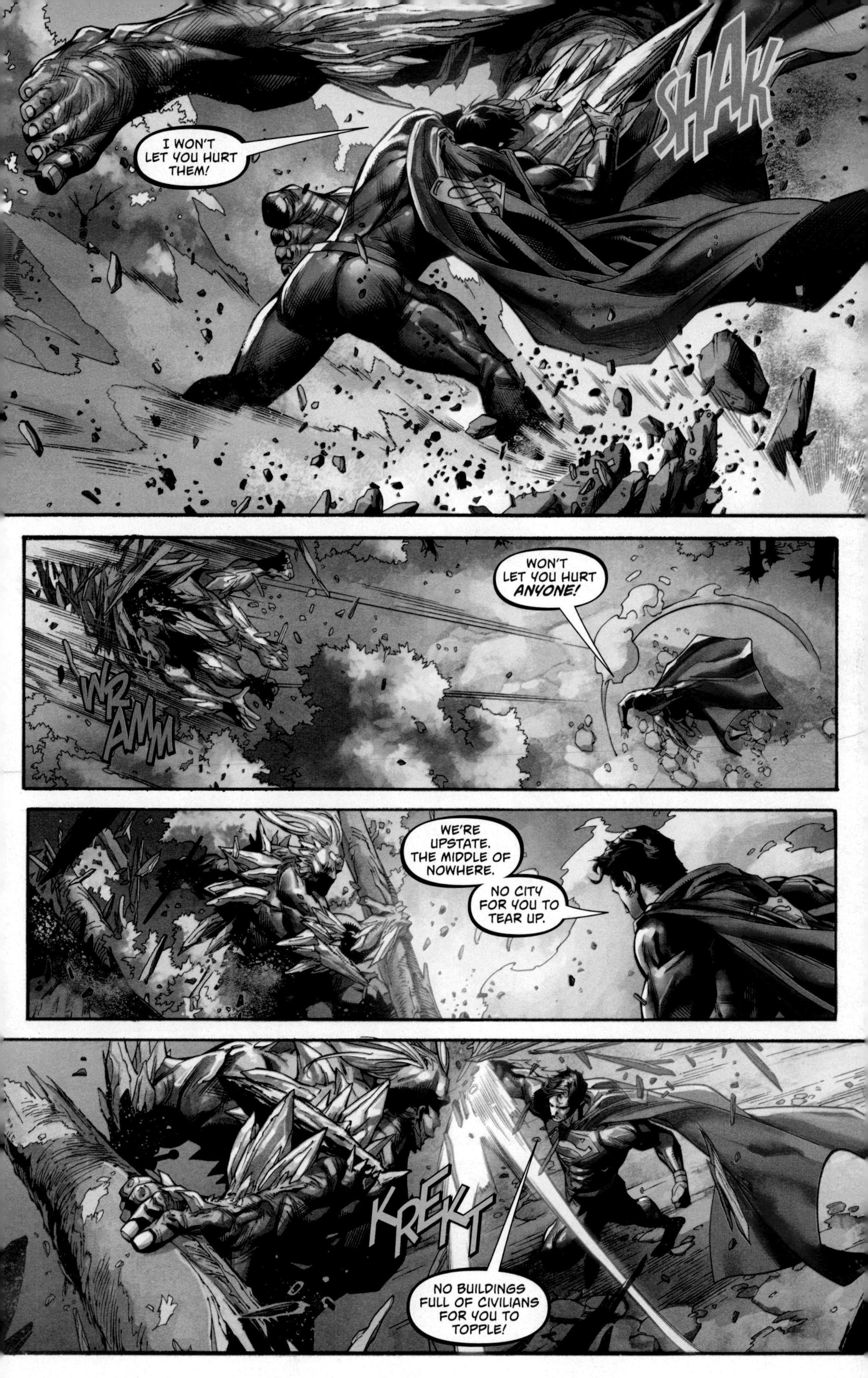
SHAK
I WON'T LET YOU HURT THEM!
WON'T LET YOU HURT *ANYONE!*
WRAMM
WE'RE UPSTATE. THE MIDDLE OF NOWHERE.
NO CITY FOR YOU TO TEAR UP.
KREKT
NO BUILDINGS FULL OF CIVILIANS FOR YOU TO TOPPLE!

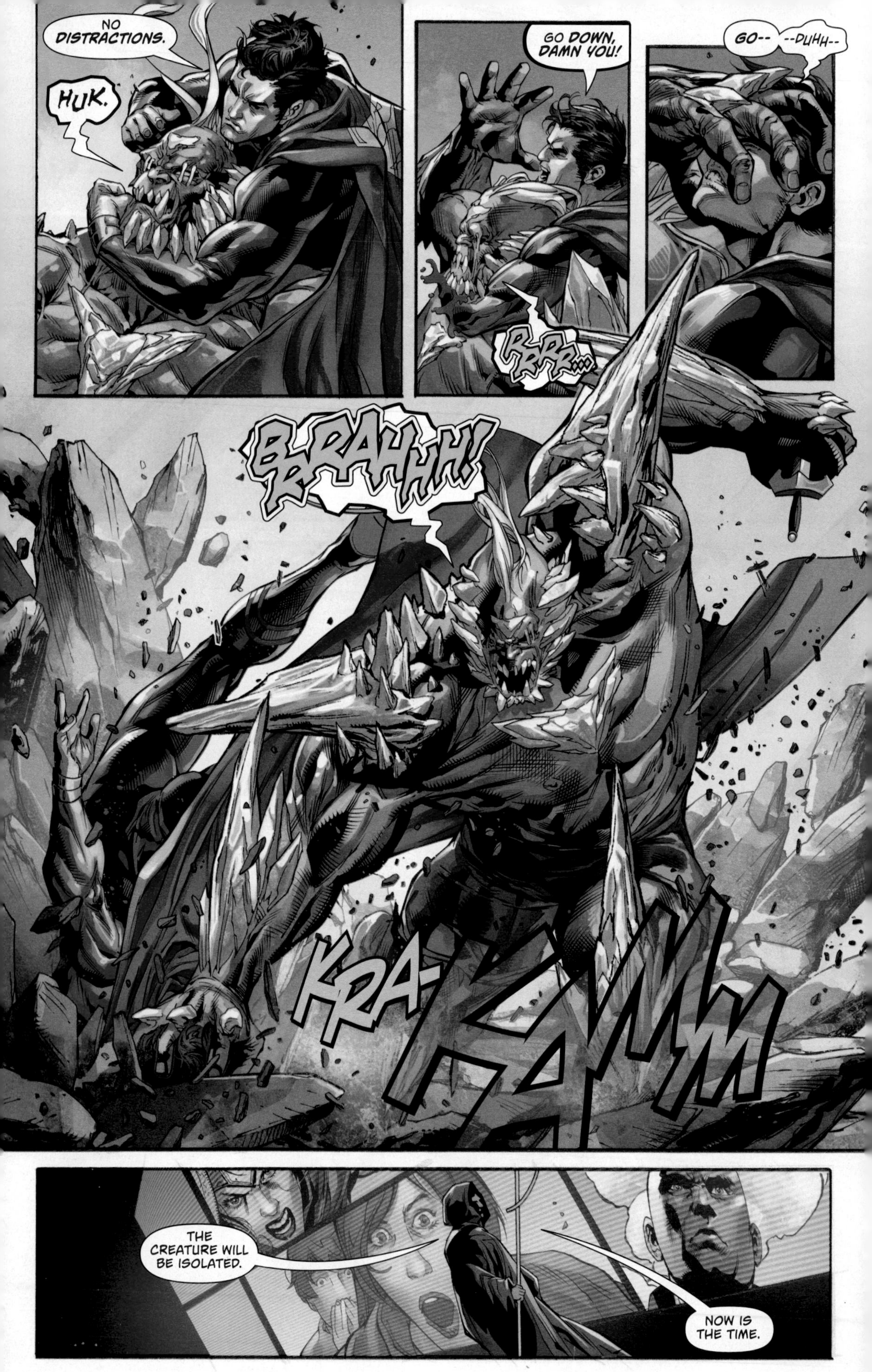
NO DISTRACTIONS.
HUK.
GO DOWN, DAMN YOU!
RRRR...
GO--
--DUHH--
BRRAHHH!
KRA-KAMM
THE CREATURE WILL BE ISOLATED.
NOW IS THE TIME.

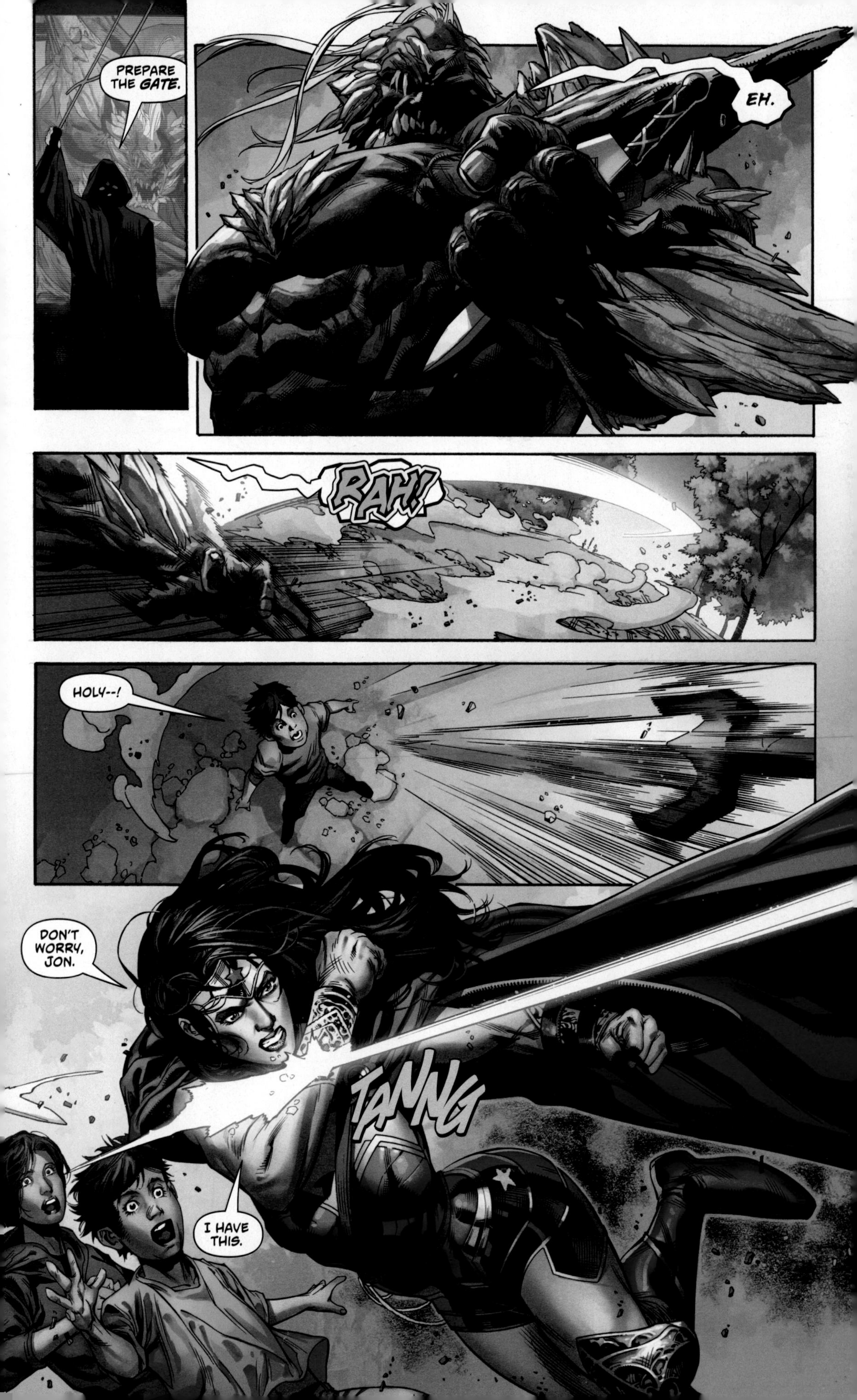
PREPARE THE GATE.
EH.
RAH!
HOLY--!
DON'T WORRY, JON.
TANNG
I HAVE THIS.

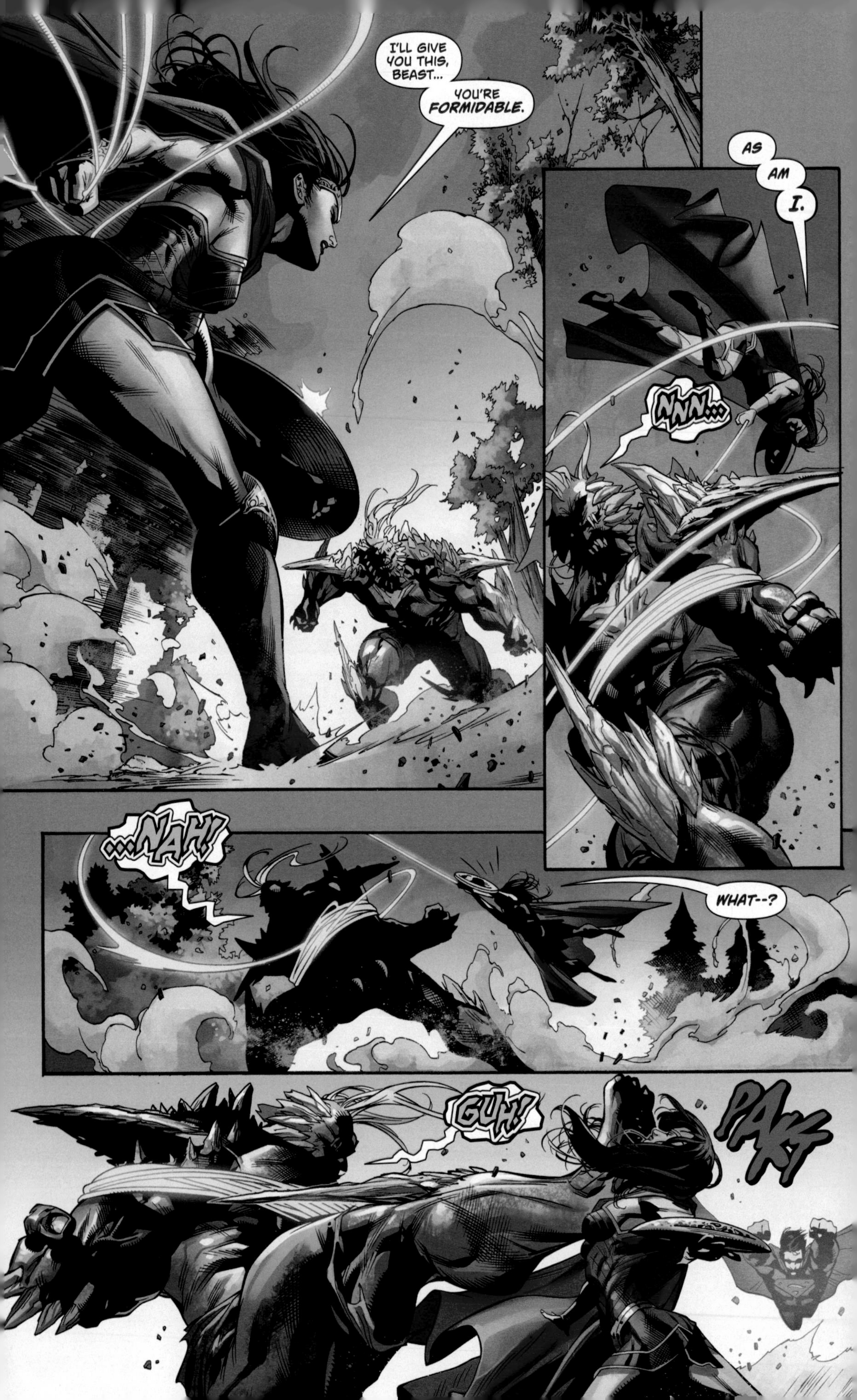
I'LL GIVE YOU THIS, BEAST...
YOU'RE FORMIDABLE.
AS AM I.
NNN...
...NAH!
WHAT--?
GUH!
PAKT

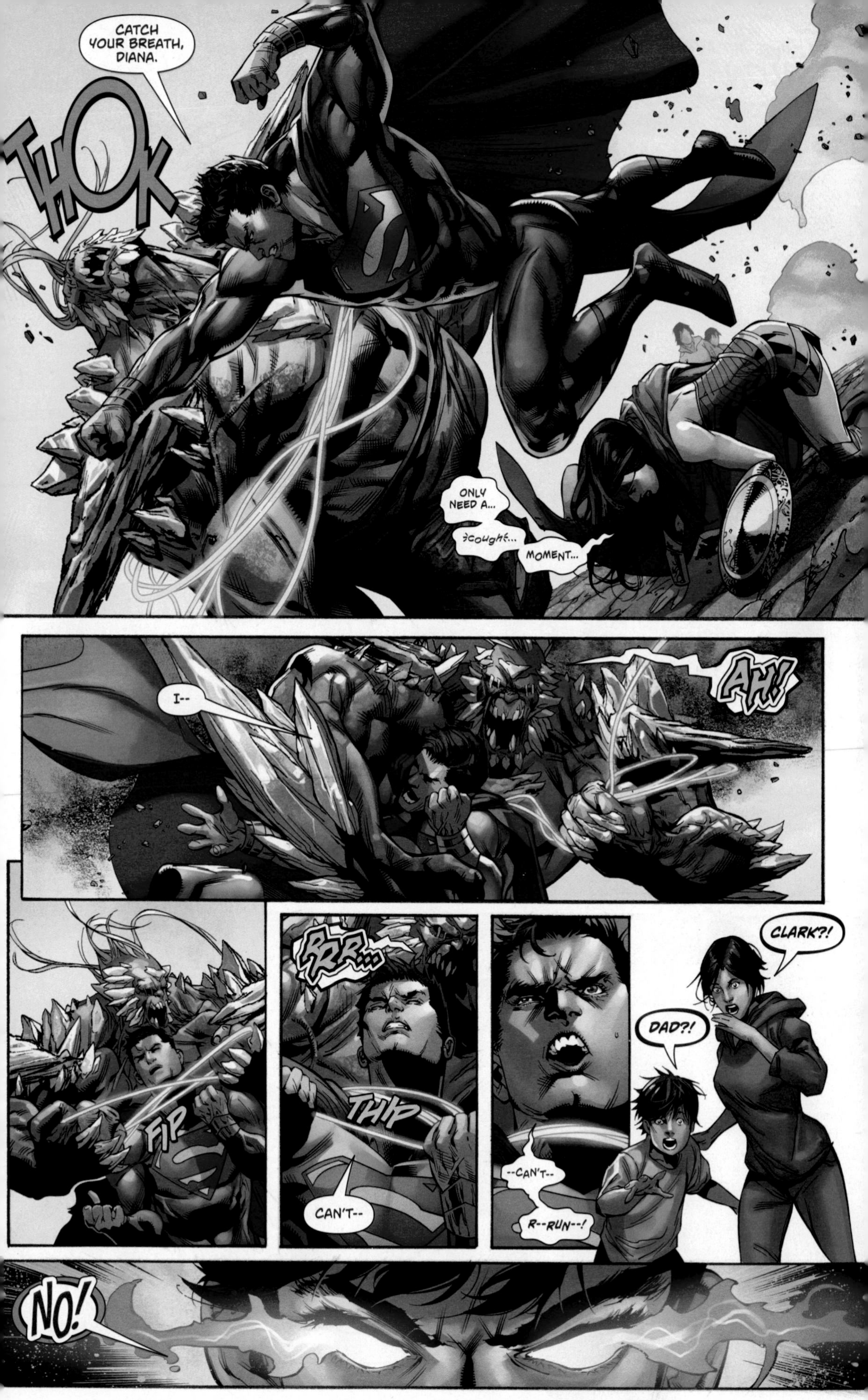
CATCH YOUR BREATH, DIANA.
THOK
ONLY NEED A...
cough...
MOMENT...
I--
AH!
FIP
RRR...
THIP
CAN'T--
--CAN'T--
R--RUN--!
CLARK?!
DAD?!
NO!

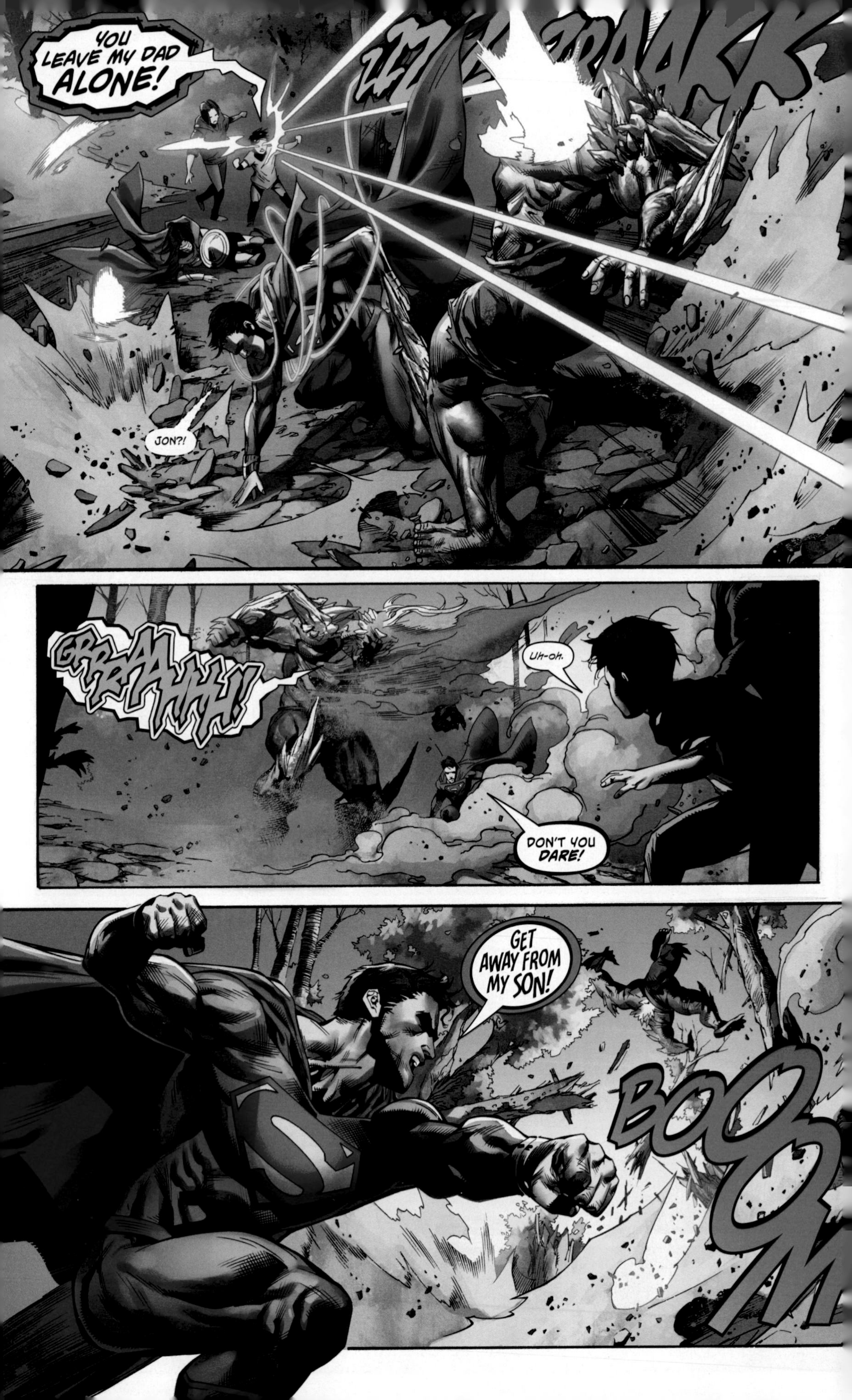
YOU LEAVE MY DAD ALONE!
JON?!
Uh-oh.
DON'T YOU DARE!
GET AWAY FROM MY SON!
BOOM

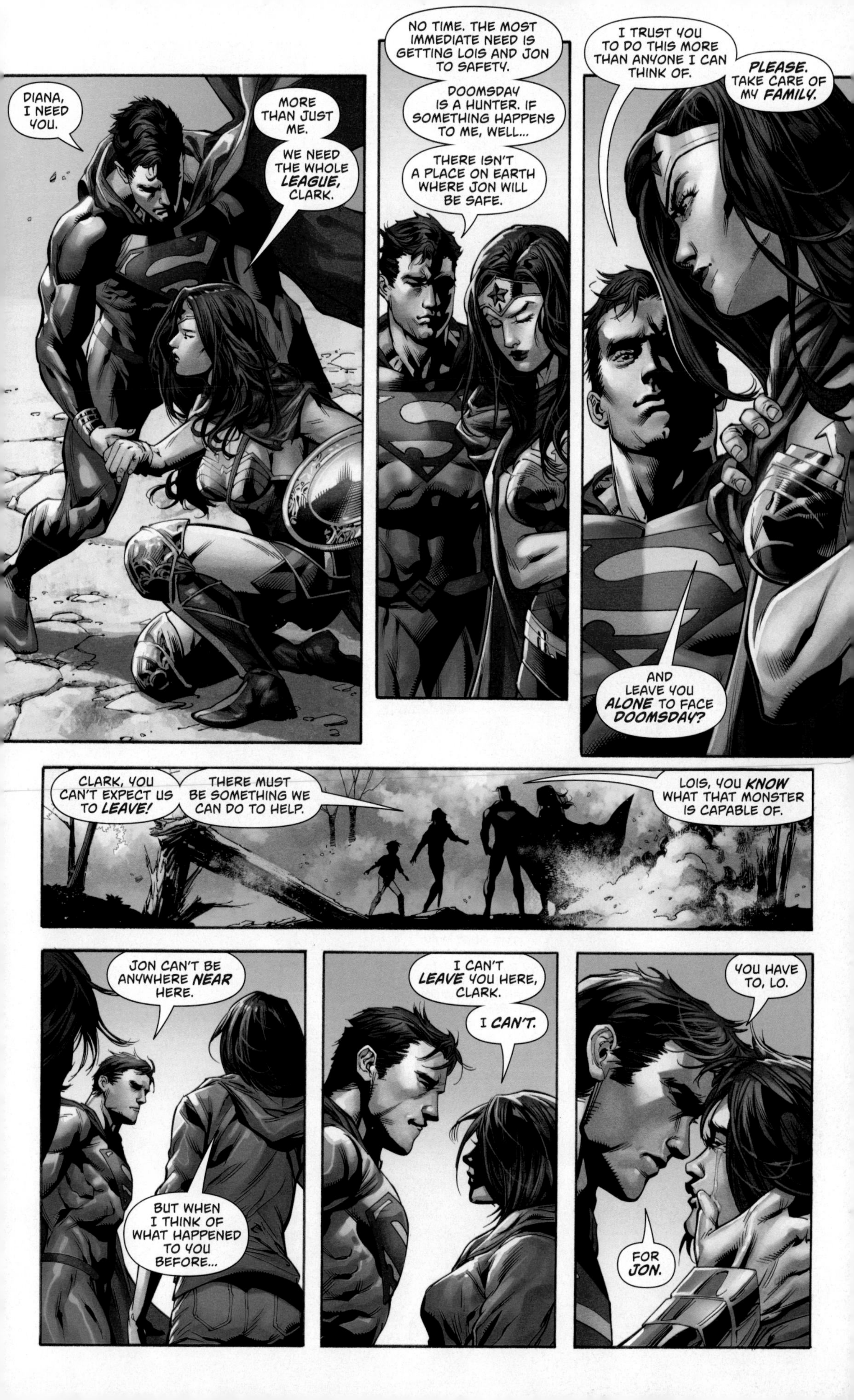
DIANA, I NEED YOU.
MORE THAN JUST ME.
WE NEED THE WHOLE LEAGUE, CLARK.
NO TIME. THE MOST IMMEDIATE NEED IS GETTING LOIS AND JON TO SAFETY.
DOOMSDAY IS A HUNTER. IF SOMETHING HAPPENS TO ME, WELL...
THERE ISN'T A PLACE ON EARTH WHERE JON WILL BE SAFE.
I TRUST YOU TO DO THIS MORE THAN ANYONE I CAN THINK OF.
PLEASE. TAKE CARE OF MY FAMILY.
AND LEAVE YOU ALONE TO FACE DOOMSDAY?
CLARK, YOU CAN'T EXPECT US TO LEAVE!
THERE MUST BE SOMETHING WE CAN DO TO HELP.
LOIS, YOU KNOW WHAT THAT MONSTER IS CAPABLE OF.
JON CAN'T BE ANYWHERE NEAR HERE.
BUT WHEN I THINK OF WHAT HAPPENED TO YOU BEFORE...
I CAN'T LEAVE YOU HERE, CLARK.
I CAN'T.
YOU HAVE TO, LO.
FOR JON.

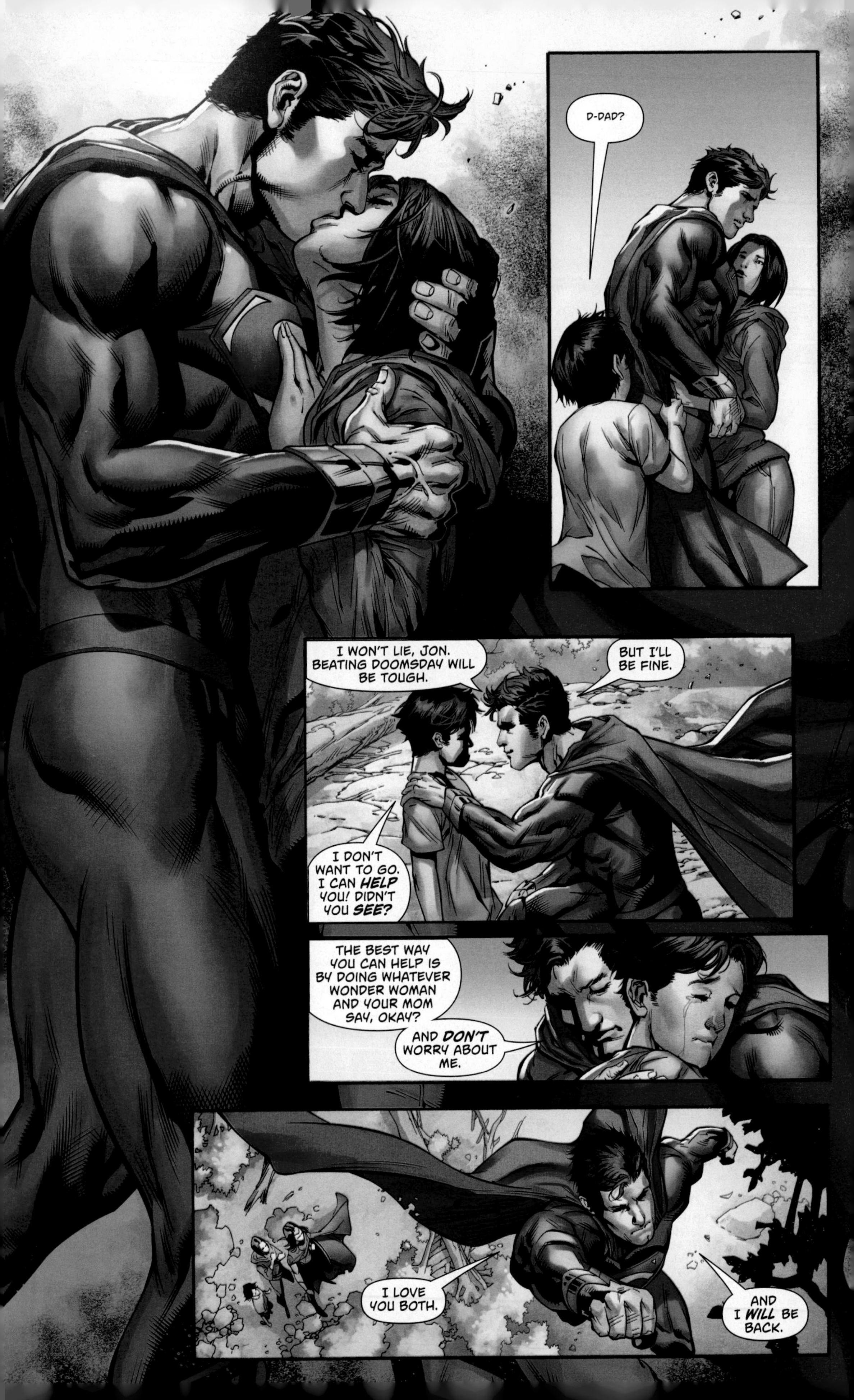
D-DAD?
I WON'T LIE, JON. BEATING DOOMSDAY WILL BE TOUGH.
BUT I'LL BE FINE.
I DON'T WANT TO GO. I CAN HELP YOU! DIDN'T YOU SEE?
THE BEST WAY YOU CAN HELP IS BY DOING WHATEVER WONDER WOMAN AND YOUR MOM SAY, OKAY?
AND DON'T WORRY ABOUT ME.
I LOVE YOU BOTH.
AND I WILL BE BACK.

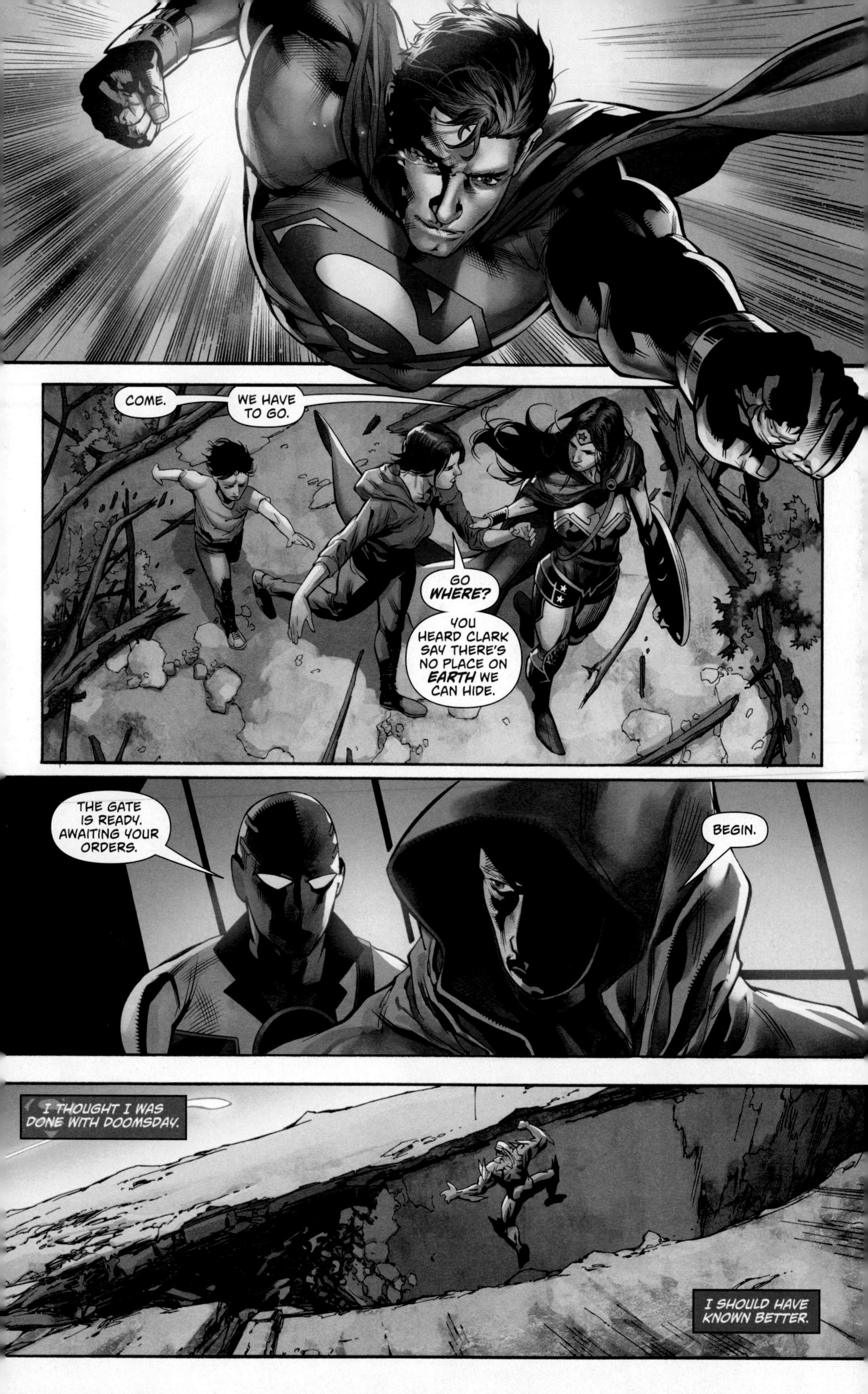
COME.
WE HAVE TO GO.
GO WHERE?
YOU HEARD CLARK SAY THERE'S NO PLACE ON EARTH WE CAN HIDE.
THE GATE IS READY. AWAITING YOUR ORDERS.
BEGIN.
I THOUGHT I WAS DONE WITH DOOMSDAY.
I SHOULD HAVE KNOWN BETTER.

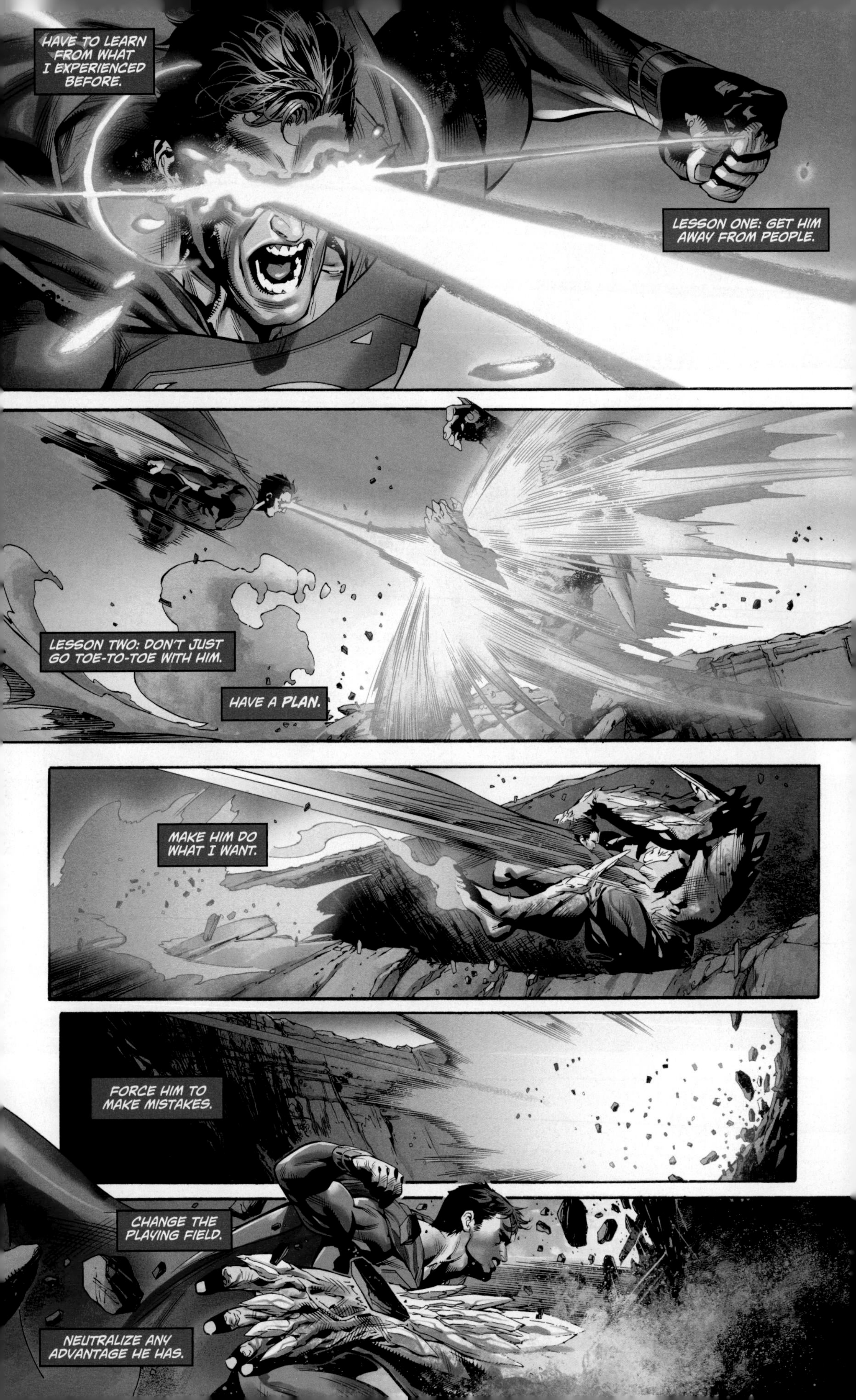
HAVE TO LEARN FROM WHAT I EXPERIENCED BEFORE.
LESSON ONE: GET HIM AWAY FROM PEOPLE.
LESSON TWO: DON'T JUST GO TOE-TO-TOE WITH HIM.
HAVE A PLAN.
MAKE HIM DO WHAT I WANT.
FORCE HIM TO MAKE MISTAKES.
CHANGE THE PLAYING FIELD.
NEUTRALIZE ANY ADVANTAGE HE HAS.

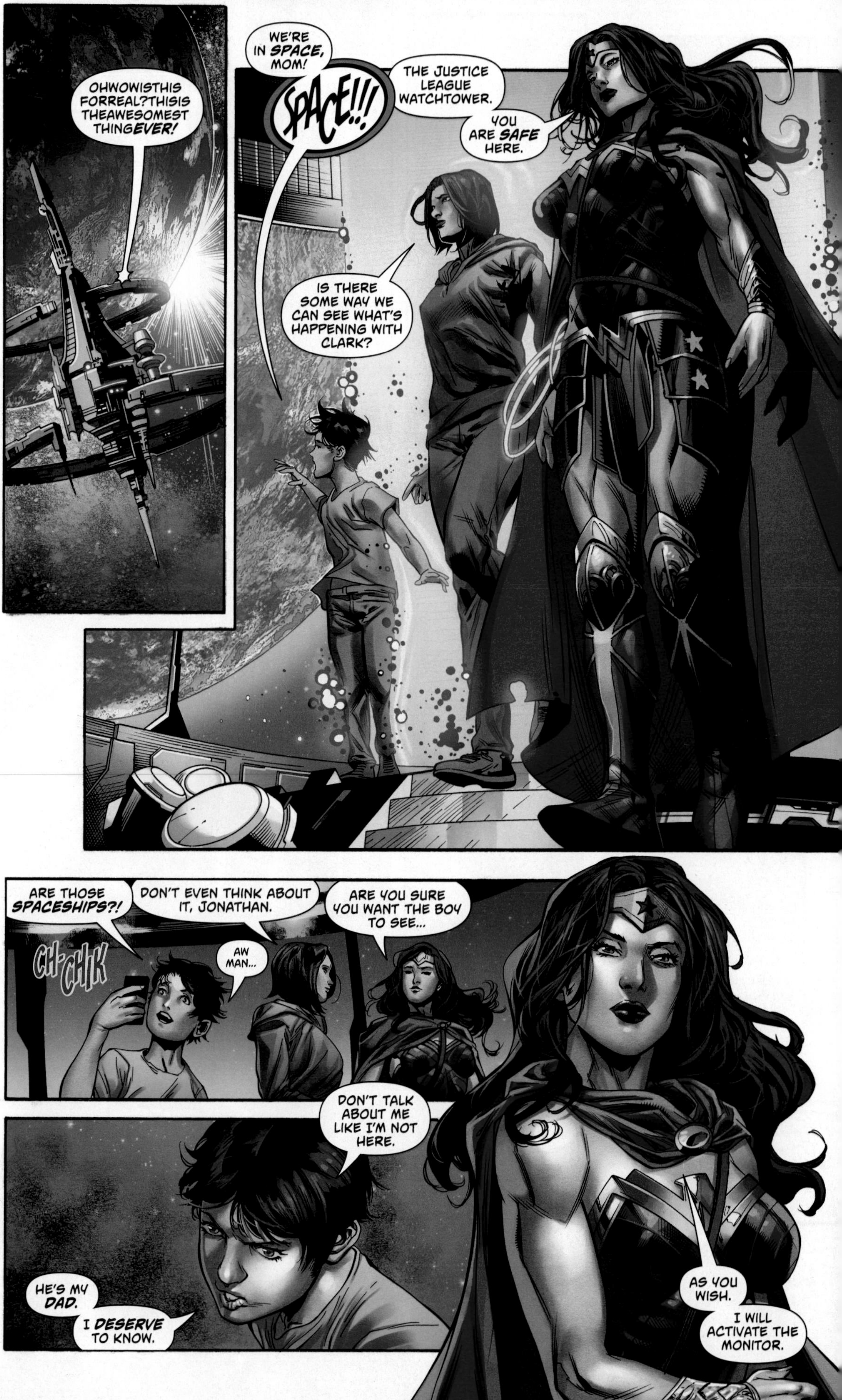
OHWOWISTHIS FORREAL?THISIS THEAWESOMEST THINGEVER!
WE'RE IN SPACE, MOM!
SPACE!!!
THE JUSTICE LEAGUE WATCHTOWER.
YOU ARE SAFE HERE.
IS THERE SOME WAY WE CAN SEE WHAT'S HAPPENING WITH CLARK?
ARE THOSE SPACESHIPS?!
CH-CHIK
DON'T EVEN THINK ABOUT IT, JONATHAN.
AW MAN...
ARE YOU SURE YOU WANT THE BOY TO SEE...
DON'T TALK ABOUT ME LIKE I'M NOT HERE.
HE'S MY DAD.
I DESERVE TO KNOW.
AS YOU WISH.
I WILL ACTIVATE THE MONITOR.

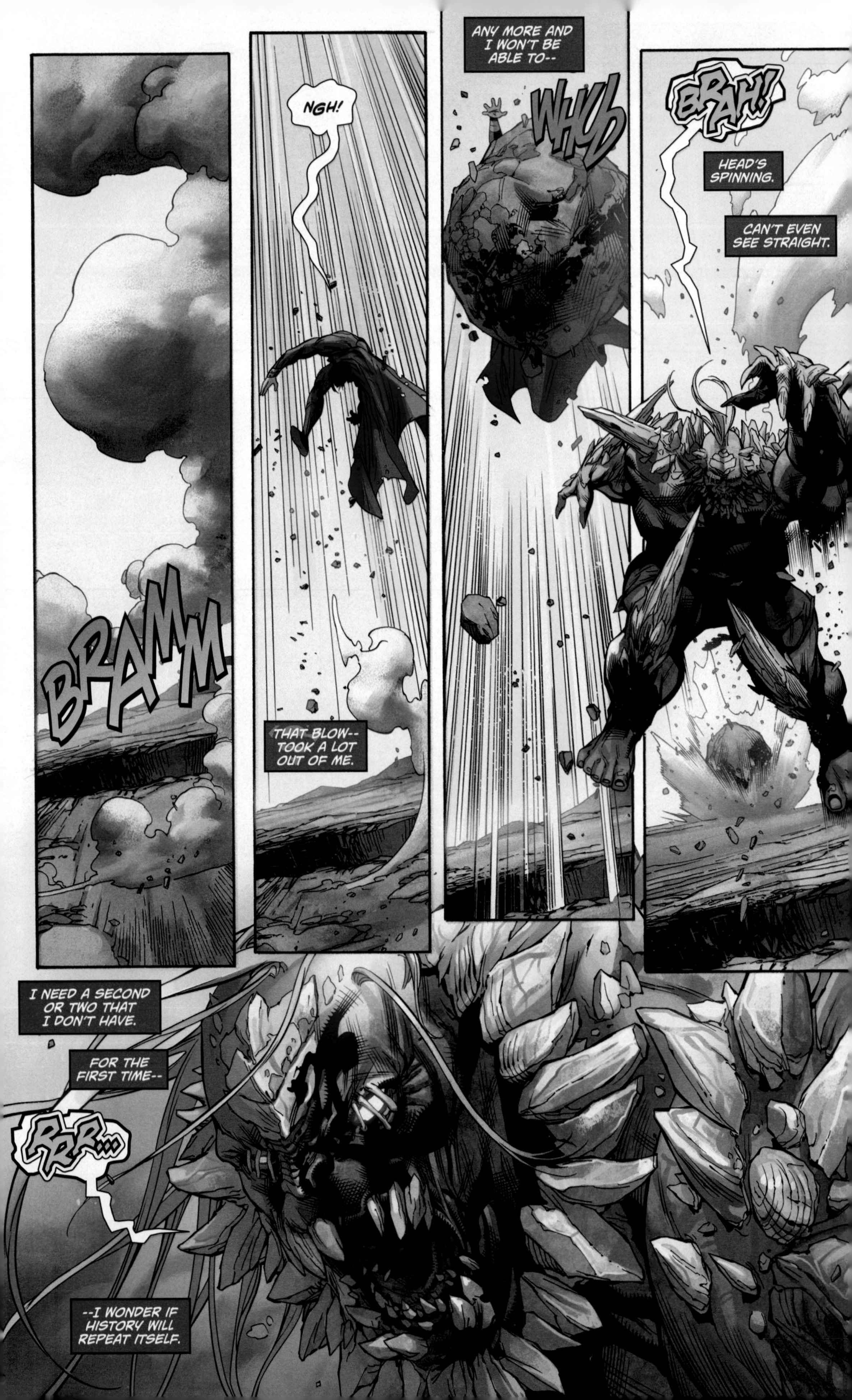
BRAMM
NGH!
THAT BLOW--
TOOK A LOT
OUT OF ME.
ANY MORE AND
I WON'T BE
ABLE TO--
WHUB
BRAH!
HEAD'S
SPINNING.
CAN'T EVEN
SEE STRAIGHT.
I NEED A SECOND
OR TWO THAT
I DON'T HAVE.
FOR THE
FIRST TIME--
RRRR...
--I WONDER IF
HISTORY WILL
REPEAT ITSELF.

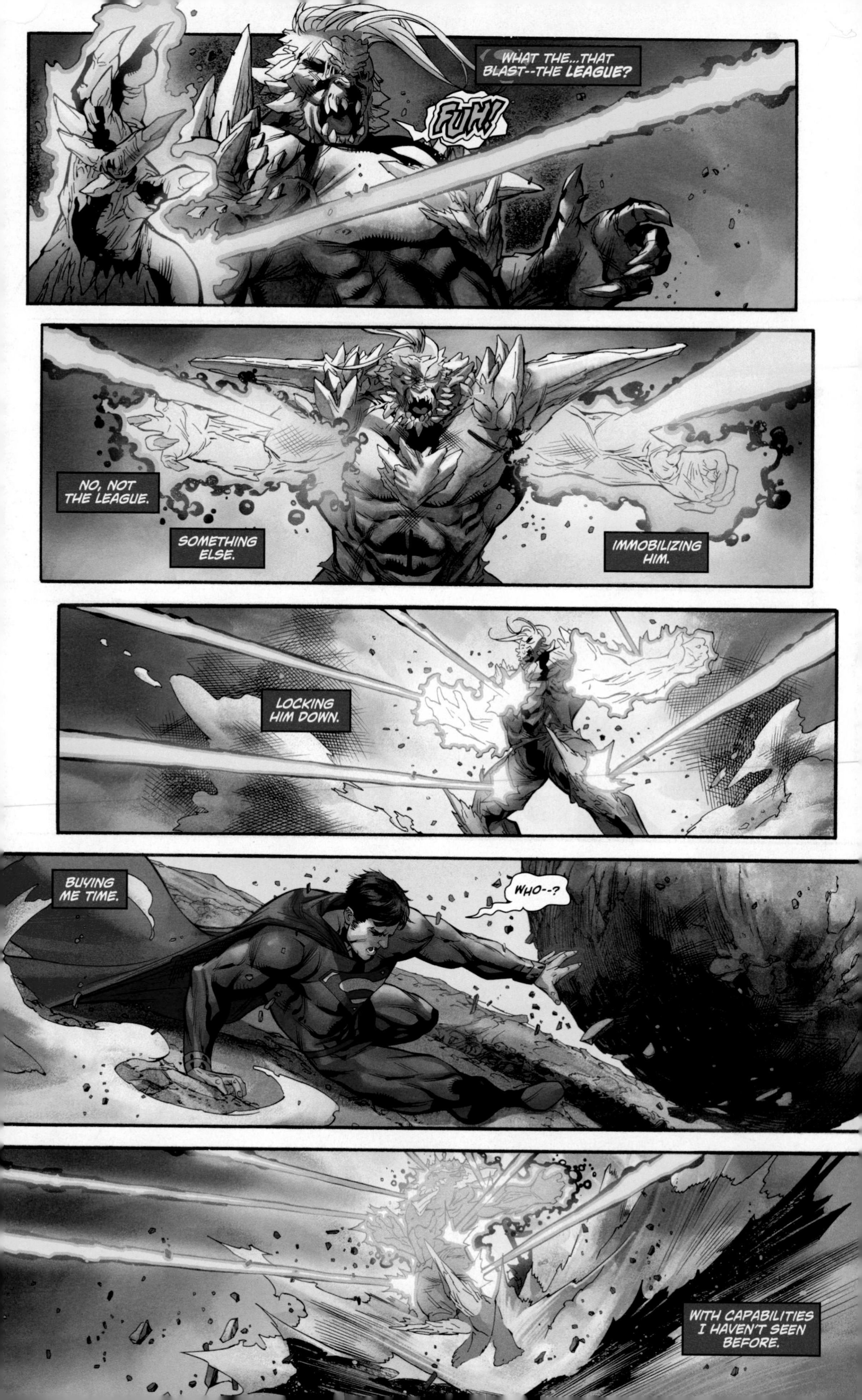
WHAT THE...THAT BLAST--THE LEAGUE?
FUH!
NO, NOT THE LEAGUE.
SOMETHING ELSE.
IMMOBILIZING HIM.
LOCKING HIM DOWN.
BUYING ME TIME.
WHO--?
WITH CAPABILITIES I HAVEN'T SEEN BEFORE.

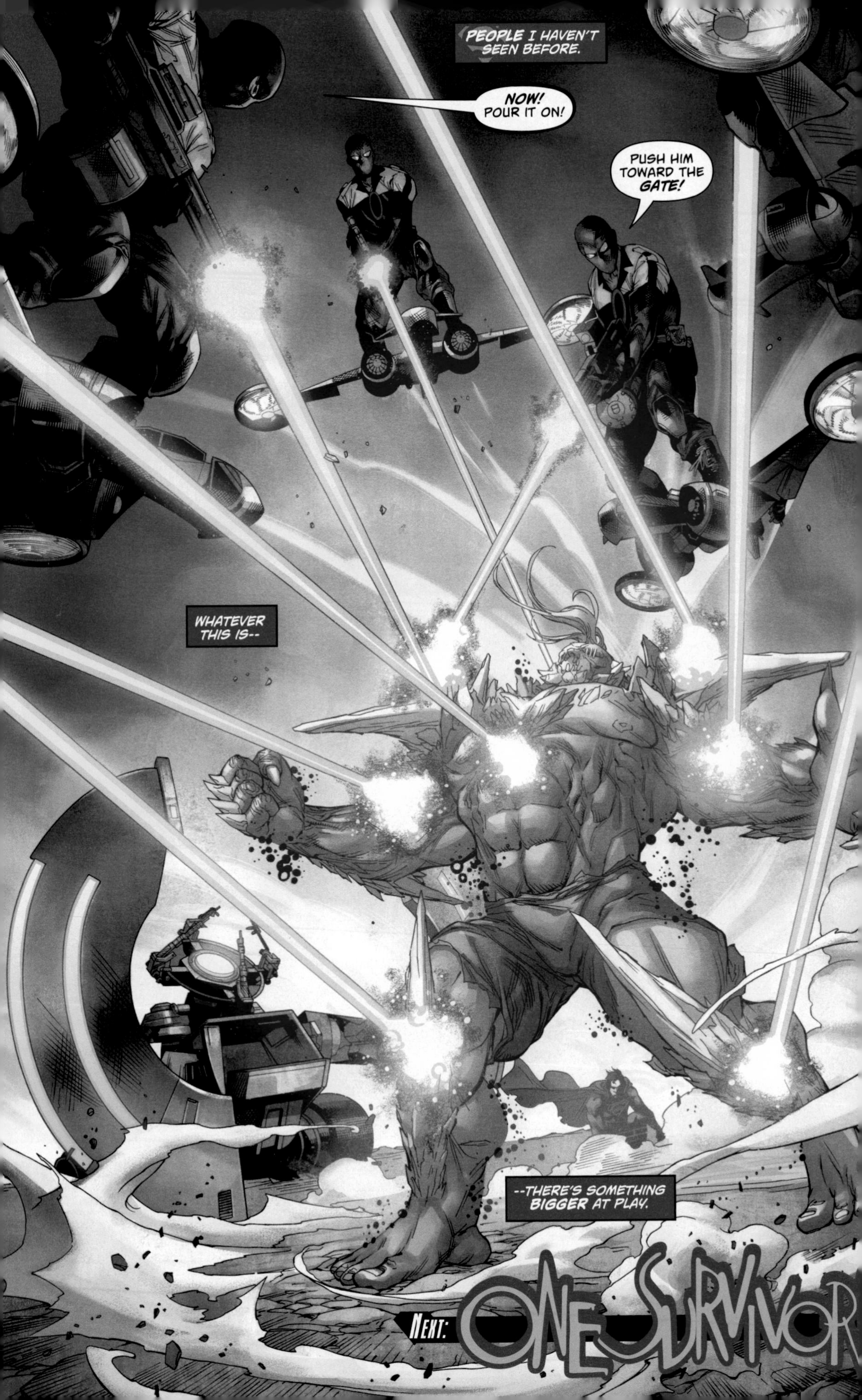
PEOPLE I HAVEN'T SEEN BEFORE.
NOW! POUR IT ON!
PUSH HIM TOWARD THE GATE!
WHATEVER THIS IS--
--THERE'S SOMETHING BIGGER AT PLAY.
NEXT: ONE SURVIVOR

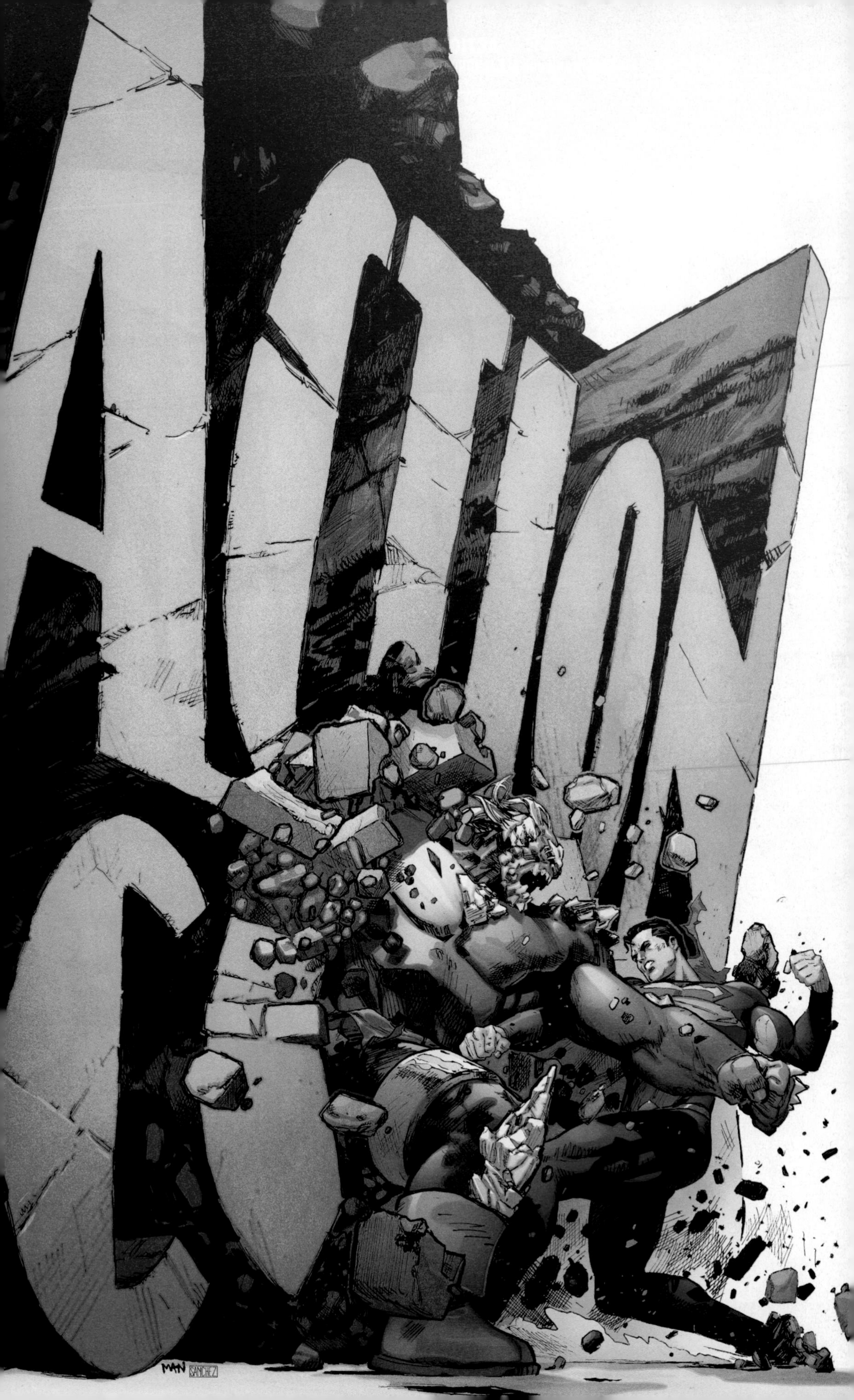
ACTION
MAN
SANCHEZ

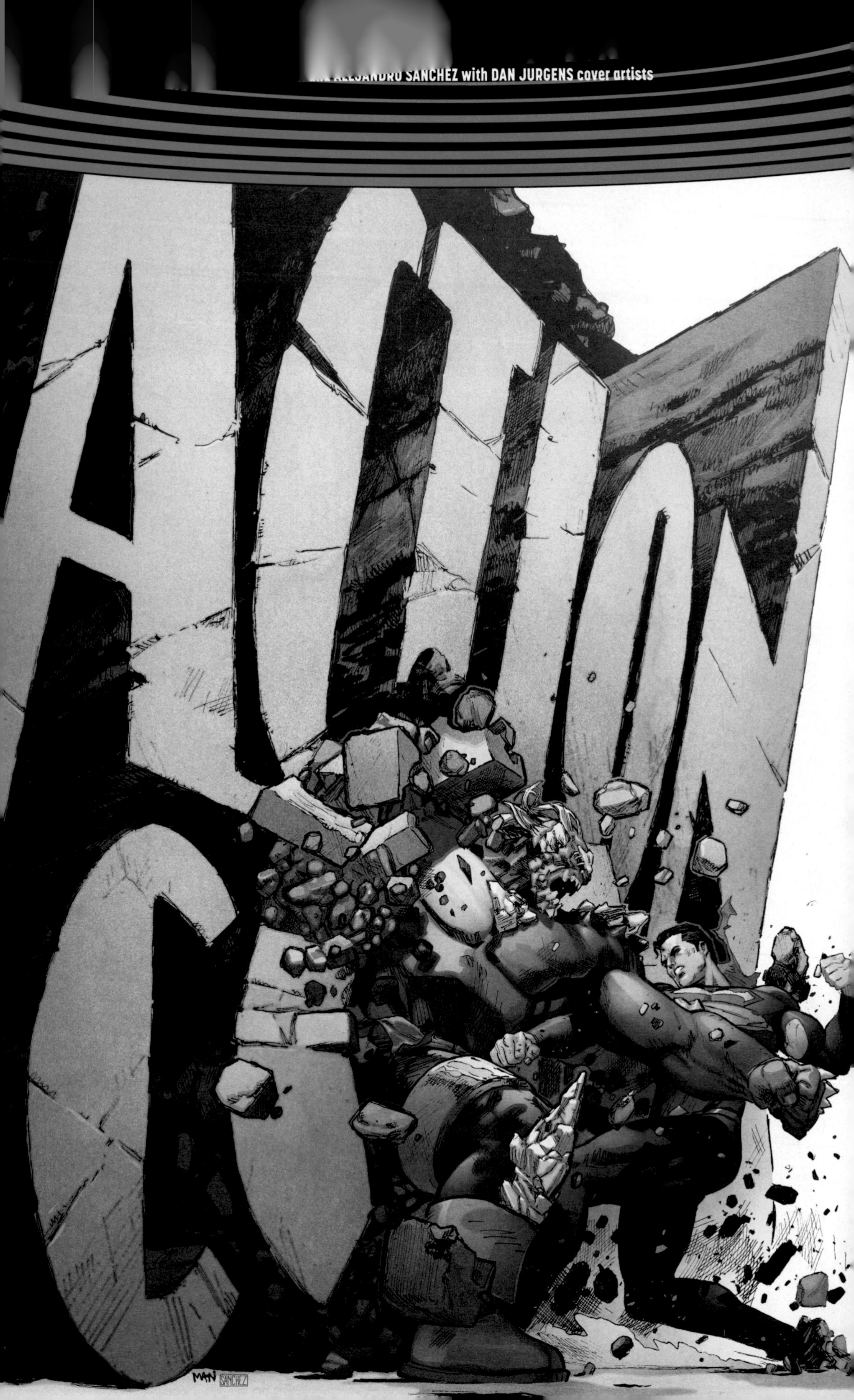
ALEJANDRO SANCHEZ with DAN JURGENS cover artists

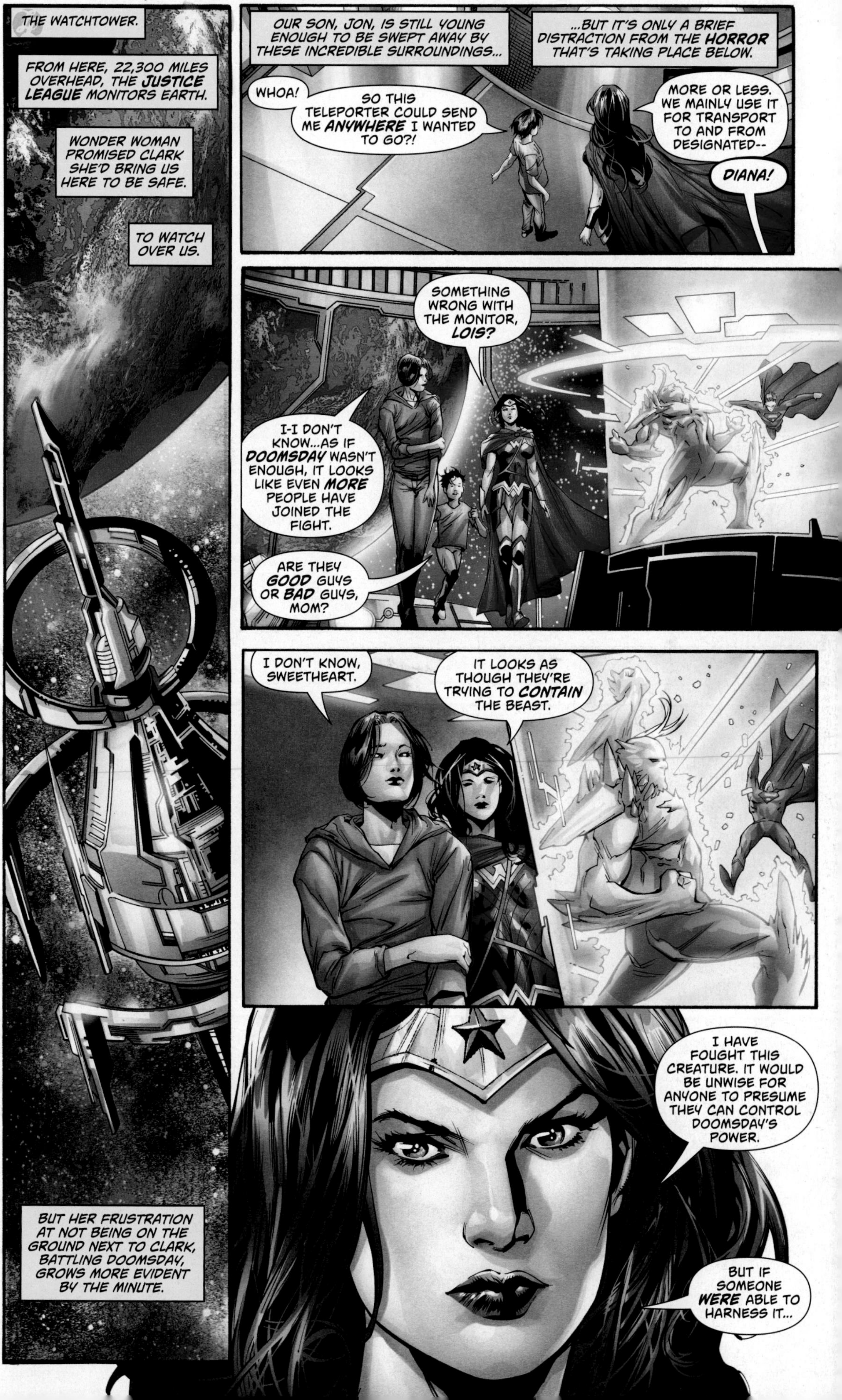
THE WATCHTOWER.
FROM HERE, 22,300 MILES OVERHEAD, THE JUSTICE LEAGUE MONITORS EARTH.
WONDER WOMAN PROMISED CLARK SHE'D BRING US HERE TO BE SAFE.
TO WATCH OVER US.
OUR SON, JON, IS STILL YOUNG ENOUGH TO BE SWEPT AWAY BY THESE INCREDIBLE SURROUNDINGS...
...BUT IT'S ONLY A BRIEF DISTRACTION FROM THE HORROR THAT'S TAKING PLACE BELOW.
WHOA!
SO THIS TELEPORTER COULD SEND ME ANYWHERE I WANTED TO GO?!
MORE OR LESS. WE MAINLY USE IT FOR TRANSPORT TO AND FROM DESIGNATED--
DIANA!
SOMETHING WRONG WITH THE MONITOR, LOIS?
I-I DON'T KNOW...AS IF DOOMSDAY WASN'T ENOUGH, IT LOOKS LIKE EVEN MORE PEOPLE HAVE JOINED THE FIGHT.
ARE THEY GOOD GUYS OR BAD GUYS, MOM?
I DON'T KNOW, SWEETHEART.
IT LOOKS AS THOUGH THEY'RE TRYING TO CONTAIN THE BEAST.
I HAVE FOUGHT THIS CREATURE. IT WOULD BE UNWISE FOR ANYONE TO PRESUME THEY CAN CONTROL DOOMSDAY'S POWER.
BUT HER FRUSTRATION AT NOT BEING ON THE GROUND NEXT TO CLARK, BATTLING DOOMSDAY, GROWS MORE EVIDENT BY THE MINUTE.
BUT IF SOMEONE WERE ABLE TO HARNESS IT...

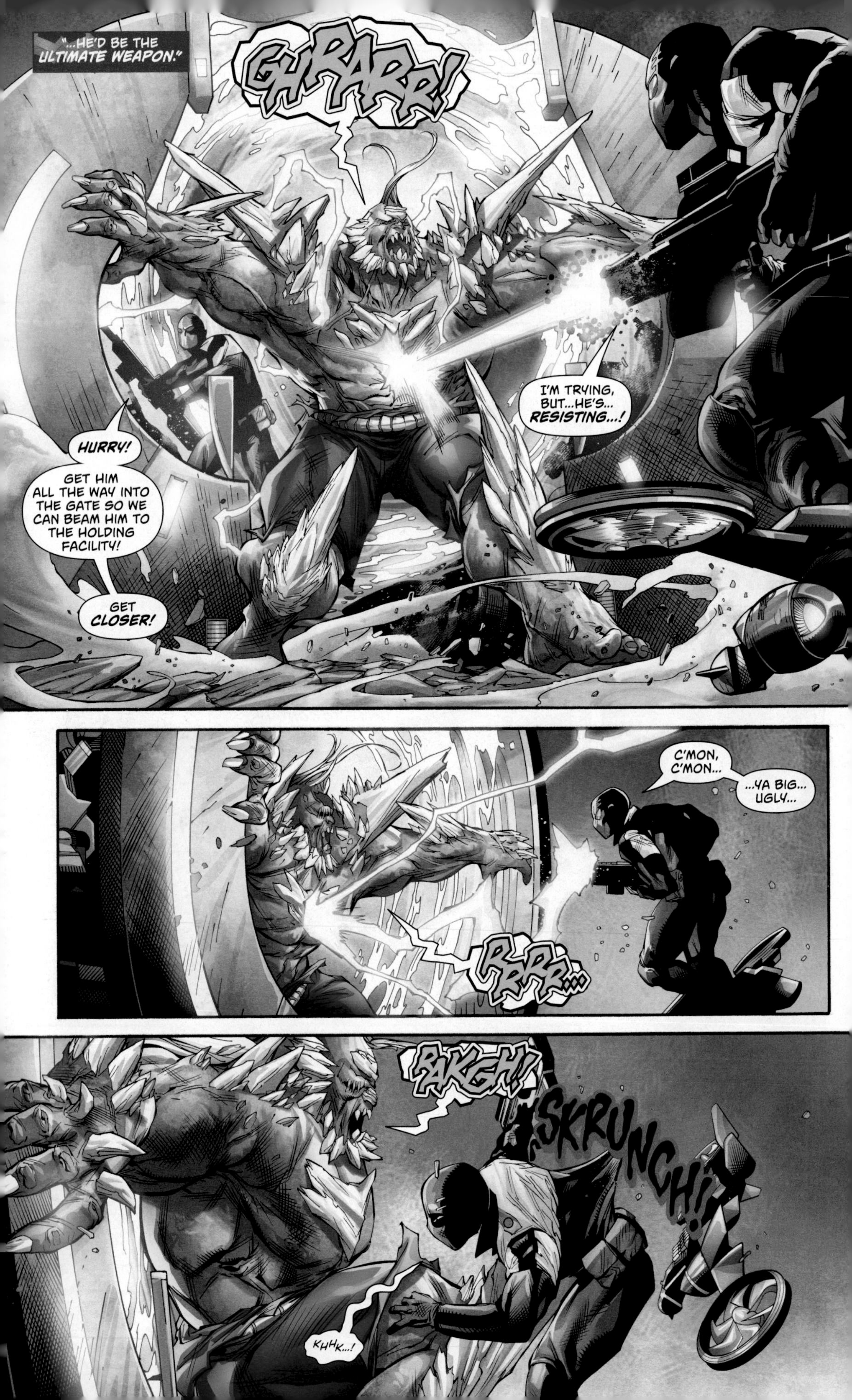
"...HE'D BE THE ULTIMATE WEAPON."
GHRARR!
HURRY!
GET HIM ALL THE WAY INTO THE GATE SO WE CAN BEAM HIM TO THE HOLDING FACILITY!
GET CLOSER!
I'M TRYING, BUT...HE'S... RESISTING...!
C'MON, C'MON...
...YA BIG... UGLY...
RRRR...
RAKGH!
SKRUNCH!
KHHK...!

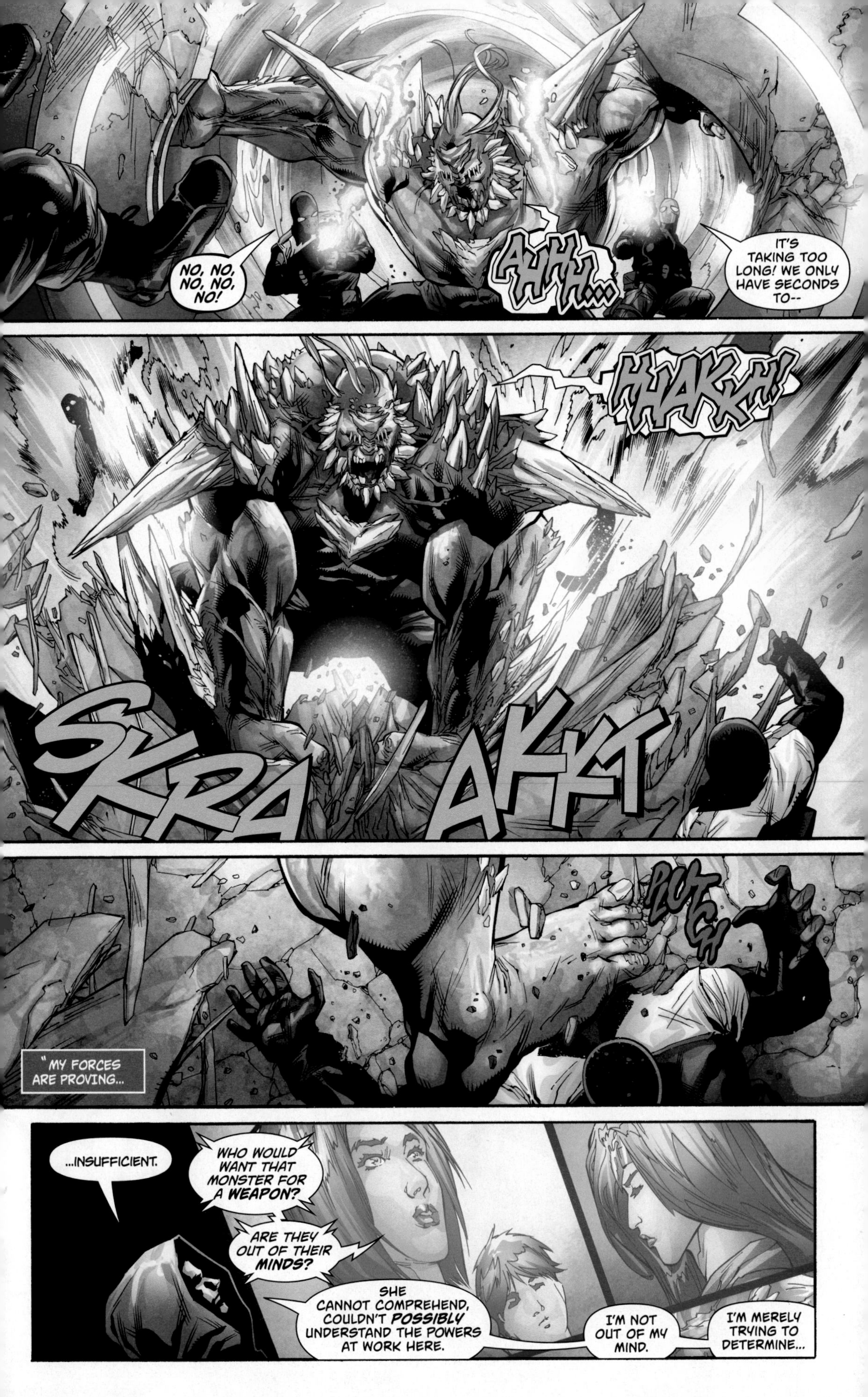
NO, NO, NO, NO, NO!
AHHH...
IT'S TAKING TOO LONG! WE ONLY HAVE SECONDS TO--
HHAKKH!
SKRAAKKT
PLOTCH
"MY FORCES ARE PROVING...
...INSUFFICIENT.
WHO WOULD WANT THAT MONSTER FOR A WEAPON?
ARE THEY OUT OF THEIR MINDS?
SHE CANNOT COMPREHEND, COULDN'T POSSIBLY UNDERSTAND THE POWERS AT WORK HERE.
I'M NOT OUT OF MY MIND.
I'M MERELY TRYING TO DETERMINE...

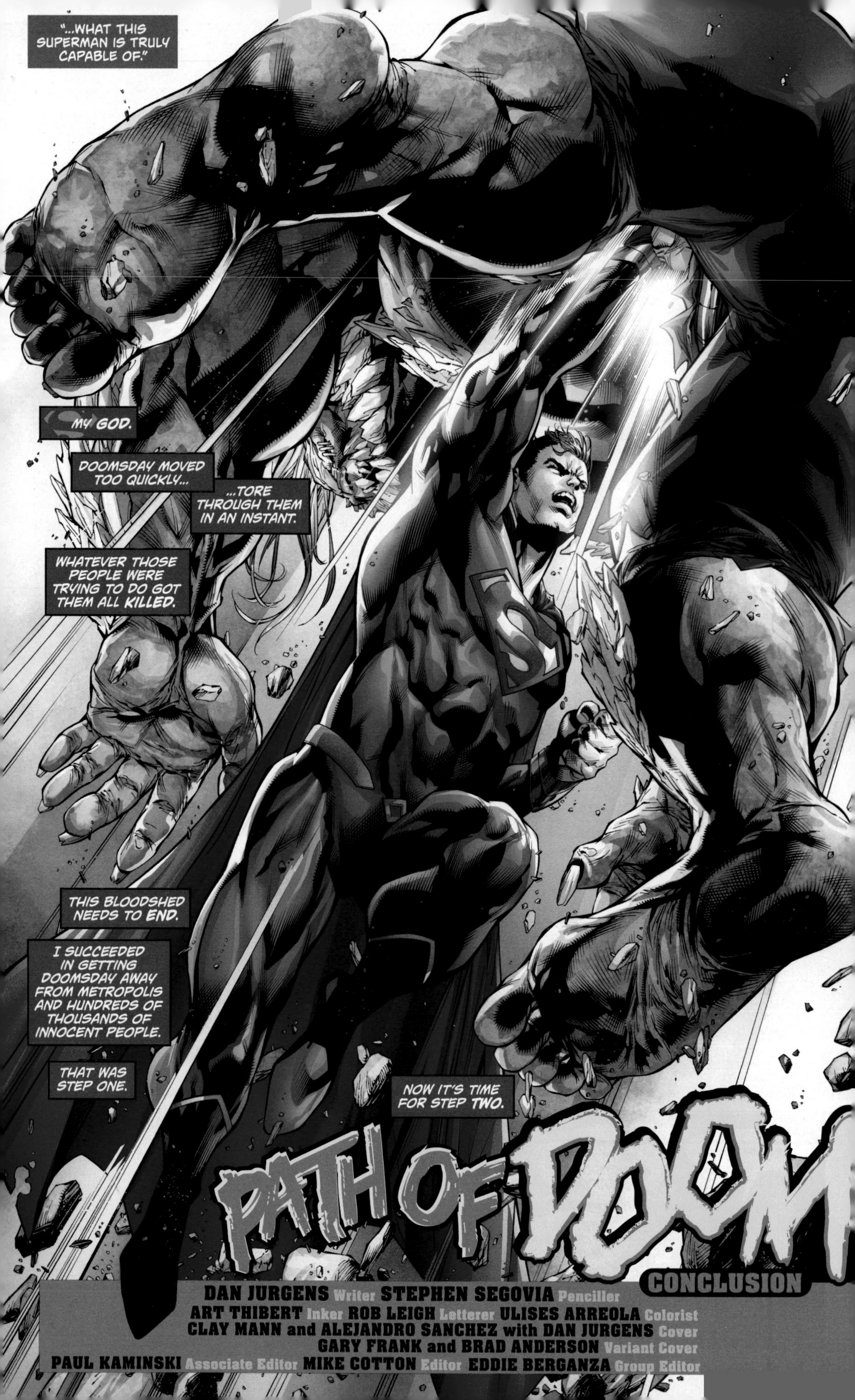
"...WHAT THIS SUPERMAN IS TRULY CAPABLE OF."
MY GOD.
DOOMSDAY MOVED TOO QUICKLY...
...TORE THROUGH THEM IN AN INSTANT.
WHATEVER THOSE PEOPLE WERE TRYING TO DO GOT THEM ALL KILLED.
THIS BLOODSHED NEEDS TO END.
I SUCCEEDED IN GETTING DOOMSDAY AWAY FROM METROPOLIS AND HUNDREDS OF THOUSANDS OF INNOCENT PEOPLE.
THAT WAS STEP ONE.
NOW IT'S TIME FOR STEP TWO.
PATH OF DOOM
CONCLUSION
DAN JURGENS Writer STEPHEN SEGOVIA Penciller
ART THIBERT Inker ROB LEIGH Letterer ULISES ARREOLA Colorist
CLAY MANN and ALEJANDRO SANCHEZ with DAN JURGENS Cover
GARY FRANK and BRAD ANDERSON Variant Cover
PAUL KAMINSKI Associate Editor MIKE COTTON Editor EDDIE BERGANZA Group Editor

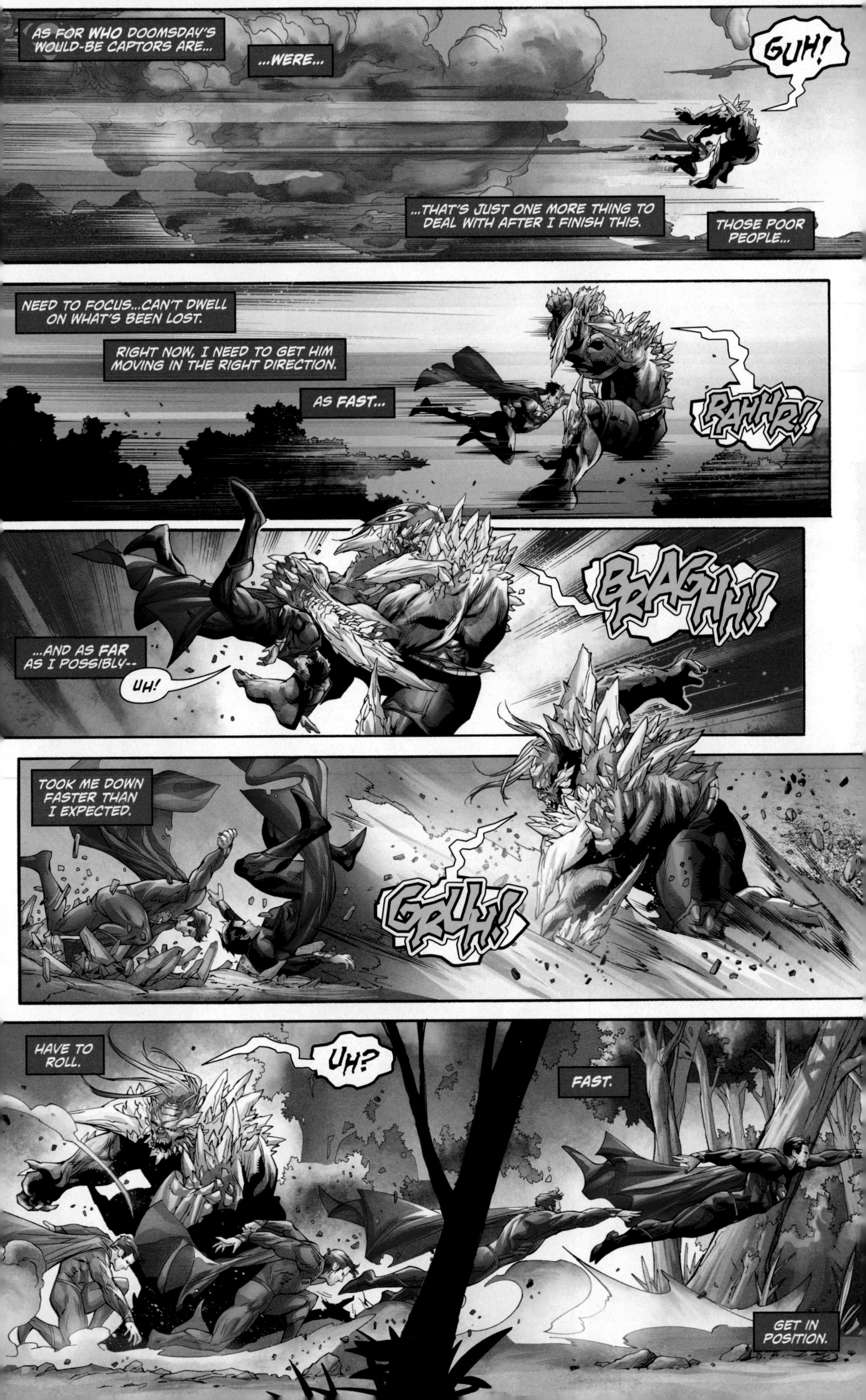
AS FOR WHO DOOMSDAY'S WOULD-BE CAPTORS ARE...
...WERE...
GUH!
...THAT'S JUST ONE MORE THING TO DEAL WITH AFTER I FINISH THIS.
THOSE POOR PEOPLE...
NEED TO FOCUS...CAN'T DWELL ON WHAT'S BEEN LOST.
RIGHT NOW, I NEED TO GET HIM MOVING IN THE RIGHT DIRECTION.
AS FAST...
RAHHR!
BRAGHH!
...AND AS FAR AS I POSSIBLY--
UH!
TOOK ME DOWN FASTER THAN I EXPECTED.
GRUH!
HAVE TO ROLL.
UH?
FAST.
GET IN POSITION.

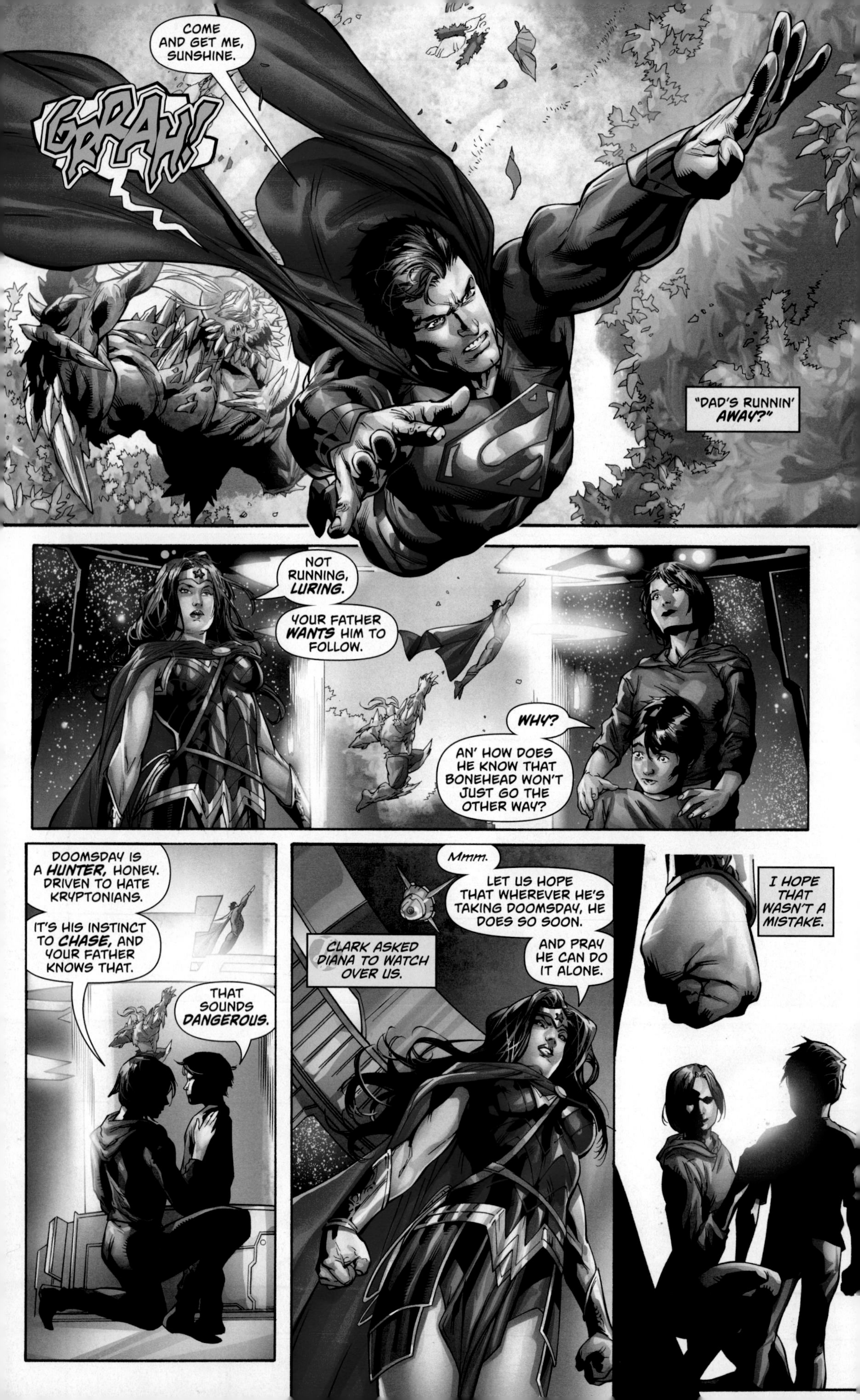
COME AND GET ME, SUNSHINE.
GRRAH!
"DAD'S RUNNIN' AWAY?"
NOT RUNNING, LURING.
YOUR FATHER WANTS HIM TO FOLLOW.
WHY?
AN' HOW DOES HE KNOW THAT BONEHEAD WON'T JUST GO THE OTHER WAY?
DOOMSDAY IS A HUNTER, HONEY. DRIVEN TO HATE KRYPTONIANS.
IT'S HIS INSTINCT TO CHASE, AND YOUR FATHER KNOWS THAT.
THAT SOUNDS DANGEROUS.
Mmm.
LET US HOPE THAT WHEREVER HE'S TAKING DOOMSDAY, HE DOES SO SOON.
AND PRAY HE CAN DO IT ALONE.
CLARK ASKED DIANA TO WATCH OVER US.
I HOPE THAT WASN'T A MISTAKE.

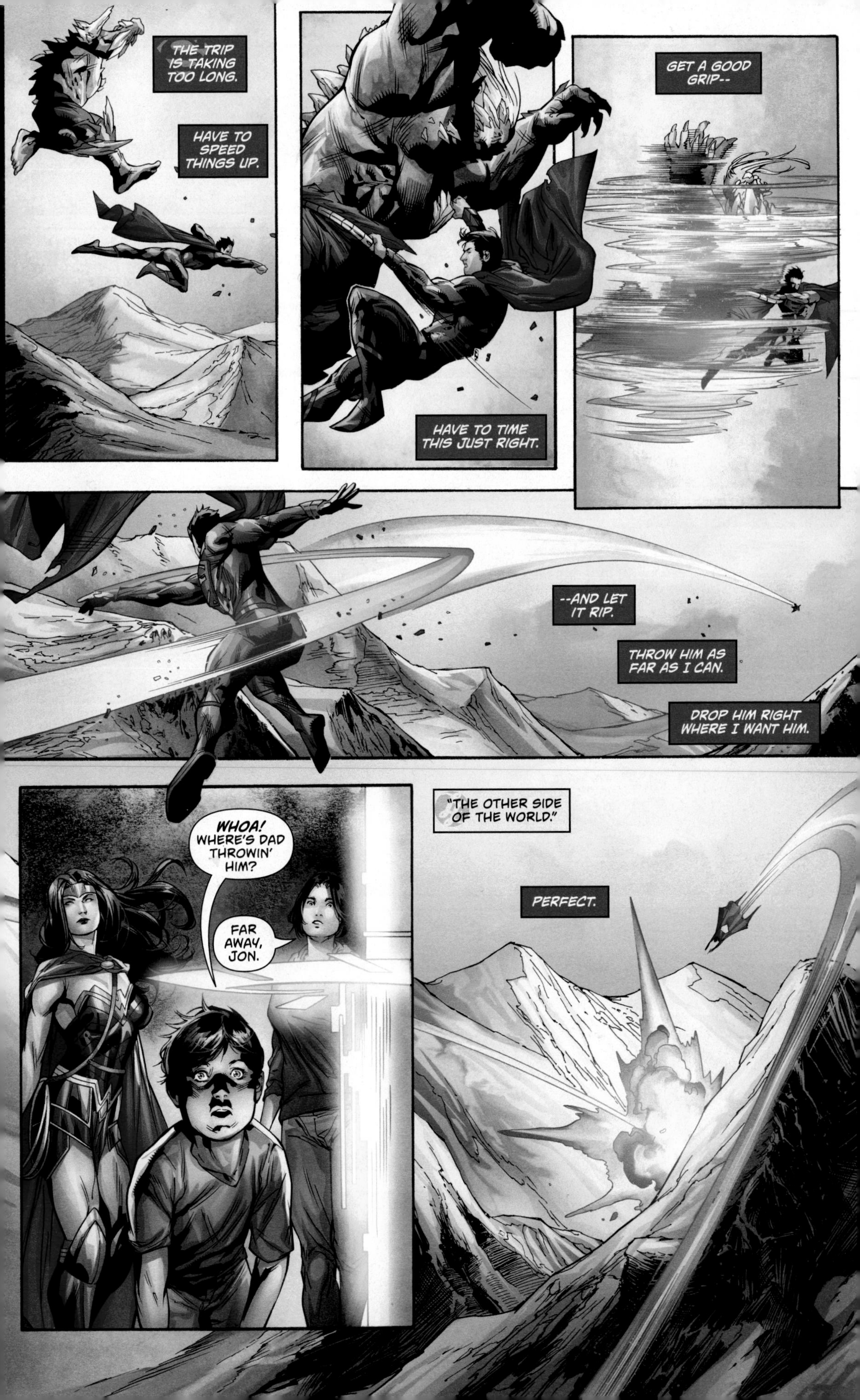
THE TRIP IS TAKING TOO LONG.
HAVE TO SPEED THINGS UP.
HAVE TO TIME THIS JUST RIGHT.
GET A GOOD GRIP--
--AND LET IT RIP.
THROW HIM AS FAR AS I CAN.
DROP HIM RIGHT WHERE I WANT HIM.
WHOA! WHERE'S DAD THROWIN' HIM?
FAR AWAY, JON.
"THE OTHER SIDE OF THE WORLD."
PERFECT.

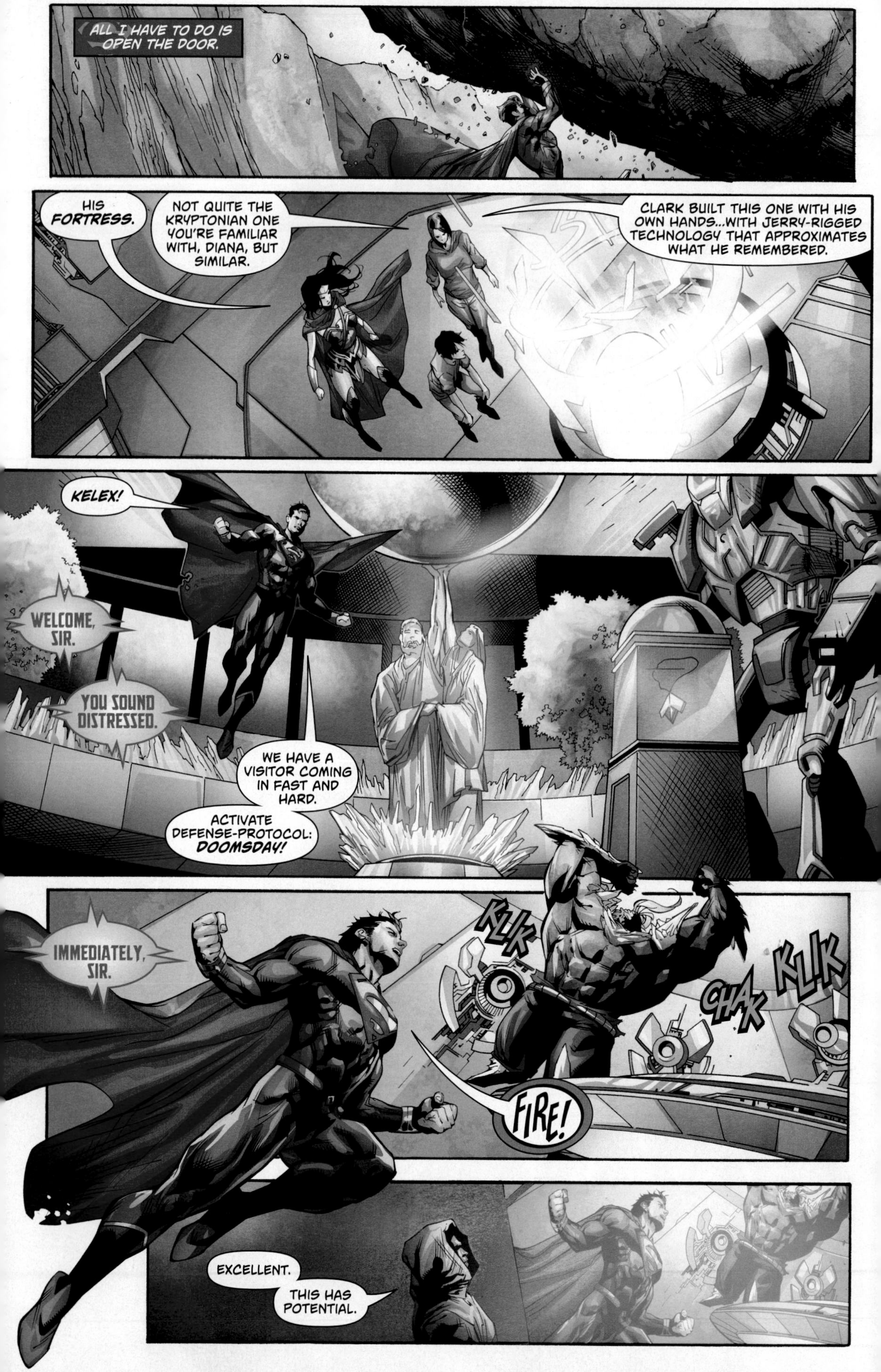
ALL I HAVE TO DO IS OPEN THE DOOR.
HIS FORTRESS.
NOT QUITE THE KRYPTONIAN ONE YOU'RE FAMILIAR WITH, DIANA, BUT SIMILAR.
CLARK BUILT THIS ONE WITH HIS OWN HANDS...WITH JERRY-RIGGED TECHNOLOGY THAT APPROXIMATES WHAT HE REMEMBERED.
KELEX!
WELCOME, SIR.
YOU SOUND DISTRESSED.
WE HAVE A VISITOR COMING IN FAST AND HARD.
ACTIVATE DEFENSE-PROTOCOL: DOOMSDAY!
IMMEDIATELY, SIR.
KLIK
CHAK
KLIK
FIRE!
EXCELLENT.
THIS HAS POTENTIAL.

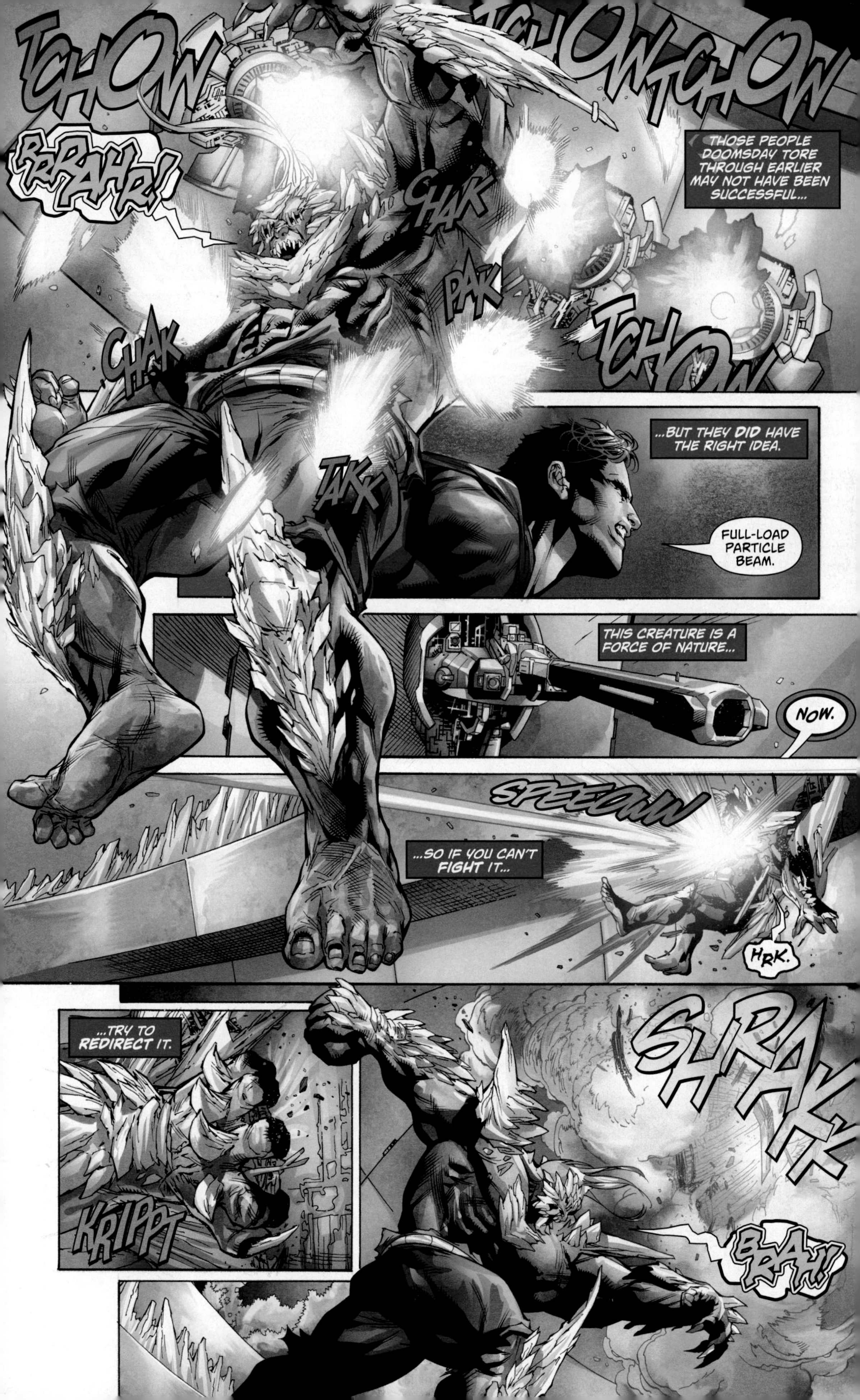

TCHOW
RRRAHR!
TCHOWTCHOWTCHOW
THOSE PEOPLE DOOMSDAY TORE THROUGH EARLIER MAY NOT HAVE BEEN SUCCESSFUL...
CHAK
PAK
CHAK
TCHOW
...BUT THEY DID HAVE THE RIGHT IDEA.
TAKK
FULL-LOAD PARTICLE BEAM.
THIS CREATURE IS A FORCE OF NATURE...
NOW.
SPEEOWW
...SO IF YOU CAN'T FIGHT IT...
HRK.
...TRY TO REDIRECT IT.
SHRAKK
KRIPPT
BRAH!

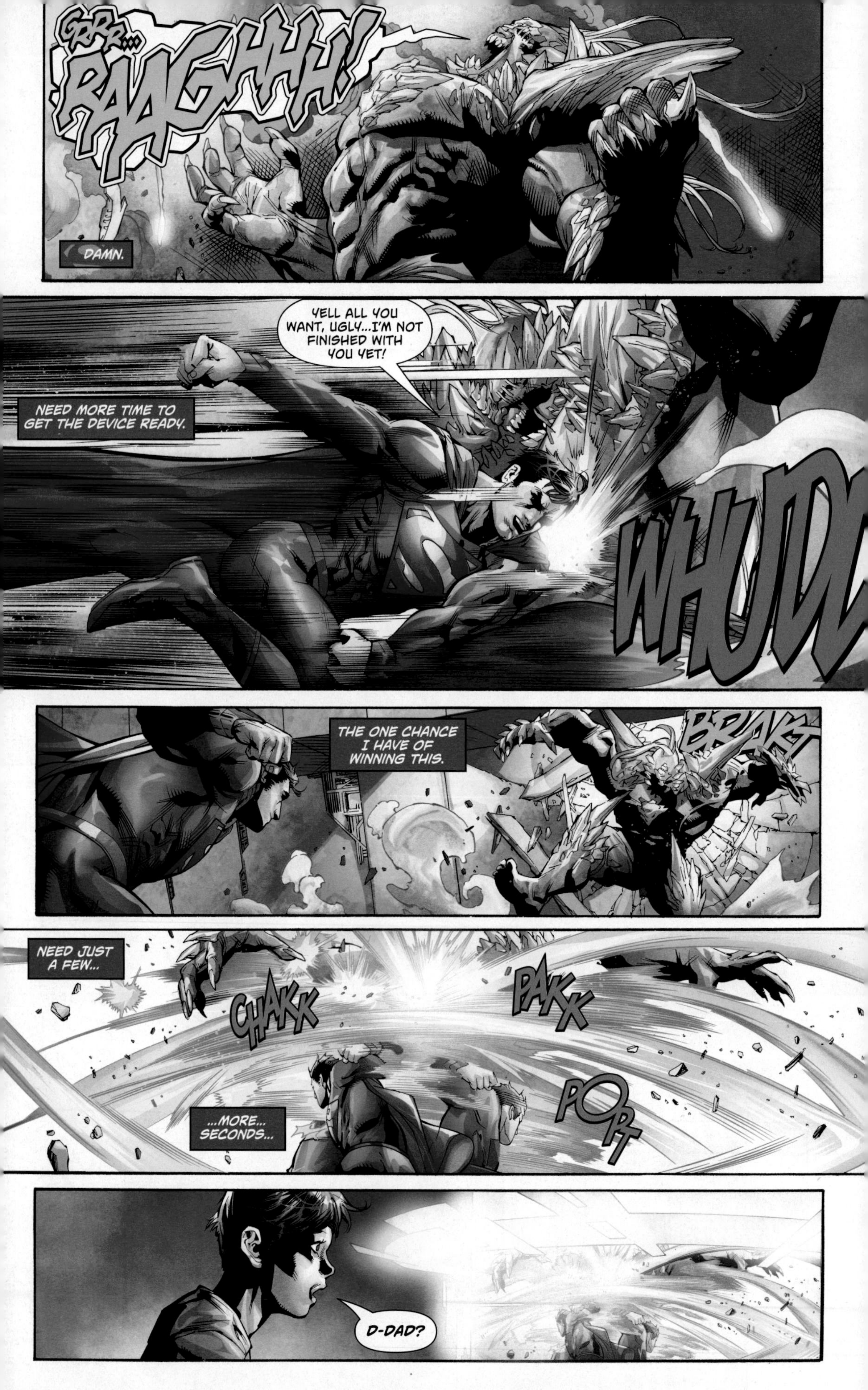
GRR... RAAGHHH!
DAMN.
YELL ALL YOU WANT, UGLY...I'M NOT FINISHED WITH YOU YET!
NEED MORE TIME TO GET THE DEVICE READY.
WHUDD
THE ONE CHANCE I HAVE OF WINNING THIS.
BRAKT
NEED JUST A FEW...
CHAKK
PAKK
POPT
...MORE... SECONDS...
D-DAD?

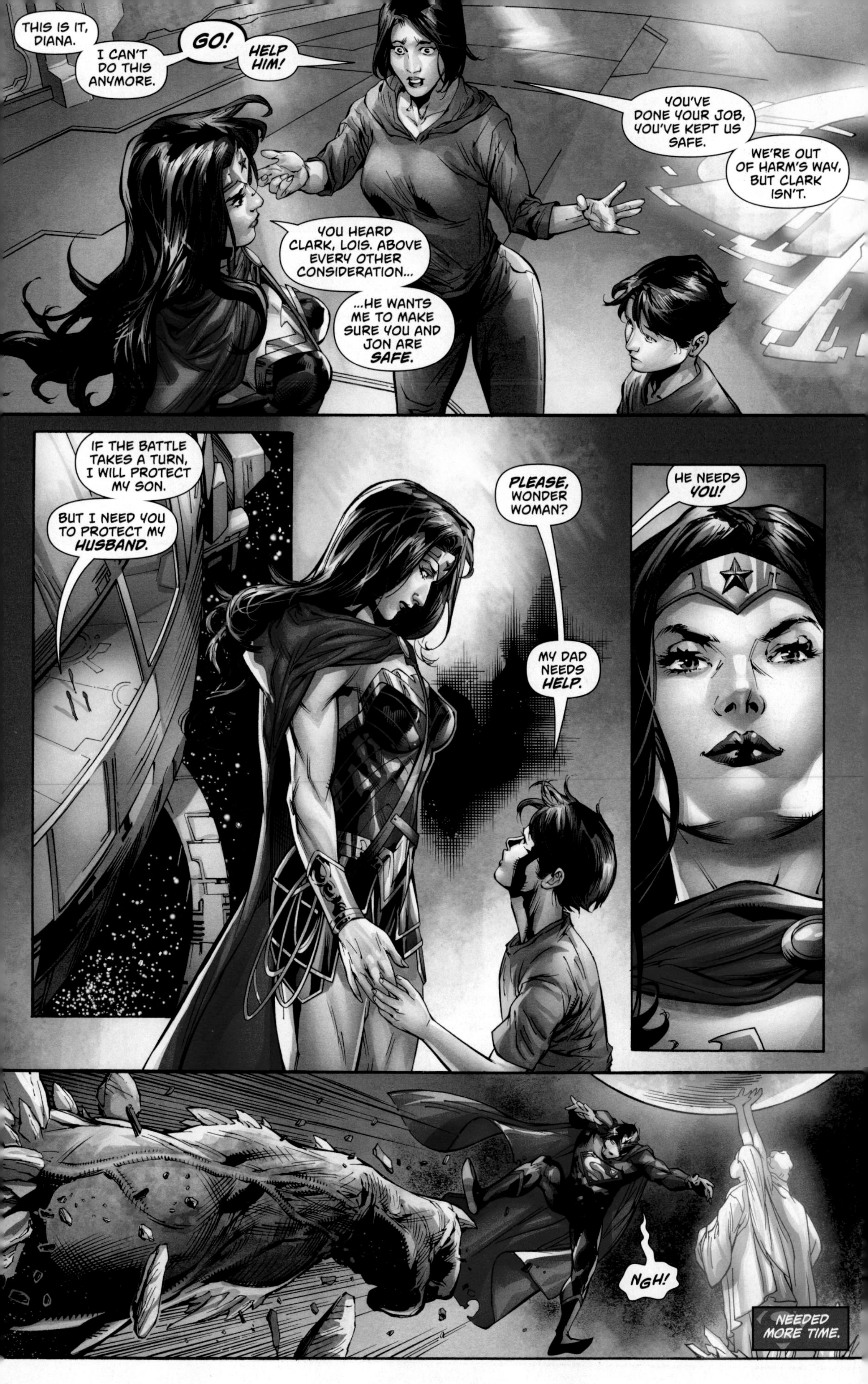
THIS IS IT, DIANA.
I CAN'T DO THIS ANYMORE.
GO!
HELP HIM!
YOU'VE DONE YOUR JOB, YOU'VE KEPT US SAFE.
WE'RE OUT OF HARM'S WAY, BUT CLARK ISN'T.
YOU HEARD CLARK, LOIS. ABOVE EVERY OTHER CONSIDERATION...
...HE WANTS ME TO MAKE SURE YOU AND JON ARE SAFE.
IF THE BATTLE TAKES A TURN, I WILL PROTECT MY SON.
BUT I NEED YOU TO PROTECT MY HUSBAND.
PLEASE, WONDER WOMAN?
MY DAD NEEDS HELP.
HE NEEDS YOU!
NGH!
NEEDED MORE TIME.

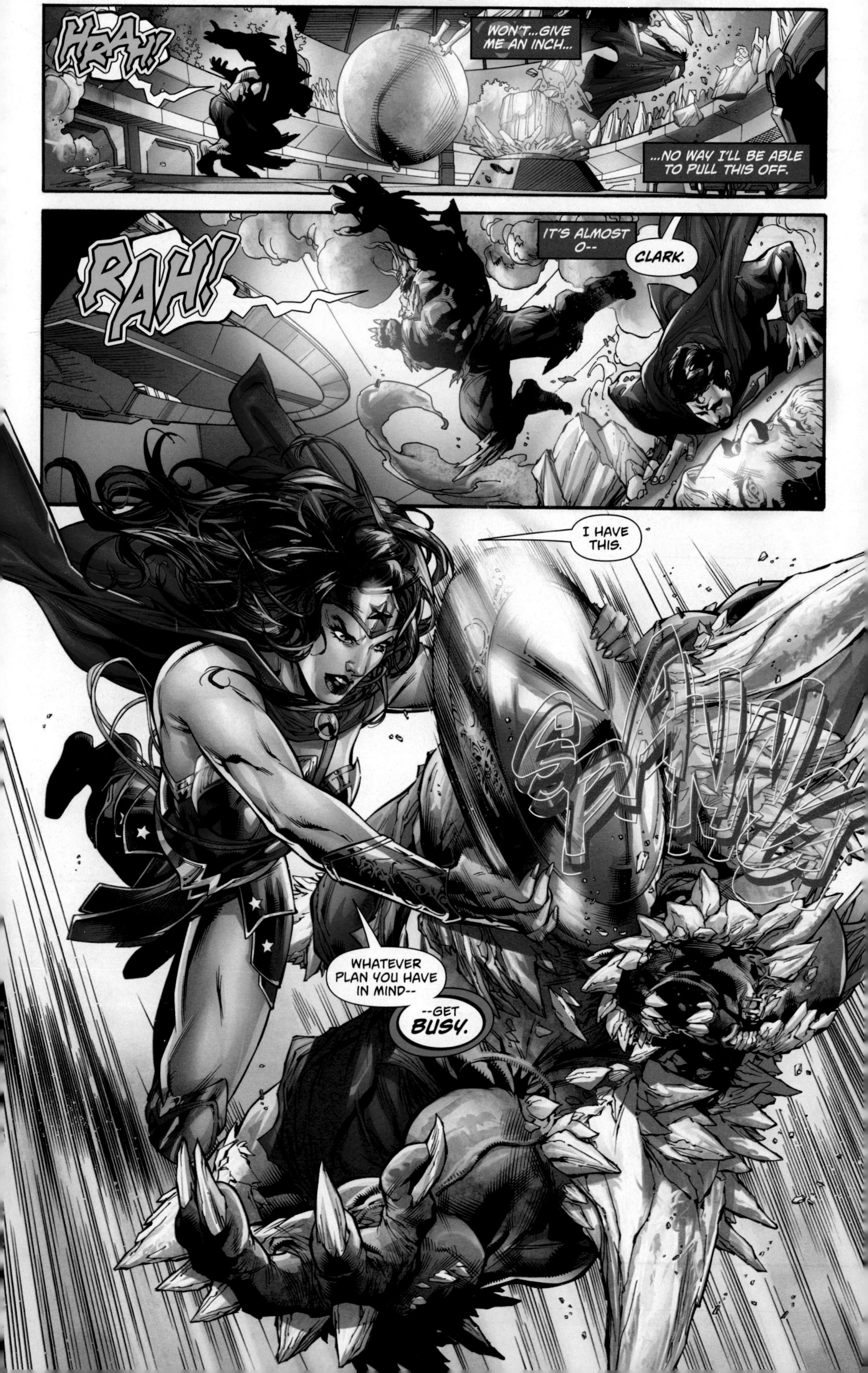
HRAH!
WON'T...GIVE ME AN INCH...
...NO WAY I'LL BE ABLE TO PULL THIS OFF.
RAH!
IT'S ALMOST O--
CLARK.
I HAVE THIS.
WHATEVER PLAN YOU HAVE IN MIND--
--GET BUSY.

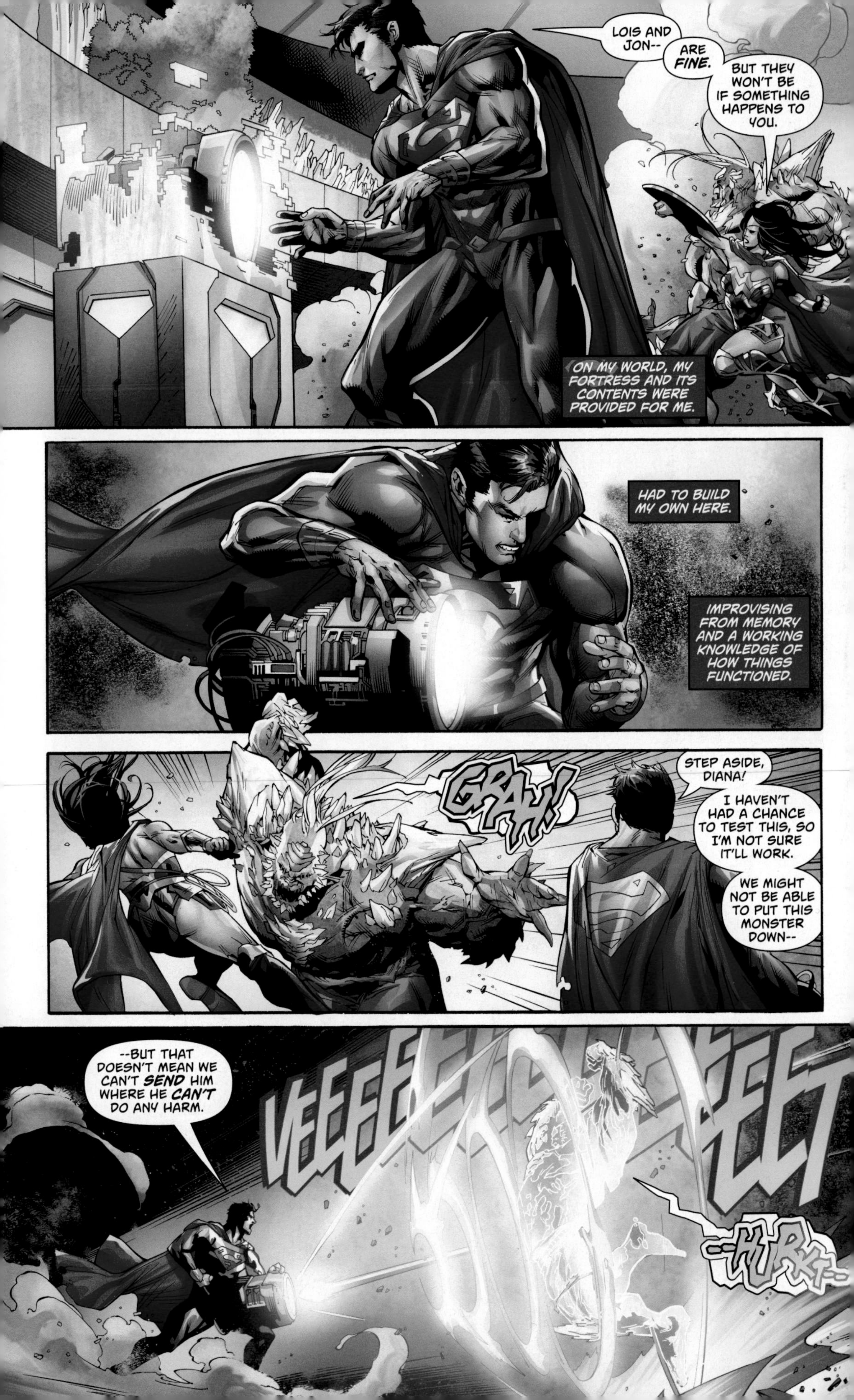
LOIS AND JON--
ARE *FINE.*
BUT THEY WON'T BE IF SOMETHING HAPPENS TO YOU.
ON MY WORLD, MY FORTRESS AND ITS CONTENTS WERE PROVIDED FOR ME.
HAD TO BUILD MY OWN HERE.
IMPROVISING FROM MEMORY AND A WORKING KNOWLEDGE OF HOW THINGS FUNCTIONED.
GRAH!
STEP ASIDE, DIANA!
I HAVEN'T HAD A CHANCE TO TEST THIS, SO I'M NOT SURE IT'LL WORK.
WE MIGHT NOT BE ABLE TO PUT THIS MONSTER DOWN--
--BUT THAT DOESN'T MEAN WE CAN'T *SEND* HIM WHERE HE *CAN'T* DO ANY HARM.
VEEEEEEEEEEEEEET
HURK

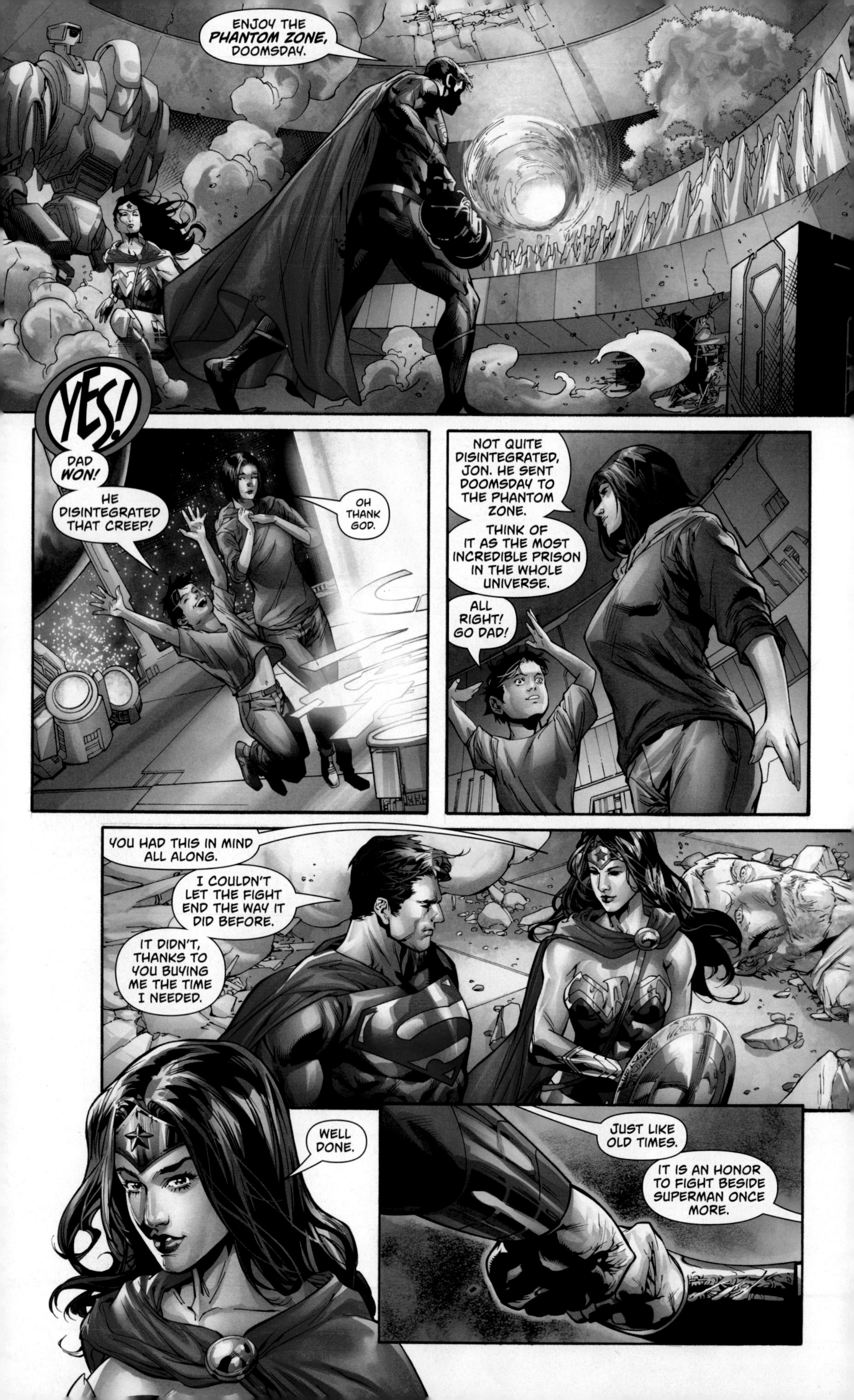
ENJOY THE PHANTOM ZONE, DOOMSDAY.
YES!
DAD WON!
HE DISINTEGRATED THAT CREEP!
OH THANK GOD.
NOT QUITE DISINTEGRATED, JON. HE SENT DOOMSDAY TO THE PHANTOM ZONE.
THINK OF IT AS THE MOST INCREDIBLE PRISON IN THE WHOLE UNIVERSE.
ALL RIGHT! GO DAD!
YOU HAD THIS IN MIND ALL ALONG.
I COULDN'T LET THE FIGHT END THE WAY IT DID BEFORE.
IT DIDN'T, THANKS TO YOU BUYING ME THE TIME I NEEDED.
WELL DONE.
JUST LIKE OLD TIMES.
IT IS AN HONOR TO FIGHT BESIDE SUPERMAN ONCE MORE.

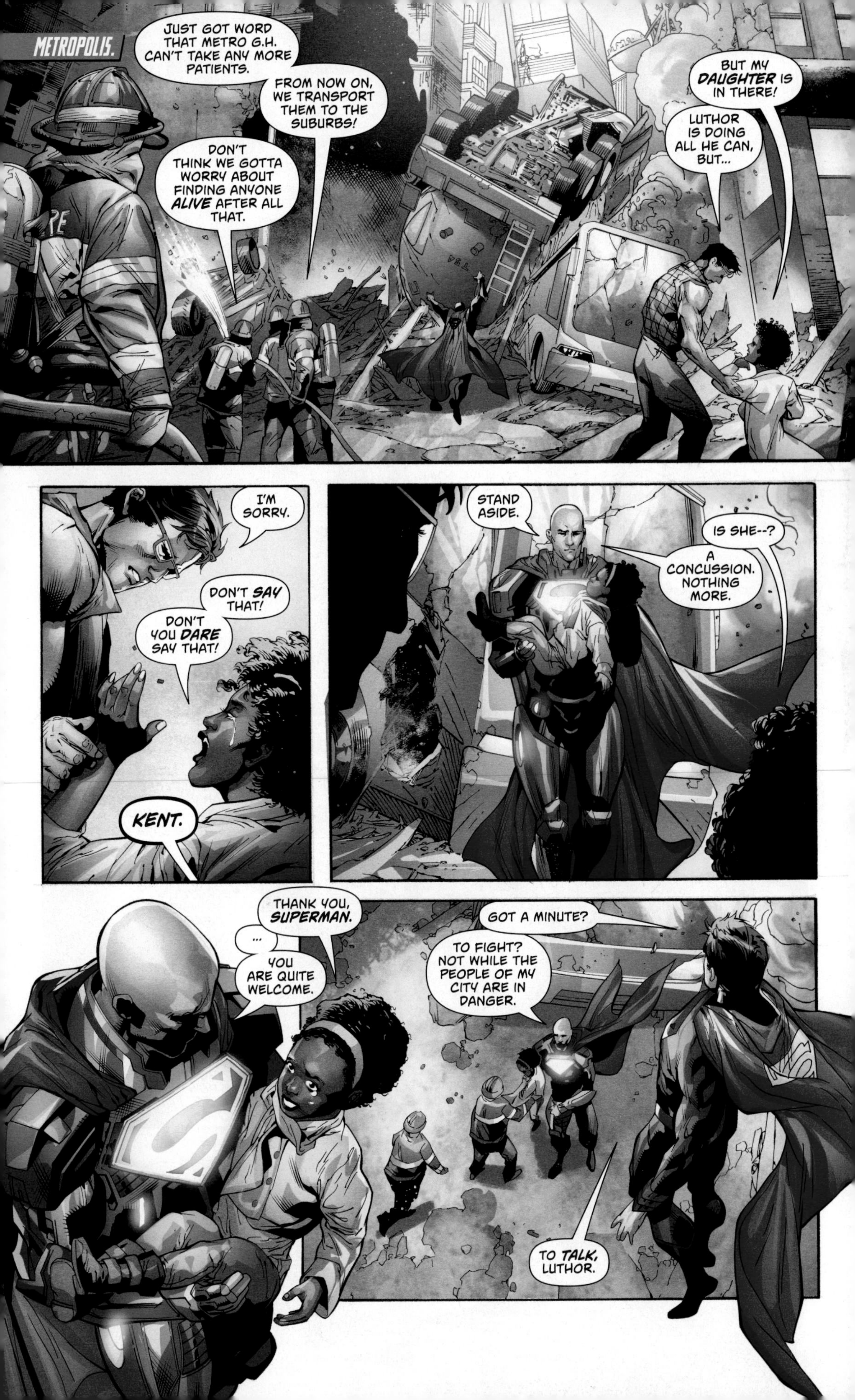
METROPOLIS.
JUST GOT WORD THAT METRO G.H. CAN'T TAKE ANY MORE PATIENTS.
FROM NOW ON, WE TRANSPORT THEM TO THE SUBURBS!
DON'T THINK WE GOTTA WORRY ABOUT FINDING ANYONE ALIVE AFTER ALL THAT.
BUT MY DAUGHTER IS IN THERE!
LUTHOR IS DOING ALL HE CAN, BUT...
I'M SORRY.
DON'T SAY THAT!
DON'T YOU DARE SAY THAT!
KENT.
STAND ASIDE.
IS SHE--?
A CONCUSSION. NOTHING MORE.
THANK YOU, SUPERMAN.
...
YOU ARE QUITE WELCOME.
GOT A MINUTE?
TO FIGHT? NOT WHILE THE PEOPLE OF MY CITY ARE IN DANGER.
TO TALK, LUTHOR.

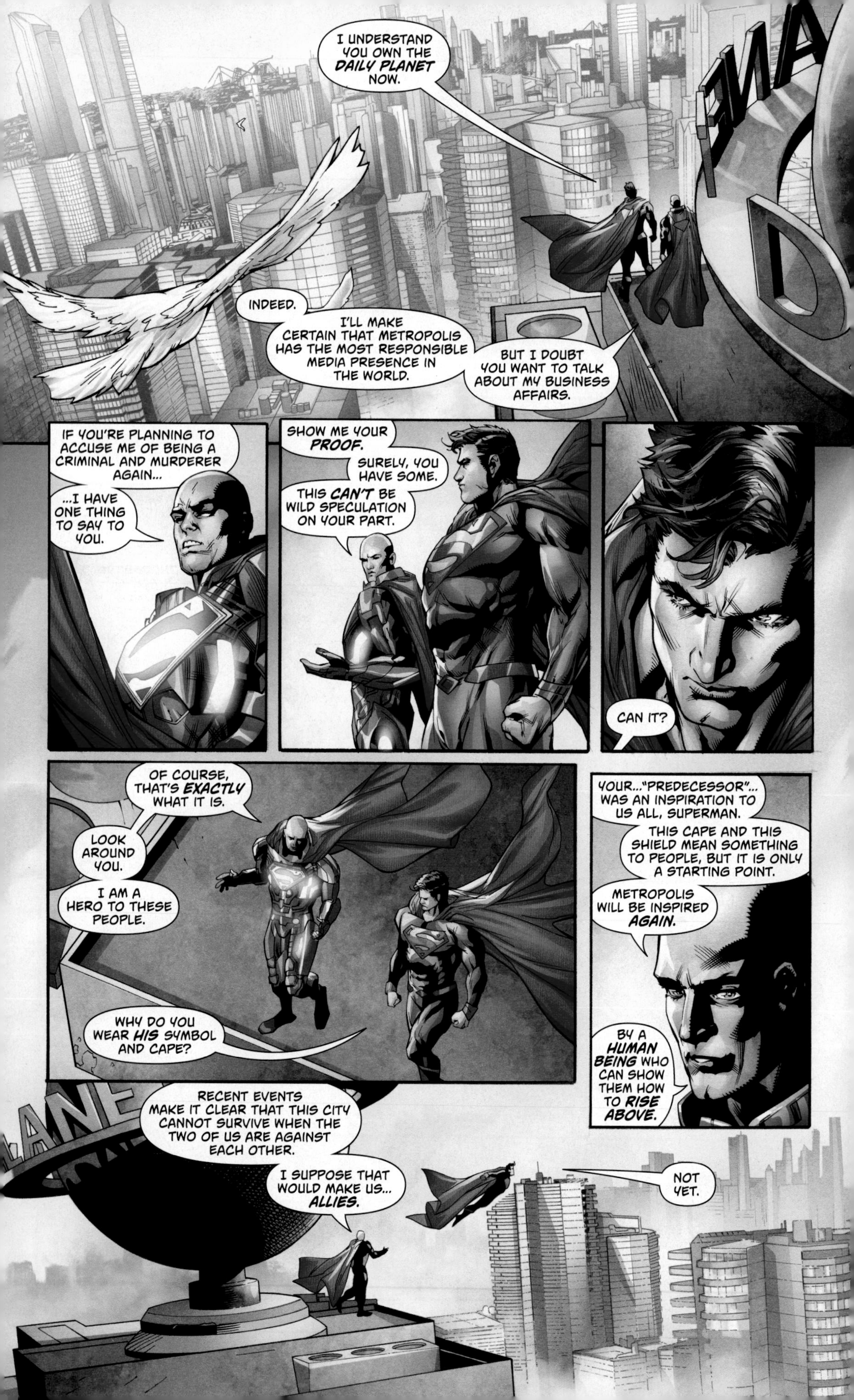
I UNDERSTAND YOU OWN THE DAILY PLANET NOW.
INDEED.
I'LL MAKE CERTAIN THAT METROPOLIS HAS THE MOST RESPONSIBLE MEDIA PRESENCE IN THE WORLD.
BUT I DOUBT YOU WANT TO TALK ABOUT MY BUSINESS AFFAIRS.
IF YOU'RE PLANNING TO ACCUSE ME OF BEING A CRIMINAL AND MURDERER AGAIN...
...I HAVE ONE THING TO SAY TO YOU.
SHOW ME YOUR PROOF.
SURELY, YOU HAVE SOME.
THIS CAN'T BE WILD SPECULATION ON YOUR PART.
CAN IT?
OF COURSE, THAT'S EXACTLY WHAT IT IS.
LOOK AROUND YOU.
I AM A HERO TO THESE PEOPLE.
WHY DO YOU WEAR HIS SYMBOL AND CAPE?
YOUR..."PREDECESSOR"... WAS AN INSPIRATION TO US ALL, SUPERMAN.
THIS CAPE AND THIS SHIELD MEAN SOMETHING TO PEOPLE, BUT IT IS ONLY A STARTING POINT.
METROPOLIS WILL BE INSPIRED AGAIN.
BY A HUMAN BEING WHO CAN SHOW THEM HOW TO RISE ABOVE.
RECENT EVENTS MAKE IT CLEAR THAT THIS CITY CANNOT SURVIVE WHEN THE TWO OF US ARE AGAINST EACH OTHER.
I SUPPOSE THAT WOULD MAKE US... ALLIES.
NOT YET.

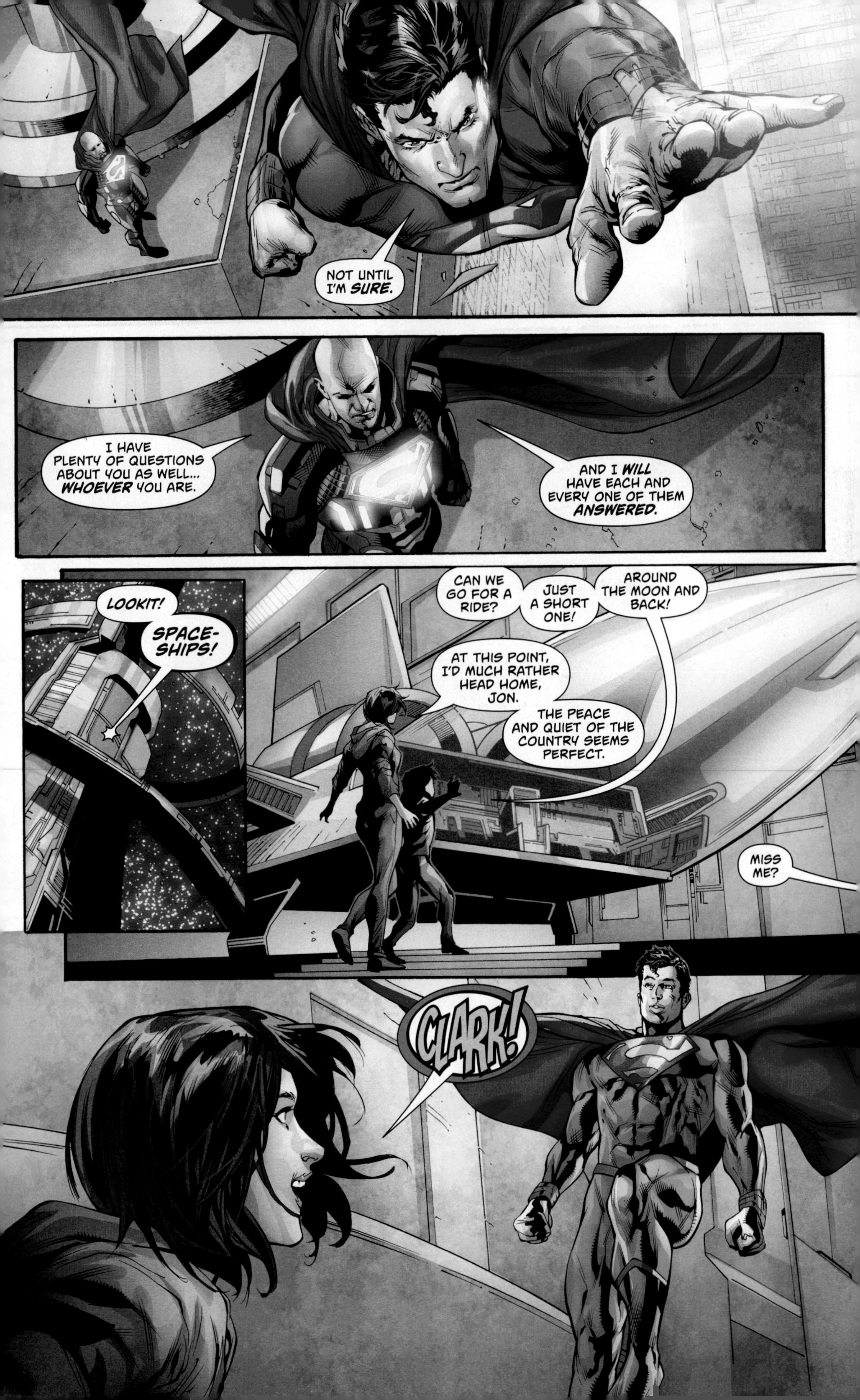
NOT UNTIL I'M SURE.
I HAVE PLENTY OF QUESTIONS ABOUT YOU AS WELL... WHOEVER YOU ARE.
AND I WILL HAVE EACH AND EVERY ONE OF THEM ANSWERED.
LOOKIT!
SPACE-SHIPS!
CAN WE GO FOR A RIDE?
JUST A SHORT ONE!
AROUND THE MOON AND BACK!
AT THIS POINT, I'D MUCH RATHER HEAD HOME, JON.
THE PEACE AND QUIET OF THE COUNTRY SEEMS PERFECT.
MISS ME?
CLARK!

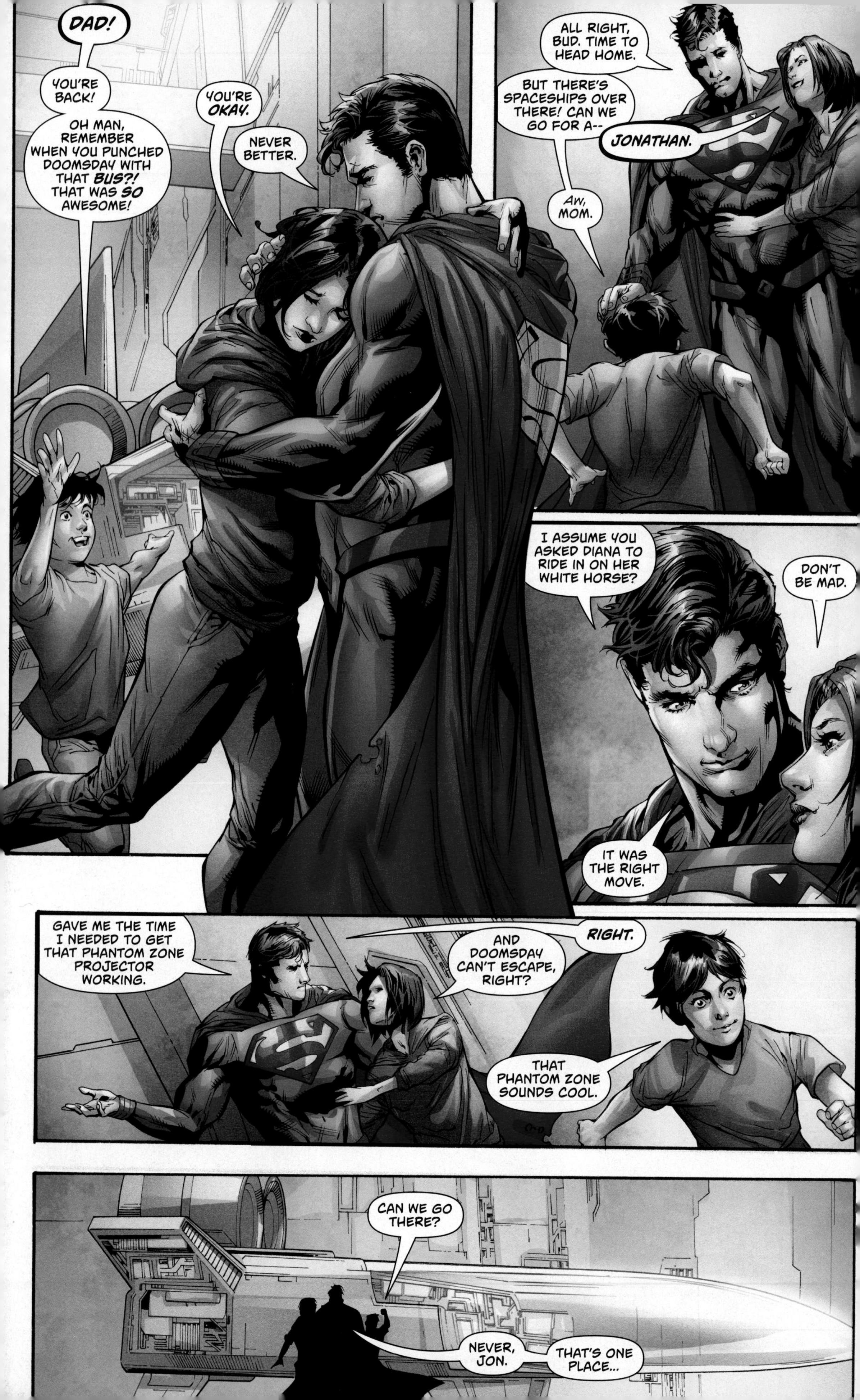
DAD!
YOU'RE BACK!
OH MAN, REMEMBER WHEN YOU PUNCHED DOOMSDAY WITH THAT BUS?! THAT WAS SO AWESOME!
YOU'RE OKAY.
NEVER BETTER.
ALL RIGHT, BUD. TIME TO HEAD HOME.
BUT THERE'S SPACESHIPS OVER THERE! CAN WE GO FOR A--
JONATHAN.
AW, MOM.
I ASSUME YOU ASKED DIANA TO RIDE IN ON HER WHITE HORSE?
DON'T BE MAD.
IT WAS THE RIGHT MOVE.
GAVE ME THE TIME I NEEDED TO GET THAT PHANTOM ZONE PROJECTOR WORKING.
AND DOOMSDAY CAN'T ESCAPE, RIGHT?
RIGHT.
THAT PHANTOM ZONE SOUNDS COOL.
CAN WE GO THERE?
NEVER, JON.
THAT'S ONE PLACE...

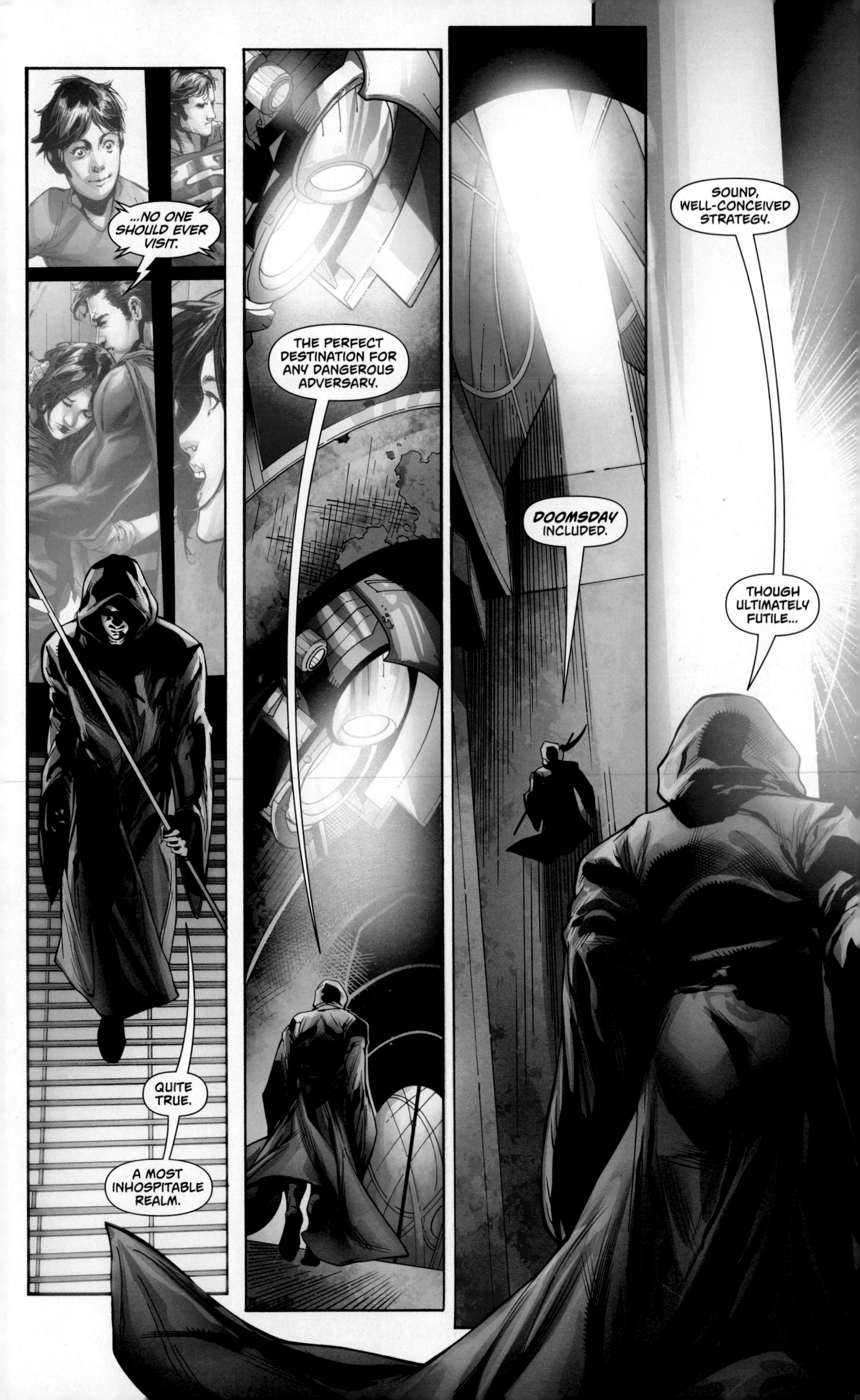
...NO ONE SHOULD EVER VISIT.
QUITE TRUE.
A MOST INHOSPITABLE REALM.
THE PERFECT DESTINATION FOR ANY DANGEROUS ADVERSARY.
DOOMSDAY INCLUDED.
SOUND, WELL-CONCEIVED STRATEGY.
THOUGH ULTIMATELY FUTILE...

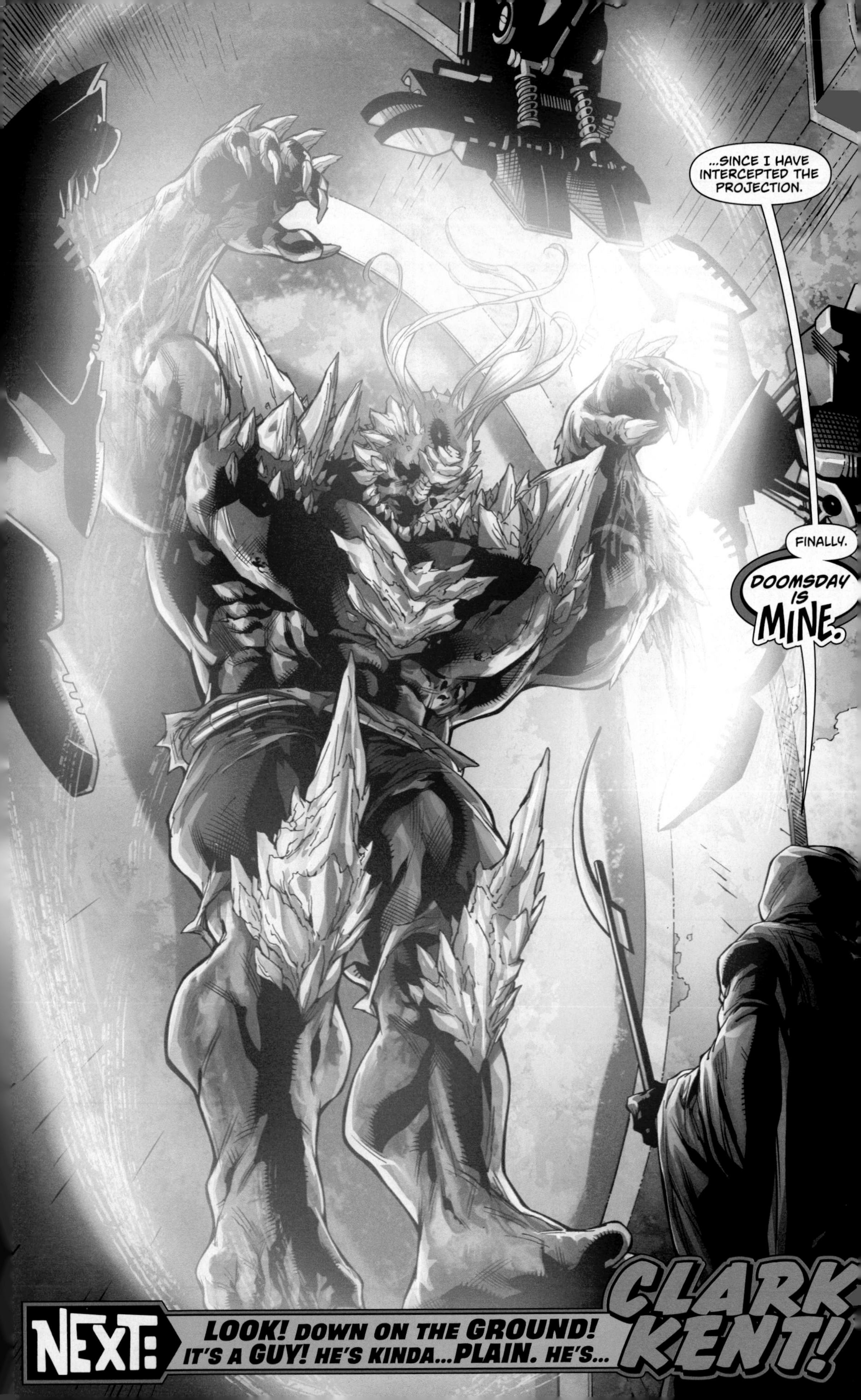
...SINCE I HAVE INTERCEPTED THE PROJECTION.
FINALLY.
DOOMSDAY IS MINE.
NEXT: LOOK! DOWN ON THE GROUND! IT'S A GUY! HE'S KINDA...PLAIN. HE'S... CLARK KENT!

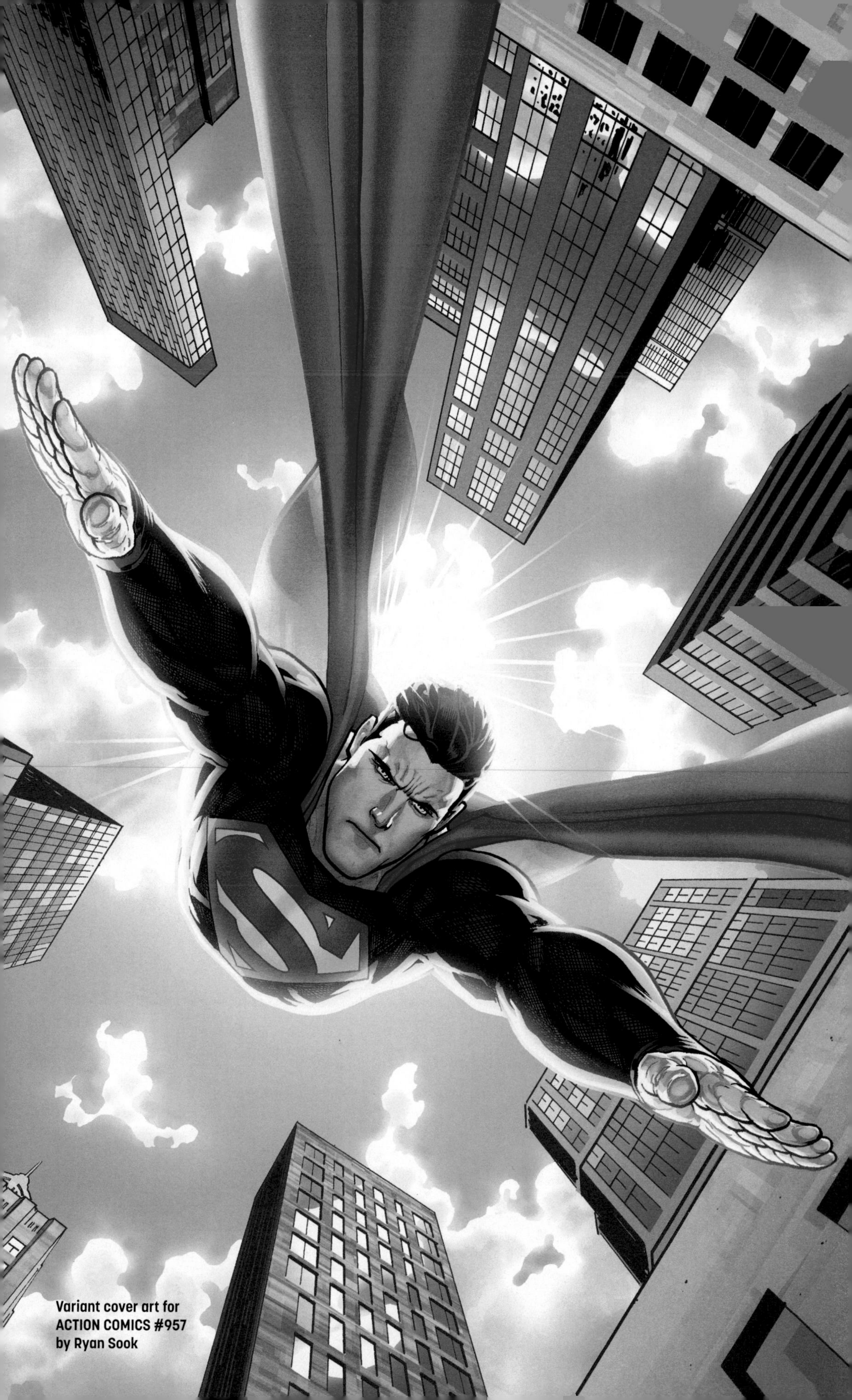

Variant cover art for
ACTION COMICS #957
by Ryan Sook

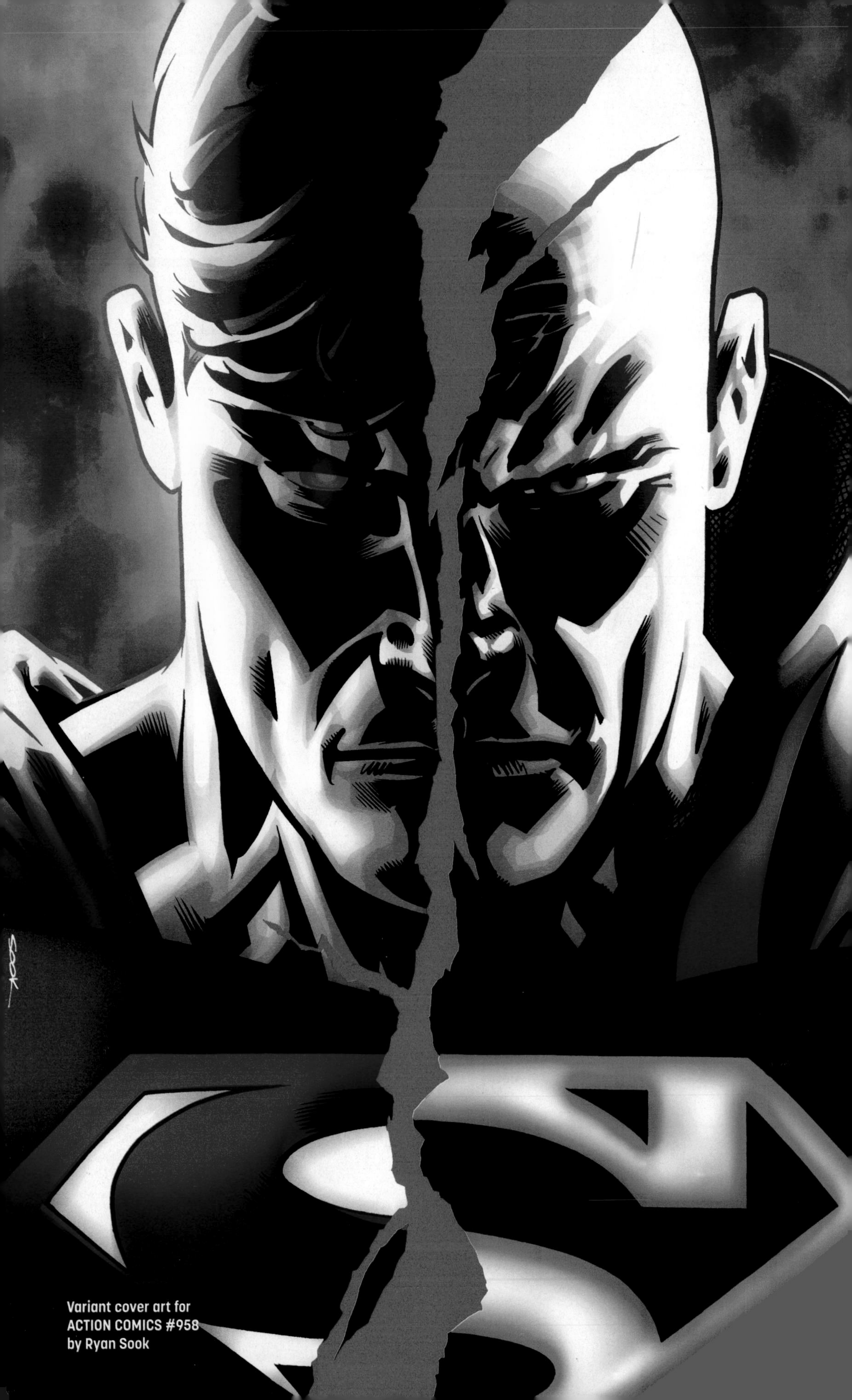
SOOK

Variant cover art for
ACTION COMICS #958
by Ryan Sook

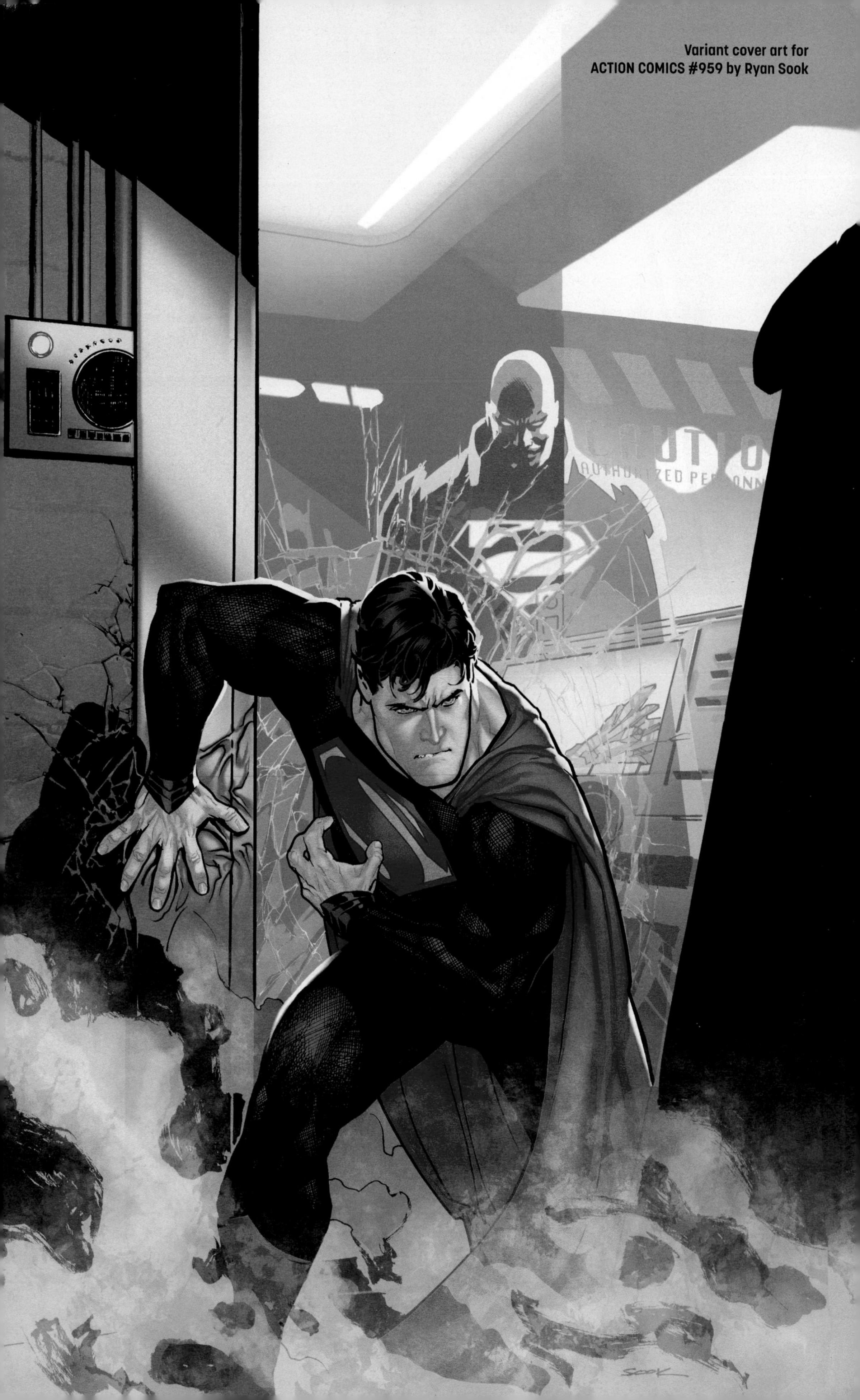

Variant cover art for
ACTION COMICS #959 by Ryan Sook

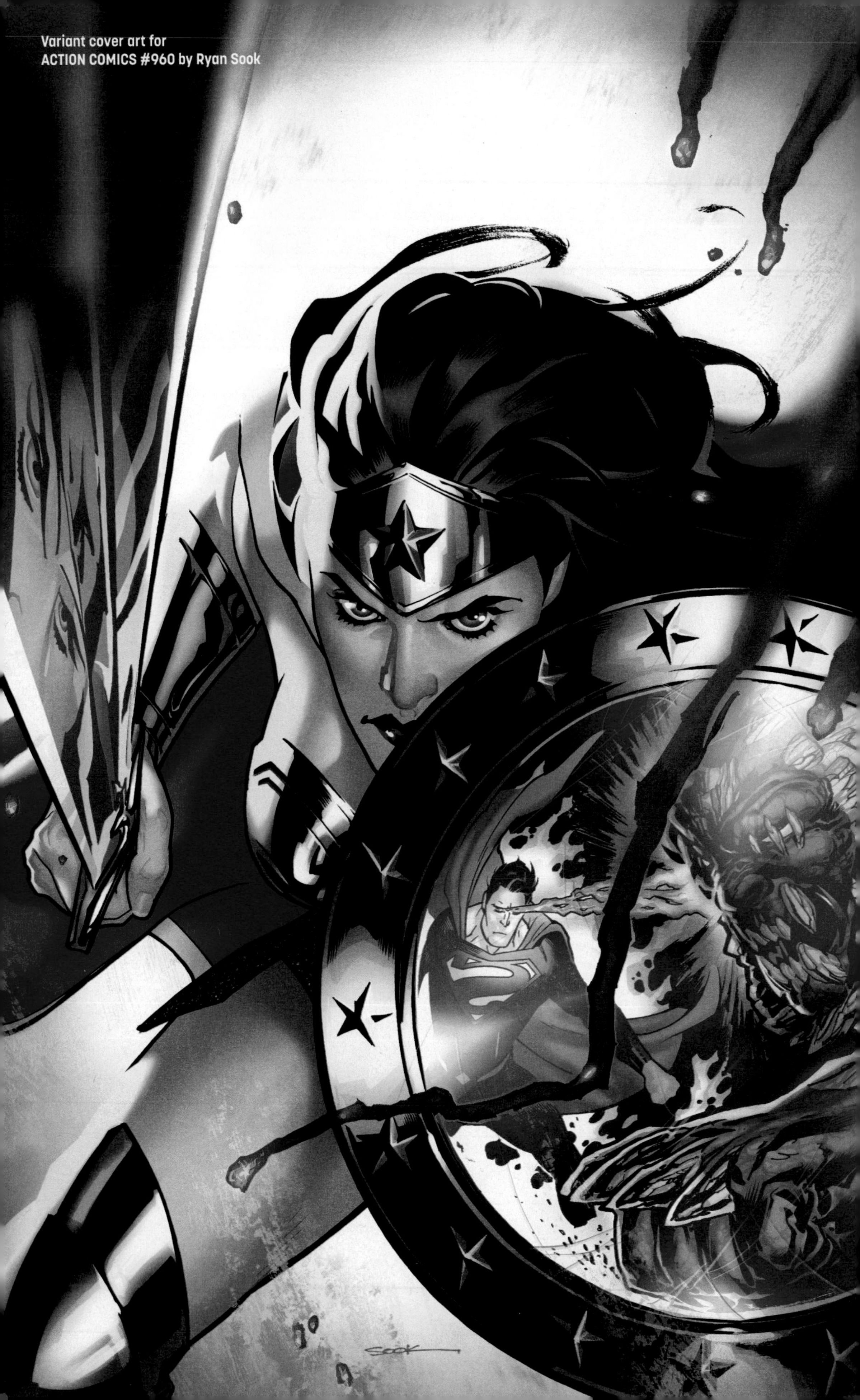
SOOK

Variant cover art for
ACTION COMICS #960 by Ryan Sook

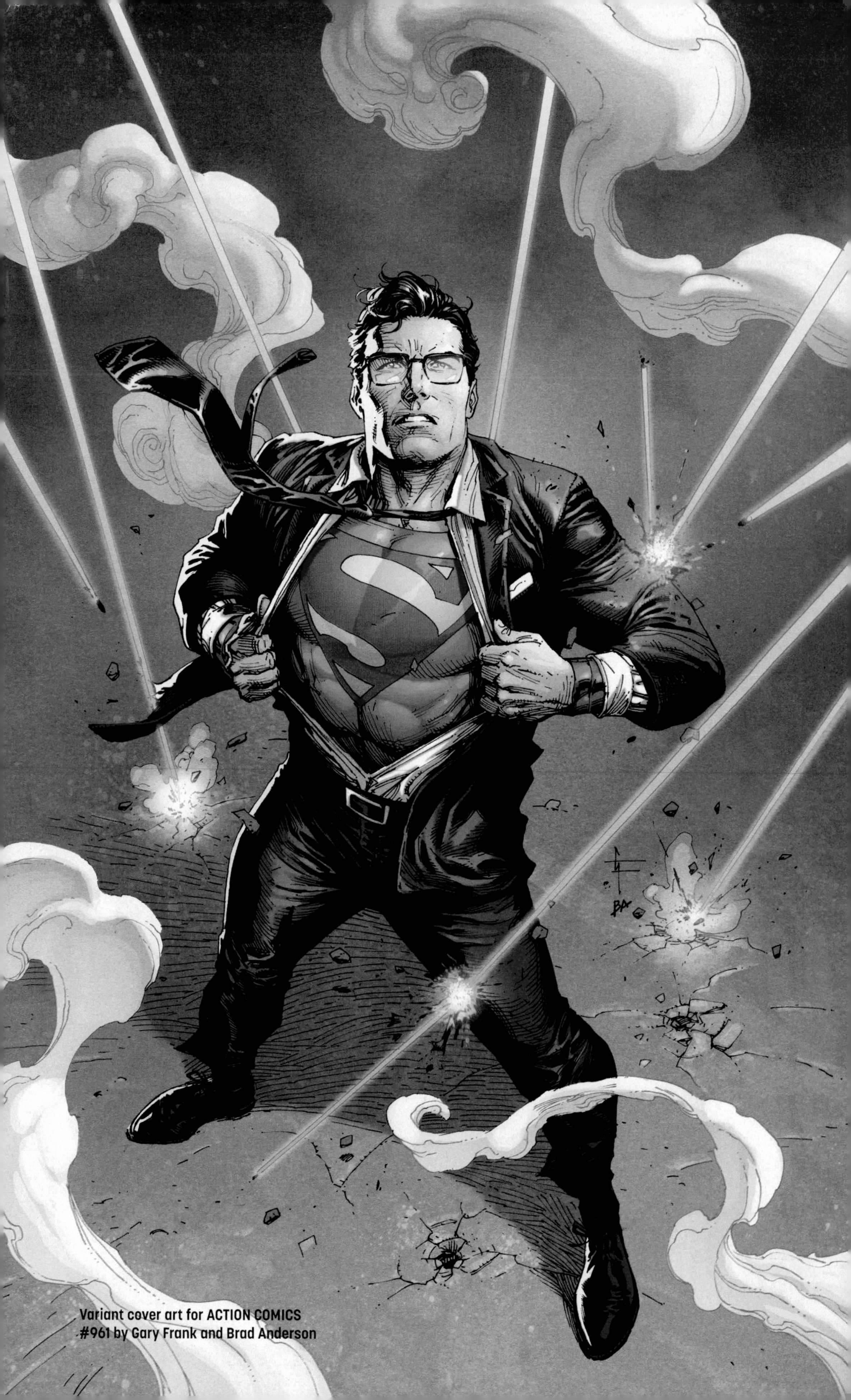

Variant cover art for ACTION COMICS
#961 by Gary Frank and Brad Anderson

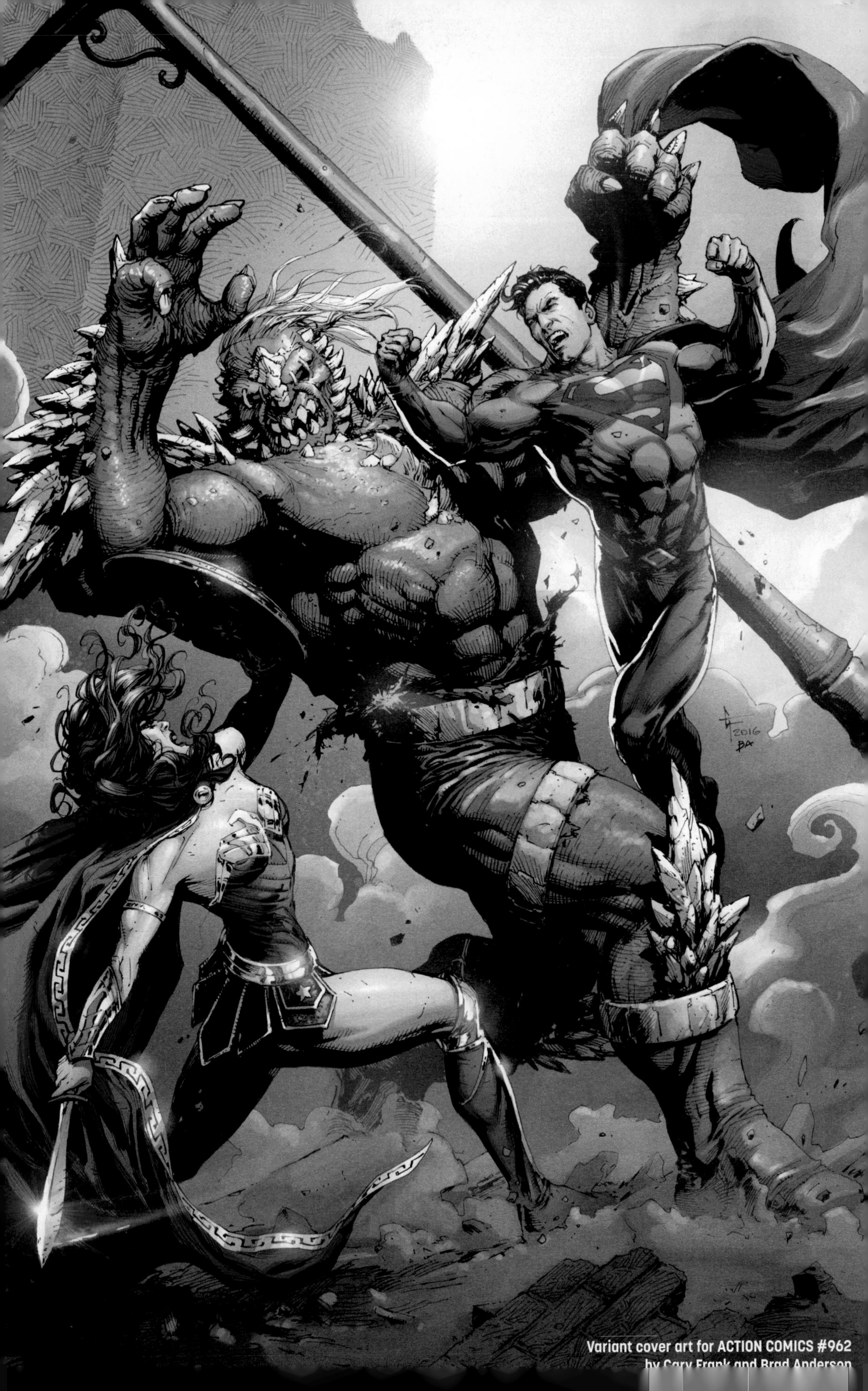

Variant cover art for ACTION COMICS #962
by Gary Frank and Brad Anderson

DC UNIVERSE REBIRTH
SUPERMAN
VOL. 1: SON OF SUPERMAN

PETER J. TOMASI with PATRICK GLEASON, DOUG MAHNKE & JORGE JIMENEZ

DC UNIVERSE REBIRTH
SUPERMAN
VOL. 1 SON OF SUPERMAN
PETER J.TOMASI * PATRICK GLEASON * DOUG MAHNKE * JORGE JIMENEZ * MICK GRAY

SUPERGIRL
VOL.1 REIGN OF THE SUPERMEN
STEVE ORLANDO • BRIAN CHING • MIKE ATIYEH

SUPERMAN ACTION COMICS
VOL.1 PATH OF DOOM
DAN JURGENS • PATRICK ZIRCHER • TYLER KIRKHAM • STEPHEN SEGOVIA • TOM GRUMMETT

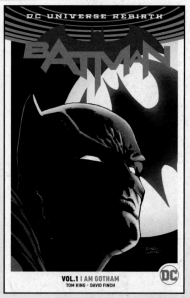

BATMAN
VOL.1 I AM GOTHAM
TOM KING • DAVID FINCH

SUPERGIRL VOL. 1:
REIGN OF THE SUPERMEN

ACTION COMICS VOL. 1:
PATH OF DOOM

BATMAN VOL. 1:
I AM GOTHAM

JUN 19 2018

SUPERMAN: ACTION COMICS

VOL. 1: SUPERMAN AND
THE MEN OF STEEL
GRANT MORRISON
with RAGS MORALES

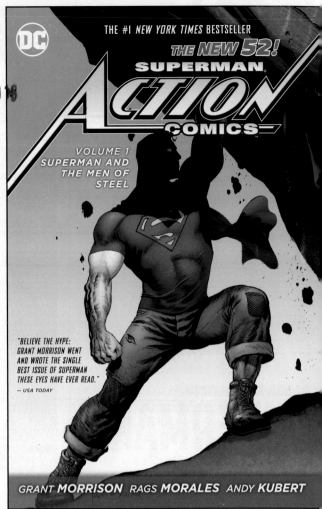

THE #1 *NEW YORK TIMES* BESTSELLER

THE NEW 52!

SUPERMAN

ACTION COMICS

VOLUME 1
SUPERMAN AND
THE MEN OF
STEEL

"BELIEVE THE HYPE: GRANT MORRISON WENT AND WROTE THE SINGLE BEST ISSUE OF SUPERMAN THESE EYES HAVE EVER READ." – USA TODAY

GRANT **MORRISON** RAGS **MORALES** ANDY **KUBERT**

THE NEW YORK TIMES BEST-SELLING SERIES THE NEW 52!

SUPERMAN

ACTION COMICS

VOLUME 2
BULLETPROOF

THE NEW YORK TIMES BESTSELLER THE NEW 52!

SUPERMAN

ACTION COMICS

VOLUME 3
AT THE END
OF DAYS

...RRISON RAGS **MORALES** BRAD **WALKER**

SUPER...
VO...

...ERMAN: ACTION COMICS
... 3: AT THE END OF DAYS

6-15-18
2-18-22 - 1-4-20
9(CING) 8
12(12142g)1

Get more DC graphic novels wherever comics and books are sold!